BURREN

BURREN
Dinners

Trevis L. Gleason is an award-winning chef, writer, culinarian, consultant and instructor, diagnosed with multiple sclerosis in 2001. His memoir, *Chef Interrupted*, won the Prestige Award of the International Jury at the Gourmand International World Cookbook Awards, and *Dingle Dinners* represented Ireland in the 2018 World Cookbook Awards. Gleason is an ambassador of the Blas na hÉireann Irish Food Awards, a senior judge and panel chair of the Irish Quality Food Awards, judge of the Irish Hotel Awards and senior judge for the Yes Chef Magazine Awards. He has been published in *The Irish Times*, *Irish Examiner*, *Irish Independent*, *The Lancet* and *The New England Journal of Medicine* among others.

An American by birth, Gleason lives in the west of County Kerry with his wife Caryn and their two Wheaten Terriers, Sadie and Maggie.

BURREN
Dinners

FROM THE CHEFS
AND ARTISAN FOOD PRODUCERS
OF NORTH CLARE

TREVIS L. GLEASON

THE O'BRIEN PRESS
DUBLIN

First published 2019 by The O'Brien Press Ltd,
12 Terenure Road East, Rathgar, Dublin 6, D06 HD27, Ireland.
Tel: +353 1 4923333; Fax: +353 1 4922777
E-mail: books@obrien.ie; Website: www.obrien.ie
The O'Brien Press is a member of Publishing Ireland.

ISBN: 978-1-78849-102-0

Food and prop styling by Jette Virdi (www.jettevirdi.com)
Food photography by Joanne Murphy (www.joanne-murphy.com)
Profile photography by Carsten Krieger (www.carstenkrieger.photography)
Additional photography by Elaine Kennedy (www.elainekennedy.com)

6 5 4 3 2 1
23 22 21 20 19

Printed by L&C Printing Group, Poland.
The paper in this book is produced using pulp from managed forests.

Published in

DUBLIN
UNESCO
City of Literature

From the Chefs and Producers of The Burren, European Destination of Excellence for Tourism & Local Gastronomy.

The Burren Ecotourism Network is a tourism network whose objective is to establish the Burren as a premier internationally recognised sustainable destination. The network is dedicated to the conservation of the Burren as a natural habitat, and to the preservation of sustainable tourism and farming practices. The Burren Food Trail is a celebration of the Fertile Rock and was established by members of the Burren Ecotourism Network, who are passionate about the Burren food story and committed to building a sustainable future for the region.

This project received funding from the European Maritime and Fisheries Fund. We are grateful to Bord Iascaigh Mhara and the Fisheries Local Action Group (FLAG) West for their support in making this project possible.

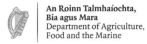

DEDICATED TO THE MEMORY OF KEADY CLIFFORD

CONTENTS

Foreword by Neven Maguire   12

Introduction   13

THE CHAMPIONS   16

Hugh Robson – Glencarn Farm   19

A Farmhouse Supper

'Craggy Island' lamb and almond tagine   22

Roast Glencarn suckling pig with herb and apple pan sauce   23

        Cider-glazed potatoes   24

        Baked chutney apples   25

Lemon and redcurrant posset with Scottish shortbreads   27

Birgitta Hedin-Curtin – Burren Smokehouse   29

Midsummer's Eve

Oyster and smoked salmon rumaki   33

Grilled lobsters with lemon mayonnaise   34

Mum's apple crumble   36

Peter Jackson – Armada Hotel   37

Catch of the Day

Grilled mackerel with smoked salmon and cucumber salad   41

Herb-crusted fillet of cod with mussels and peas   42

Blackberry crème brûlée with hazelnut shortbreads   44

Katherine Webster – Kittiwake Solutions   47

Make-Ahead Feast

Smoked mackerel and goat cheese pâté   50

Don's treacle bread   51

Lamb shanks in spiced blackberries and port   53

        Tian of summer vegetables   54

Blackberry and apple compote with honeysuckle-lavender yogurt   56

THE CHEFS 58

Loic Truffaut – Hylands Burren Hotel 61

A Chef at Play

Carpaccio of smoked haddock and kumquat 65

Duck sausages with Puy lentils 66

Szechuan pepper chocolate fondant with eucalyptus cream 67

Lesley McSweeney – Hazelwood Lodge 69

From the Kitchen Garden

Homemade lemon ricotta with golden beetroot salad 72

Sweet potato and courgette fritters, peperonata stew and dukkah spice 74

Roasted peaches with meadowsweet ice cream and pistachio-cranberry biscotti 76

Robbie McCauley – Gregans Castle 79

Game On!

Prawns with fresh mayonnaise and sourdough bread 82

Venison Wellington with game sauce 84

    Bacon-roasted Brussels sprouts 88

    Glazed parsnips 88

    Braised red cabbage 89

    Boulangère potatoes 89

Pear and almond tart 90

Vivian 'Viv' Kelly – The Burren Storehouse 93

A Taste of Gran's Table

Gran's smoked haddock and potato chowder 97

Slow-roasted lamb belly with potato-sage stuffing and Madeira cream 98

    'Beer-pura' fried cabbage 99

Pecan and maple baked cheesecake 100

John Sheedy – Sheedy's Hotel 103

A Rare Evening Off

Slow-cooked leg of duck with celeriac salad and pickled plums 106

Herb-crusted rack of lamb with confit belly 107

Lemon posset 110

Fabiola Tombo – The Copper Pot 112

A Bohemian Rhapsody

Buckwheat-beetroot risotto with goat cheese and duck egg 115

Crispy braised pork belly with pan-seared scallops ... 116

    Smoked parsnip purée ... 117

Coconut panna cotta with passion fruit and mango mousse

    and cocoa-ginger shortbreads ... 118

Daniel Craughwell – Hotel Doolin ... 121

Autumnal Spread

Wild garlic and bacon stuffed mussels ... 124

Folk Festival jambalaya ... 126

    Dooliner brown bread ... 127

    Red pepper pickle ... 128

Doolin bog pie ... 129

Ronan Kelly – The Falls Hotel ... 130

Winner, Winner, Chicken Dinner

Heirloom tomato and buffalo mozzarella salad with soused vegetables ... 134

Lemon-garlic roasted chicken with lemon and thyme stuffing and Madeira jus ... 136

    Honey-roasted carrots and parsnips ... 138

    Smoked-garlic fondant potatoes ... 139

Blackberry crème brûlée with blackberry and Cointreau sorbet ... 140

David McCann – Dromoland Castle ... 142

Not Your Mother's Pot Roast

Kale and quinoa salad with feta ... 145

Braised feather blade of beef in red wine with purée of braised vegetables ... 146

    Buttered mashed potatoes ... 148

    Oven-roasted broccoli ... 150

Pineapple pudding ... 151

THE PRODUCERS ... 152

Ciara O'Halloran – The Redbank Food Company ... 155

Shell Cottage Kitchen

Garlic breaded clams ... 158

Grilled oysters with chorizo and Parmesan ... 160

Shellfish linguini in white wine cream ... 161

Apple, berry and hazelnut crumble ... 162

Donal Monaghan – Gleninagh Burren Lamb   165
Farmhouse Posh

   Smoked salmon and shrimp 'ravioli'   168
   Farmhouse lamb and barley stew   169
      Cheese scones   170
   Irish coffee cupcakes   172

Brian O'Briain – Anam Coffee   175
That's Entertainment!

   Mackerel salad with beetroot and dill crème fraîche   178
   Grilled rib-eye steaks with duck-fat chips   179
   Trio of steak sauces: Argentine chimichurri, spicy tomato, whiskey-peppercorn   181
   Blackberry, almond and cardamom cake with black fruits 183

Peter Curtin – Burren Brewery   184
A Few of His Favourite Things

   Pouldoody Bay oysters au naturel   187
   Shellfish boil with garlic butter   188
   Irish whiskey and sherry trifle   191

Siobhán Ní Gháirbhith – St Tola Irish Goat Cheese   192
Burren Barbecue

   Foraged periwinkles with chilli-lime butter   195
   Yogurt-marinated kid goat kebabs with roasted aubergine dip   196
      Romanian cabbage slaw   198
      Potato salad   199
   Chocolate cheesecake   200

Eva Hegarty – Burren Free Range Pork Farm   202
Cross-Culture Comfort Food

   Courgette soup with seaweed crackers   206
   Confit of pork belly with rhubarb and rose-petal subh   208
      Hasselback potatoes   210
   Goat cheese panna cotta with bacon syrup and toasted hazelnuts   211

Oonagh O'Dwyer – Wild Kitchen   213
Take a Meal on the Wild Side

   Wild crudités of beetroot carpaccio, samphire salsa verde and radishes with
     seaweed butter and dandelion oil   216

Railway cake · 219

Bacon-roasted rabbits with sloe-gin giblet gravy · 220

Nettle colcannon · 221

Blackberry bread and butter pudding with gorse-flower sorbet · 222

THE KEEPERS · 223

Paul Haugh – The Wild Atlantic Lodge · 224

For a Cold, Dark Night

Chilli shrimp with guacamole salad · 229

Beef cheeks in red wine · 230

Scallion mashed potatoes · 231

Mary's ultimate chocolate celebration cake · 232

Cathleen Connole – Burren Fine Wine and Food · 234

A Proper Sunday Roast

Crab and smoked salmon salad · 239

Roast leg of lamb with vegetable gravy · 240

Minted marrowfat peas · 241

Rosemary-roasted potatoes · 242

Rhubarb crumble · 243

Niall Hughes – Seaview House · 244

Brunch or Lunch or Tea, Oh My!

Apple fritters with spiced orange syrup · 247

Niall's goat cheese frittata · 248

Darra's tomato chutney · 250

Spiced figs with marmalade ice cream · 251

Fiona Haugh – The Market House · 252

A Butcher's Kitchen

Fresh tomato soup · 255

Braised shin of beef with rocket gremolata · 256

Olivada mash · 257

Farm-fresh strawberry meringue · 258

THE LONG TABLE   260

STARTERS

Bríd Fahy – Café Linnalla   262
   Steamed mussels with white wine and cream   264
Sinéad Ní Gháirbhith – The Cheese Press   266
   Local cheese board   268
   Tomato and blood orange sorbet   270
   Sloke cakes   271

MAINS

Conor Graham – Linnane's Lobster Bar   272
   Roast fillet of hake with chorizo, mussels and clams   275
Kieran O'Halloran – Kieran's Kitchen in the Roadside Tavern   276
   Hot-smoked salmon with spring onion mash, creamed cabbage and
     leeks with mustard cream sauce   278
Neil Hawes – The Burren Craft Butcher   280
   Roast rib of beef with Yorkshire puddings   282
Helen Browne – Doolin Cave   284
   Baked wild salmon with herb crust and sorrel sauce   286

SIDE

Roy Bermingham – The Burren Nature Sanctuary   288
   Burren Nature Sanctuary savoury scones with walnuts, spinach and cheddar   290

DESSERTS

Diarmuid O'Callaghan – Burren Gold Cheese   291
   Aunt Esther's apple pie with cheesy crust   293
Karen Courtney – Stonecutters Kitchen   294
   Banana and maple upside-down toffee cake   296

Acknowledgements   298
Index   299

FOREWORD

NEVEN MAGUIRE

• •

I am delighted to have been asked to write a few words about the Burren to celebrate the publication of this wonderful book, which tells you more about the food and people of the Burren than I ever could. These recipes feature the interest in food, the landscape, the fine local produce and the seasonality of this wonderful part of the world. If I'm in Galway with my family we always take a trip out to enjoy the peace of the area, the drama of the Wild Atlantic Way and the uniqueness of places like Aillwee Cave. We are now very familiar with the bears that were happily living there long before gastropubs were ever thought of.

As you would expect, the food is my first passion, and there are so many quality, passionate producers and chefs in the Burren who work their magic! I always enjoy eating food from the local chefs, where the use of wild berries, seafood and meats of the area is influenced by the changing seasons. These are chefs who understand how special the place and its produce is.

One of my favourite artisan producers is Birgitta in the Burren Smokehouse. She has been one of the most iconic people in Irish food over the years, plus she is an absolutely fantastic businesswoman and, as any of us who work in the industry know, that is an important side of the work. We have been using her produce in MacNean for a long time and customers love it. She is excellent at what she does and, in my mind, one of the pioneers of showcasing our great produce.

We have also been proud to use St Tola cheese in the restaurant, which we source through Sheridan's. I love their goat cheese because it is all hand-made. They have a fantastic, delicious creamy cheese rubbed in ash – the Ash Log – which is always consistent and has picked up a well-deserved Gold Blas na hÉireann award.

Gregans Castle near Doolin is another unique place in a special part of the world. I love the attention that Simon, the owner, and Chef Robbie bring to the arts of inn keeping and cookery.

Then there is the great siopa búistéara of Neil Hawes, the Burren Craft Butcher, Ireland's Number 1 rural butcher. He is very active on Twitter, which is part of all our businesses these days. Follow him – I do.

The Burren has it all. Food is best eaten with friends in a beautiful environment and cooked by people who care for the sustainability of our industry and our planet. There is a lot to care for in the Burren and this book captures a great sample of what is special about this part of our country.

INTRODUCTION

· ·

To say that the Burren is a karst landscape of glacial limestone in north Clare would be like saying that hurling is a stick-and-ball sport played in Ireland. Neither statement is wrong – both are factually irrefutable – but both miss the spirit, the soul and the passion of the people who live here (and who fervently follow the sport). It was the people and their passions I went in search of over three seasons of the year: spring, summer and autumn.

At first glance, the Burren seems a rugged, desolate place, the kind of landscape – both literal and metaphoric – that takes a special kind of organism to survive there, let alone thrive. But linger awhile and you will notice that an astonishing variety of life has found niches and crevices in which to do just that. And just as a mixture of Arctic–Alpine and Mediterranean plant species have been swept here by the forces of nature, so too have a diverse array of people settled in and around the Burren. One chef said it best: 'There have been people on the Burren as long as there have been people in Ireland.' They have always made their lives and their livelihoods in connection with the health of the land.

From Dublin and London, Sweden and France, from Finland and from the north Clare land their families have lived on for centuries, they have come to the Burren. Like those seeds scattered by the forces of nature – relying on their own tenacity to survive – they have found a crack in the crag, put down roots and been nourished by the soil and spirit of their surroundings.

The names and faces and stories in this book are of the people of the Burren who create food in the Burren. It's a place that has been renowned for the quality of its produce for as long as people have cared about what they eat.

Tudor banquets of King Henry VIII are said to have been stocked with Pouldoody Bay oysters, where cold limestone-filtered water enters the salty tidal flats of Galway Bay. Cromwell's general Edmund Ludlow infamously said of the Burren in 1651 that 'it is a country where there is not enough water to drown a man, wood enough to hang one, nor earth enough to bury him'. What has been forgotten, however, is that he continued by lauding the quality of its lamb and the fatness of its cattle, attributing this to 'the grass growing in turfs of earth, of two- or three-foot square, that lie between the rocks, which are of limestone', that is 'very sweet and nourishing'.

Even to this day, heads of state and visiting royalty are served organically farmed salmon smoked in Lisdoonvarna. Ireland's first pub to earn a coveted Michelin star happens to be in the Burren.

Oysters from the Flaggy Shore are a sought-after delicacy all over the globe. The weight of awards, trophies, plaques and placards lauding artisan producers, local foods and places to enjoy them could sink a Galway hooker.

These things are no secret. Many people know the food, know the restaurants and know the places, but few know the people behind the produce. That's the book you hold in your hand.

As a follow-on to my book *Dingle Dinners*, the Burren EcoTourism Network, the Burren Food Trail and LEADER provided me with the opportunity to tell the stories of the people behind the swinging doors. You'll meet farmers and shopkeepers, chefs and artisan producers in these pages. You'll get to know whence they came, why they came and, importantly, why they stay in the Burren. What follows are snapshots of people in their homes, talking about their food and expounding their love of the place.

We then offer you an even rarer opportunity: to prepare, taste and share with your family and friends meals and dishes these Clare foodies make for their own friends and family. This isn't 'chef's food' per se. Rather, these are the dishes that people who make food for the public make in private. We settled on menus for a party of six people in all of the recipes, but everyone's appetite is different and you may have a few leftovers. For those times when group cookery is the plan for the day, we have also included suggestions for the wonderful north Clare tradition of a Long Table supper – a shared communal meal.

It was a privilege to sit down and share a cup of tea (or a pint) in homes, farms, shops, pubs, restaurants, inns and production facilities in the Burren. It is an honour to have been asked to relate the stories they shared with me within the pages that follow. You'll read of dishes from mothers' and grandmothers' kitchens, of meals prepared to welcome home loved ones, of suppers they throw together after a long day working or meticulously prepare for special occasions. They are foods that bring the Burren to mind for the foodies of one of Ireland's finest culinary destinations, foods from the heart and soul of the place they call home.

TLG, 2019

NOTE ON MEASUREMENTS

As visitors to the Burren come from all corners of the world, we have to assume that this book will make its way into the hands of cooks around the globe. We have, therefore, offered all of our recipes in standard imperial and metric measurements. The same for temperatures and ingredient names.

We hope you enjoy these wonderful menus and recipes no matter where you call home.

THE CHAMPIONS

Advocates, proponents, promoters, supporters, standard-bearers, torch-bearers, defenders, protectors, upholders, backers, exponents, patrons and sponsors: the four people profiled here are all of the above, and then some. They are champions.

Along with the Burren Food Trail, we determined to represent the farming community who raise their produce here; producers who create a food product representing the Burren; chefs who use and extol foods raised, grown, caught, shot, foraged in or otherwise connected to the place; and advocates who help to promote the previous three legs of the figurative long table that is the Burren food scene.

Just as importantly as representing the Burren locally, our four champions have brought Burren food to the world and offered it when the world has come to the Burren.

People from here and people who have moved here know that Burren food tastes a certain way, that it's simply better than elsewhere. They trust the impeccable quality, knowing that the food has all been sourced locally. Eating Burren food is essential to experiencing the place to its fullest.

The champions of *Burren Dinners* are four people who know all of those things and have spread the word near and far. It's safe to say that far fewer people would know of the Burren as a culinary destination had our champions not sung its praises at the top of their lungs.

AN ACRE FOR EVERY DAY OF THE YEAR

HUGH ROBSON

GLENCARN FARM

• •

We begin where every good chef, every good producer, every person who wants to serve impeccable food must begin: at the farm and with the farmer. Hugh Robson's Glencarn Farm is cradled in a north–south valley that neighbours Father Ted's home. No, Hugh doesn't live on Craggy Island; rather, the house used as the priests' home in the beloved Channel 4 comedy series is just up the hill and over a bit from his 365 organic acres.

Neither 'farmer' nor 'chef' might have been what was expected of the son of a Dutch nurse and an Irish doctor who met in London during the Second World War. Though an admittedly good student, Hugh bridled at the institutionalised brutality of boarding schools in England and the USA. Though Trinity College Dublin called him to study natural sciences, he had no intention of following his father – by now a respected researcher in the field of tuberculosis – into medicine, nor in pursuing a teaching career after his experiences at school.

It was cooking that fuelled Hugh's imagination from an early age. He reckons the passion was sparked by his mother, an expert cook, who died when he and his four brothers were still quite young. It might have also had something to do with the food at those boarding schools. Whatever the reason, Hugh excelled at catering college in Geneva, Switzerland.

Requisite placements during college brought him to Scotland and then back to Ireland, where he worked in various management roles in hotels around the country. Then, when an opportunity arose in Bettystown, County Meath, Hugh and his new wife, Mary, purchased a former coastguard station and set out to run it as an upmarket seafood restaurant.

Their reputation flourished, and The Coast Guard restaurant became the 1970s destination for high-end fish, shellfish and hand-cut steaks.

Mary died and Hugh left the restaurant business and moved to farm sheep in Portarlington.

Hugh married again, to Isabell. They wanted to make the leap from high-intensity farming (they bred some 350 ewes for lamb) to organics, and his brother lived in Corofin. So enamoured with the area were Hugh and Isabell that they spent the bulk of two years searching out a place to establish their dream of setting up an organic farm upon which to retire.

The economic crisis of the 1980s, however, saw their mortgage interest shoot well into the double digits and the hobby farm had to turn a profit and turn it quickly.

The pine marten made farming sheep next to impossible, so they shifted from sheep to suckler cattle and pigs for producing organic beef and pork. It is the basis of the farm's business to this day, though the next-generation Robsons may have something to say about that: glamping, horse training and adventure tourism are on their minds. Meanwhile, one of Hugh's older sons, Eric, is working in Dublin at the ever-expanding Ely family of restaurants and wine bars in the city.

Organic beef and pork (as well as sourced organic lamb from the Burren), raised and processed by Hugh and supplied to Ely, may be how many people know of the Burren's reputation for quality meats now. A few decades ago, however, Hugh was evangelising about the quality of its product at Dublin's open-air markets.

From night-shift-working South African immigrants taking home specially made Boerewors sausages to the D4 crowd's hand-cut steaks and chops, Hugh filled Dublin's belly with exquisite Burren meat while filling their ears with stories of why and how the product is so very good. With one or, occasionally, two extra pairs of hands, Hugh was selling more on a Saturday than most butchers outside of urban Dublin were selling in a week.

Hugh plans to get to that long-awaited, well-earned retirement in the not-too-distant future. He's making fewer of the delivery trips to Dublin these days and aims to spend more time in the flower gardens and to build up a vegetable bed or two. He is concerned that climate change will alter the way that the farm is run and whether the next generation will be able to make a living on the land.

IT WAS COOKING THAT FUELLED HUGH'S IMAGINATION FROM AN EARLY AGE

It is the remoteness that Hugh has come to love about the Burren. It's the sort of place where a man can put his mind and his back into his work of choice without interruptions or expectations from others. And while for a good few days of the year his valley is neither above nor below but actually *in* the clouds, he finds a beauty about the place that transcends weather, and season, and hopefully will remain.

A FARMHOUSE SUPPER

. . . .

Suckling pig for 6? Don't worry, it's not even half a pig! You'll need to contact your butcher a few days in advance to get the right cuts, but this is a dinner party your guests will talk about for a long time. The addition of Robbie McCauley's braised red cabbage (page 89) would beat Banagher.

STARTER
'Craggy Island' lamb and almond tagine
MAIN
Roast Glencarn suckling pig with herb and apple pan sauce
SIDES
Cider-glazed potatoes
Baked chutney apples
DESSERT
Lemon and redcurrant posset with Scottish shortbreads

'CRAGGY ISLAND' LAMB AND ALMOND TAGINE

Serves 6, with plenty to spare

2 pinches saffron threads

1 tbsp whole cumin seeds

1 tsp cinnamon

1 large onion, finely chopped

2–3 cloves garlic, peeled and crushed

5 cm/2 inches fresh ginger, peeled and grated

1.2 kg/2 lb 12 oz boneless lamb shoulder, cut into 2.5 cm/1-inch cubes

110 g/4 oz/½ cup butter

50 g/1½ oz/⅓ cup nibbed almonds

110 g/4 oz/½ cup currants

1 tbsp sea salt

2 tbsp fresh mint, chopped

Crush the saffron threads and cumin seeds together with a mortar and pestle. Add the cinnamon.

Toss the spices together with onions, garlic and ginger. Place the lamb in a large bowl, add the spice and onion mixture and toss to coat evenly. Cover and leave to stand for 1 hour at room temperature.

Preheat oven to 150°C/300°F/Gas Mark 2.

Transfer the lamb to a casserole (Dutch oven) and add the butter, almonds and currants. Add cold water to come to the level of the lamb, but not to cover. Sprinkle with salt and cover with a tight-fitting lid.

Place the dish in the preheated oven for 3 hours, stirring occasionally. Add a little water if the lamb begins to stick, but only a little.

The tagine is ready when the meat is tender, but not stringy, and the sauce has thickened.

Correct the seasoning with salt if needed.

Serve in individual bowls sprinkled with the chopped mint.

ROAST GLENCARN SUCKLING PIG WITH HERB AND APPLE PAN SAUCE

Serves at least 6

½ suckling pig, cut up as follows
(your butcher can trim for you):

- Shoulder, boned and sinew
  removed, reserve bones for sauce
- Belly, trimmed, ribs removed and
  reserved
- Best end (rack), chine removed and
  reserved
- Leg, boned and sinew removed, cut
  large bones and reserve
- Skin of all pieces, scored

Sea salt and freshly ground black pepper

2 onions, peeled and chopped

1 carrot, peeled and chopped

1 stalk celery, peeled and chopped

For the sauce

30 g/1 oz/2 tbsp butter

5 shallots, finely chopped

5 sprigs thyme

0.5 litres/18 fl oz/2 cups apple juice

1 litre/1¾ pints/4 cups pork stock (from
  bones)

1 litre/1¾ pints/4 cups chicken stock

1 litre/1¾ pints/4 cups veal stock (beef
  can be substituted)

5 sprigs sage, finely chopped

5 sprigs tarragon, finely chopped

Preheat oven to 200°C/400°F/Gas Mark 6. Season the pork well with salt and pepper. Cover and refrigerate. Place the bones on a baking tray. Roast until golden, 30 to 45 minutes. Put the bones in a large stockpot, cover with cold water and place over medium–high heat.

Place roasting tin on a warm burner, deglaze with a little water or white wine. Add the drippings to the stockpot. Bring the stock to a hard simmer, reduce heat to medium and add onions, carrot and celery. Simmer for 3 hours, strain, defat and reserve for the sauce.

An hour before roasting, remove the pork from the fridge to bring it to room temperature. Place in a roasting tin and into the oven, preheated as for bones. Reduce heat to 150°C/300°F/Gas Mark 2. Roast until the internal temperature reaches 71°C/160°F. Remove, cover loosely with tinfoil and rest for 20 to 30 minutes.

To make the sauce, place a large pan over a medium heat. Melt the butter and sweat the shallots with the thyme until soft. Add the apple juice and reduce to the consistency of syrup.

Add the pork stock and chicken stock, bring to a simmer and reduce by two-thirds.

Add the veal stock and reduce to the consistency of sauce. Stir in tarragon and sage. Correct the seasoning with salt and pepper.

Slice the pork, keeping each part separate. Serve on a large preheated platter with cider-glazed potatoes (page 24) and chutney apples (page 25). Serve sauce in a large jug alongside.

CIDER-GLAZED POTATOES

Serves 6

6 large baking potatoes, washed and
  peeled

60 g/2 oz/4 tbsp butter

1 litre/1¾ pints/4 cups cider (hard cider)

1 tbsp sea salt

Cut the potatoes into 2.5 cm/1-inch slices.

Using a 5 cm/2-inch round cutter, cut each slice into a circle and reserve the scraps for another use.

Place the potatoes, butter, cider and salt into a large pan over a high heat.

Bring to a boil and reduce heat to medium–low.

Reduce the liquid to the consistency of syrup. The caramelising of the potatoes begins.

Cook until the potatoes are nicely golden and tender. If they colour too much but are not cooked, add a bit of water.

Remove, cover and keep warm until ready to serve.

CHEF'S NOTE

Cooking with cider is not unlike cooking with wine. The first rule is that you don't cook with something you wouldn't be willing to drink with the dish or meal. Use a craft cider for these potatoes rather than a mass-market beverage. It'll show itself worth the effort.

BAKED CHUTNEY APPLES

Serves 6

3 Granny Smith apples

170 g/6 oz/⅔ cup apple and sultana
   chutney

115 g/4 oz/½ cup caster (superfine) sugar

Preheat oven to 190°C/375°F/Gas Mark 5.

Top, tail and core the apples.

Fill the cavity of each apple with chutney.

Place in an ovenproof baking dish, dust with half the sugar and bake until soft (about 30 to 45 minutes).

Remove and preheat the grill (broiler) to high.

Dust the apples with the remaining sugar and place under the grill (broiler) until golden.

Keep warm until serving.

CHEF'S NOTE

Using tart Granny Smith apples means the acid from the fruit cuts through the richness of the roast pork.

LEMON AND REDCURRANT POSSET WITH SCOTTISH SHORTBREADS

. . . .

Serves 6, with plenty of extra shortbreads

For the posset

750 ml/27 fl oz/3 cups double (heavy) cream

200 g/7 oz/1 cup golden caster (raw) sugar

4 lemons, zested

80 ml/3 fl oz/⅓ cup lemon juice

For the shortbread (see Chef's Note)

650 g/23 oz salted butter

230 g/9 oz/1⅓ cups caster (superfine) sugar, plus extra for dusting

1 kg/36 oz/6⅔ cups oat flour

170 ml/6 fl oz/⅔ cup redcurrant jelly

CHEF'S NOTE

The shortbread recipe makes 36–48 biscuits, depending on the size of your cutter. Feel free to halve the recipe or make the full batch and keep the extras for coffee or tea.

To make the posset, stir the cream and sugar in a large saucepan over a medium–low heat until the sugar has melted.

Increase heat to medium–high and bring to a boil, stirring, for 1 minute.

Remove from the heat and gently stir in the lemon zest and juice.

Pour equal amounts into 6 decorative glasses or cups.

Cool to room temperature, cover with cling film and chill in the refrigerator to set for at least 4 hours or overnight.

To make the shortbread, first preheat oven to 190°C/375°F/Gas Mark 5.

In a stand mixer with the paddle attachment, cream the butter and sugar until light, scraping down often.

Gently fold in the flour on low speed.

Turn the dough out onto a lightly floured work surface.

Roll it out to 1 cm/⅜ inch.

Cut into the desired shapes using a cutter.

Place on a baking tray and sprinkle with caster sugar.

Refrigerate for 30 minutes to let the dough relax.

Bake in the middle of the preheated oven for about 20 minutes (turning the tray once) until pale golden.

Cool on a wire rack.

To serve, melt the redcurrant jelly in a small saucepan over medium heat.

Carefully spoon over the set possets and serve with shortbread.

A MARINE BIOLOGIST WALKS INTO A BAR ...

BIRGITTA HEDIN-CURTIN

BURREN SMOKEHOUSE

• •

Lisdoonvarna in County Clare may seem to be the most unlikely place in the world for a farmer's daughter from a forestry outside of Nyköping on Sweden's Baltic coast to settle. It did to me, until I sat down for a coffee with Birgitta Hedin-Curtin. Then it made perfect sense.

Now well known beyond the borders of the Burren and representing artisan Irish produce beyond the shores of this island, Birgitta wandered into Lisdoonvarna as an eighteen-year-old student in search of traditional music. She'd just finished gymnasium (the Swedish equivalent of the senior cycle and Leaving Cert) and was travelling with friends to experience Irish culture and begin her casual study of the Atlantic.

A lift from an American musician on his way to Doolin (her intended destination for music) detoured through the Roadside Tavern where publican Peter Curtin greeted the group with pints of Guinness and his now-famous banter. Mr Curtin neither remembers (nor will he admit) if he knew that he might bump into Birgitta were he to make his way to the session at O'Connor's pub, but that's where they met for the second time in one day. Neither looked back.

Their long-distance relationship was necessitated by the difference in tuition for a native Swede to study at home versus here in Ireland. Finding a way to focus her love for marine biology into a reason to get back to the west of Ireland, Birgitta landed a fellowship with NUI Galway professor Dr Michael Gormally at the university's Finavarra Field Research Station.

With 450 varieties of seaweed to study, stunning views across the bay to the Burren proper and an international community of like-minded young people who were drawn to the area in the early 1980s (let alone that she was little more than half an hour's drive from Lisdoonvarna and Peter), the phycology student found her footing in the local community and became rooted like a wild hazel in the crag.

Although far from the farm on the Baltic coast where she was raised, Birgitta found similar joys of foraging, wild game and myriad outdoor activities. One thing she did miss, however, was the hot-smoked eels of her youth.

She and her father would tend fyke nets from their small boat each eel season. The day's catch was given over to a local fisherman who ran a small smokehouse using traditional methods and live, smouldering fire. She remembered Stockholmares on holidays making their way to the fisherman's smokehouse to enjoy his wares while at their summer homes or to take back to the city to remind them of their visits. He also sold his smoked eels (and other smoked fish) alongside the day's freshly landed catch at the local farmers' market in the town. Wouldn't it be wonderful, she thought, if there were some iconic west coast of Ireland food product that could bring that same experience to Irish and international tourists to the Burren? But what product?

FAR FROM THE BALTIC COAST WHERE SHE WAS RAISED, BIRGITTA FOUND SIMILAR JOYS OF FORAGING, WILD GAME AND MYRIAD OUTDOOR ACTIVITIES

With sides of both wild and organically farmed oak-smoked Burren Smokehouse salmon now being served to visiting royalty and elected heads of state, being shipped in care packages to Irish embassies around the world for a taste of home at the holidays and even presented to the US president (along with the traditional bowl of shamrock) each Saint Patrick's Day, we now know her answer.

She and Peter began tinkering with kilns and fish in 1987 and by 1989 had opened the smokehouse, with a small visitor centre to give both a literal and figurative taste of the Burren to visitors from around the corner and around the globe.

Few in the Irish food world are unfamiliar with Birgitta from producer events and industry roundtable discussions. Many of the culinary laity will recognise her smiling face as an occasional television guest talking about the joys, merits and importance of quality Irish produce representing our nation on the world stage.

That a fish that meant so very much to the early people of the island, a method of preserving food in times of plenty for the cold winter ahead and a girl from Sweden who says she 'grew up in Ireland as much as she did in Sweden' are now synonymous with the place she calls her home speaks volumes about the legacy Birgitta Hedin-Curtin has created where the sea meets the limestone on the west coast of County Clare.

MIDSUMMER'S EVE

· ·

This menu reminds me of summer days at a seaside cottage with friends, eating lobsters on the back porch and making a game of throwing the spent shells into a bin in the garden below. Nothing blends luxury with fun like a lobster dinner with friends. Ronan Kelly's heirloom tomato and buffalo mozzarella salad (page 134) wouldn't be long for the table at Birgitta's lobster party.

STARTER
Oyster and smoked salmon rumaki
MAIN
Grilled lobsters with lemon mayonnaise
DESSERT
Mum's apple crumble

OYSTER AND SMOKED SALMON RUMAKI

Serves 6

12 large oysters

6 slices cold-smoked salmon, cut in
2 lengthwise

Cocktail skewers

For the sauce

100 g/3½ oz/½ cup granulated sugar

60 ml/2 fl oz/¼ cup soy sauce

60 ml/2 fl oz/¼ cup water

3 cloves garlic, crushed

15 ml/1 tbsp rice vinegar

1 tsp sriracha sauce

To assemble

Coarse salt for serving

1 spring onion (scallion), thinly sliced

CHEF'S NOTE

Popularised in the post-war 'tiki bar' period of American dining culture, rumaki was a westernisation of Polynesian flavours experienced by GIs in the Pacific. While recipes usually use chicken livers or water chestnuts wrapped in bacon and glazed with soy sauce, this version using oysters and smoked salmon is glazed with a sticky Korean-style sauce.

Preheat grill (broiler) to high.

Shuck the oysters over a bowl to catch the liquid. Reserve the deepest half of each shell. Scrunch a piece of tinfoil 1½ times the length of a baking tray into a loose tube, coil the tube on the tray and place the reserved shells on the foil, pressing down to keep them in place.

Lay one slice of salmon on a plate or work surface, place one oyster on the salmon, wrap the salmon around the oyster and secure in place with a skewer. Set aside and repeat with all 12 oysters.

To make the sauce, mix all ingredients in a saucepan and bring to a boil. Reduce to a simmer to thicken.

Set out 6 plates and pour a mound of salt onto each. The salt is the bed that will hold the hot oyster shells in place. Put the baking tray with the empty shells under the grill to heat for about 5 minutes. Remove the tray and, using tongs, carefully transfer two hot shells onto each salted plate. Press down on the shells to ensure that they are firmly in place. Spoon a couple of tablespoons of the sauce into each shell. Be careful as it will probably sputter. Place a skewered oyster into each sauce-filled shell. Spoon some reserved oyster liquid over each one. Garnish with spring onion and serve.

GRILLED LOBSTERS WITH LEMON MAYONNAISE

Serves 6

For the mayonnaise

3 egg yolks

20 ml/⅔ fl oz/1 tbsp + 1 tsp good white
   wine vinegar

1 tsp Dijon mustard

1 lemon, zested

100 ml/3½ fl oz/⅓ cup + 4 tsp olive oil

200 ml/7 fl oz/¾ cup + 4 tsp vegetable oil

Salt to taste

6 lobsters (500–600 g/1–1¼ lb each)

Seawater (see note)

1 bunch coriander (cilantro), minced, to
   garnish

1 lemon, cut into 6 wedges for serving

CHEF'S NOTE

The method used here for the killing of lobsters is deemed humane by the RSPCA. We also find that placing lobsters in the freezer for 10 minutes before plunging them into boiling water to be a useful method.

To make the mayonnaise, place the egg yolks, vinegar, mustard and lemon zest in a large bowl and whisk until light in colour. Season lightly. Slowly add the oils in a thin stream while whisking the egg mixture vigorously until all the oil has emulsified and the sauce is thick. Season to taste with salt.

In a large stockpot, cover the lobsters with lukewarm seawater. If you cannot use seawater, use 170 g (6 oz) of fine sea salt for every 1.8 litres (half gallon) of fresh water. It will be very salty, like the sea. Put the pot over medium heat and slowly bring to a hard simmer. The lobsters will die at about 45°C (112°F). By the time the water comes to a simmer, the lobsters will be ready for this dish.

Preheat grill (broiler) on high. Drain the water and pat the lobsters dry.

Lay a tea damp towel under a firm chopping board so it does not slip. Place one lobster at a time on its back on the board. Using a large chef's knife, cut each lobster in half from head to tail. Use the back of the knife to crack the claws. Place each half – cut side up – on a baking tray and lightly brush the meat with a bit of the mayonnaise. Place under the grill (broiler) until the meat is firm and hot.

To serve, place the lobsters on a serving tray, brush with more mayonnaise and garnish with coriander. Serve with a bowl of mayonnaise and lemon wedges.

MUM'S APPLE CRUMBLE

Serves 6

800 g/2¾ lb Granny Smith apples, peeled and sliced

50 g/1¾ oz/¼ cup caster (superfine) sugar

Butter, for greasing

For the crumble

200 g/7 oz/1⅓ cups plain (all-purpose) flour

Pinch of salt

2 tbsp caster (superfine) sugar

100 g/3½ oz/½ cup butter, cold and cut into small chunks

Preheat oven to 180°C/350°F/Gas Mark 4.

Toss the apples with the sugar and place in a buttered baking dish.

To make the crumble, mix the flour, salt and sugar in a bowl. Add the butter and rub it in with your fingertips until the mixture resembles coarse crumbs. Alternatively, pulse in a food processor until sandy (don't over-process). Spread the crumble over the apples in small lumps until they're lightly covered.

Place the dish onto a baking tray and into the preheated oven for 35 to 40 minutes, until the top is golden and the apples feel very soft when you insert a small, sharp knife. Leave to cool for at least 10 minutes. Serve with ice cream or a custard sauce, if desired.

PETER JACKSON

ARMADA HOTEL

. . . .

Chef Peter Jackson's artistry in the kitchen has him on many shortlists of best chefs in the country. The son of a construction worker and a psychiatric nurse, and eldest of his three siblings, however, he sees being a chef more as a craft or a trade than an art.

He lied about his age to get a kitchen-porter job in the summer of his fifteenth year. That position lasted two days and then he was promoted to vegetable and salad prep. It was simply a job to begin with, but he says that the buzz about the place, the manner in which staff were treated by the owners and the quality of the men and women working in the kitchen – many of whom he's still friends with these decades later – stoked a passion he tells me wasn't inherited from his mother's home cooking.

CHASING THE VISA

Perhaps, he admits, his knack for cooking came from his paternal grandmother, who had a 'magic pot' in the kitchen. With twenty-one children and scores of grandchildren (not to mention neighbours' children looking for a meal), his gran had a way of making sure no one went hungry. 'There wasn't much to be had,' Peter says, 'but everyone shared what they had to make sure everyone got what they needed.'

The summer job turned into year-round part-time employment, which led to culinary college at Limerick IT. Straight from formal training and at the ripe age of twenty, Peter accepted a position to lead a staff of sixteen at a busy tourist pub in Bunratty, not knowing that he didn't know everything in a head chef's remit. He called it the best mistake he ever made because it forced him to learn – quickly – about managing a team (most of whom were far older than him), financial responsibility and maintaining quality standards while feeding busloads of visitors who wanted their food good, hot and now.

Equally important to the experience gained as head chef, Peter met a woman from Australia called Skye. They'd become close so when, after a year, her Irish visa was about to run out and she decided to chase a UK work permit, Peter gave notice and the young couple pitched their fortunes in London.

When he looks back on that time, he realises that he hadn't grown much in his cooking skills. Sure, he was putting out quality food that tasted good and he had the top job at a London restaurant that had begun to win awards, but the life of a city chef is difficult. He felt his health being compromised and one day, about a year into his job, he took an opportunity that changed everything – he took a head-chef job at a small coach house inn in Loch Fyne, Scotland.

HE SEES BEING A CHEF MORE AS A CRAFT OR A TRADE THAN AN ART

With seafood from the loch out the back door, lamb and beef coming from the fields out the front and underused gardens and glasshouses for growing herbs and vegetables, our young Limerick city chef became fisherman and gardener while his passion for quality food bloomed. The provenance of his ingredients allowed his cooking to blossom in tandem with his passion for sourcing impeccable quality produce and treating food with a simple and respectful hand. This was a time and place that changed the chef and which he still looks back on as the most important time in his professional life.

After almost two years in the UK, however, Skye's visa was nearly up yet again. Though it pained him, they moved to Brisbane where he worked under a chef who had been the lead for the Singapore culinary team and learned new techniques, used ingredients unknown to him and was quickly promoted to chef de cuisine; within a year they had won international acclaim as the best new restaurant in Australia.

But once again, in 2004 visa issues created the need for Peter to move back to Ireland and he landed in the middle of an economic and culinary boom … and we all know how that turned out! These were dark times for the chefs of Ireland but after a year of long-distance relationship, Peter and Skye married.

Towards the end of the recession Peter was recruited to the family-owned Hotel Doolin, where he once again found the connection of food, people and place in a way that reminded him of his time in Scotland. He helped found the Burren Food Trail, worked on a low-food-miles plan for the restaurants and grew business by over 80 per cent in his first two years at the helm. Peter helped to create an identity for the hotel and for the food scene in the Burren and brought attention to the area in a way that producers alone could not.

Now doing the same for a sister hotel, The Armada, he tends a 7-acre farm, creates signature products from his kitchens and helps to recruit young chefs from around the country to experience what the Burren means to food and what food means to the Burren.

CATCH OF THE DAY

This menu is a seafood-lover's dream. Finfish, shellfish and smoked fish, oh my! Even on his days off, Peter loves to cook and eat fish for and with friends. To see how much a simple swap can change an entire menu, replace Peter's hazelnut shortbreads that accompany the blackberry crème brûlée with Fabiola Tombo's cocoa-ginger shortbreads (page 118). It's like another meal altogether.

STARTER
Grilled mackerel with smoked salmon and cucumber salad
MAIN
Herb-crusted fillet of cod with mussels and peas
DESSERT
Blackberry crème brûlée with hazelnut shortbreads

GRILLED MACKEREL WITH SMOKED SALMON AND CUCUMBER SALAD

. . . .

Serves 6

6 mackerel fillets, boned with skin on

Salt and freshly ground black pepper

30 g/1 oz/2 tbsp butter

300 g/10½ oz cold-smoked salmon

1 cucumber, peeled and deseeded

1 lemon

30 g/1 oz/2 tbsp fresh horseradish, finely
   grated

150 g/5¼ oz/⅔ cup crème fraîche

Preheat grill (broiler) to high.

Lay the mackerel fillets, skin-side down, on a baking tray.
Season with sea salt and black pepper. Dot each fillet with
a bit of butter. Set aside.

Finely dice the salmon and cucumber. Stir together in
a bowl. Squeeze in the juice of half the lemon. Toss
together.

In another bowl, fold the horseradish into the crème
fraîche.

Squeeze the remaining half lemon over the mackerel and
place under the grill for 2 minutes until firm.

To serve, divide the cucumber salad between 6 plates.
Place a mackerel fillet alongside the salad and drizzle a
bit of the cooking liquid over each fillet. Finish each plate
with a dollop of horseradish crème fraîche.

CHEF'S NOTE
Summer-caught mackerel will taste different
from winter-caught. Regardless of the time
of year, the fresher the better, as the high
oil content will cause off-flavours quickly.
The old adage is 'never let the sun go down
on a mackerel'.

HERB-CRUSTED FILLET OF COD WITH MUSSELS AND PEAS

. . . .

Serves 6

6 cod fillet portions (150 g/5¼ oz each)

Sea salt

For the herb crust

150 g/5¼ oz/1¼ cups stale breadcrumbs

1 bunch parsley, picked from stems

1 lemon, zested and juiced (keep juice and
    zest separate)

75 g/2½ oz/¾ cup ground almonds

150 g/5¼ oz/1½ cups smoked Gouda,
    finely grated

150 g/5¼ oz mussels in their shells

60 ml/2 fl oz/¼ cup white wine

1 clove garlic, smashed

1 shallot, minced

300 g/10½ oz garden peas (frozen are fine)

150 ml/5¼ fl oz/⅔ cup cooking liquid
    from the mussels

75 g/2½ oz/5 tbsp butter, cold

Rapeseed (canola) oil

75 g/2½ oz/5 tbsp butter

CHEF'S NOTE

Salting the fillets of cod well and refrigerating them isn't just about seasoning. Salt draws excess moisture from the flesh, thus firming the fillets and giving the cooked fish a pleasant 'meaty' texture.

Preheat grill (broiler) to medium.

Sprinkle the cod portions with sea salt on all sides. Place onto a plate and refrigerate for 20 minutes to firm up the fish.

Place the breadcrumbs, parsley, lemon zest, almonds and cheese in a blender. Pulse until green throughout. Put the crumb topping in a bowl and set aside.

In a saucepan over high heat, place the mussels, wine, garlic and shallot. Cover and cook until the mussels have just opened. Remove from heat. Drain 150 ml of the cooking liquid to use for the peas. Leave the remaining liquid in with the mussels.

In another saucepan, place the peas and hot mussel liquid. Bring to a boil until the peas are cooked. Transfer to the bowl of a food processor and pulse until smooth, scraping down between pulses. With the motor running, add the cold butter, 1 tablespoonful at a time. Scrape into a bowl and keep warm.

Preheat a skillet over medium–high heat. Rub each portion of cod with a bit of oil and place in the pan. After about 1 minute, add butter to the pan. Turn the fillets and sprinkle with the lemon juice. Top each fillet with a scoop of herb crumb. Place the skillet under the preheated grill (broiler) until the crumb becomes slightly toasted and fragrant.

To serve, place a smear of pea purée on each plate and top with a fillet. Arrange some mussels around the plate and drizzle with cooking juices from both mussels and cod.

BLACKBERRY CRÈME BRÛLÉE WITH HAZELNUT SHORTBREADS

Serves 6

For the crème brûlée

450 ml/16 fl oz/2 cups cream

150 ml/5¼ fl oz/⅔ cup full-fat (whole) milk

½ vanilla bean, split in half lengthwise

6 egg yolks

50 g/1¾ oz/¼ cup caster (superfine) sugar plus extra for dusting

For the compote

300 g/10½ oz fresh blackberries (frozen will weep too much liquid)

150 g/5¼ oz/¾ cup caster (superfine) sugar

150 ml/5¼ fl oz/⅔ cup water

For the shortbreads

200 g/7 oz/¾ cup + 3 tbsp butter, softened

100 g/3½ oz/½ cup caster (superfine) sugar

300 g/10½ oz/2 cups plain (all-purpose) flour

50 g/1¾ oz/⅓ cup hazelnuts, toasted and chopped

To make the crème brûlée, preheat oven to 120°C/250°F/Gas Mark ½.

Add the cream, milk and vanilla pod to a saucepan over medium heat. Heat until nearly but not quite boiling. In a heat-resistant bowl, whisk the yolks and sugar together. Slowly add the cream mixture to the yolks while whisking rapidly. Strain through a fine-mesh sieve and divide between 6 ramekins.

Set a kettle of water to boil. Place a tea towel in a deep baking dish. Put the ramekins on top of the towel, then put the dish on a baking tray and the tray in the middle of the preheated oven. Pour boiling water into the baking dish to reach halfway up the sides of the ramekins (this is easier than transferring a baking dish of boiling water into the oven). Bake for approximately 30 minutes until the custards are set, with no wobble.

Remove the baking tray from the oven and the ramekins from the water. Cool on a wire rack for 30 minutes, then refrigerate until fully chilled – 4 hours, or overnight if possible.

Put all the ingredients for the compote into a saucepan. Bring to a boil and cook for 2 minutes. Remove from heat and cool to room temperature.

To make the shortbread, first preheat oven to 160°C/320°F/Gas Mark 3. Line a baking tray with greaseproof paper.

In a stand mixer fitted with the paddle attachment, cream the butter and sugar together until light and fluffy, scraping down once or twice. Sift in the flour and mix on low speed until it just comes together.

Turn out onto a lightly floured surface, form into a ball and roll the dough to a thickness of 20 mm/¾ inch. Spread hazelnuts evenly over the dough and lightly press in with the back of a baking tray. Cut into shapes using a cutter and transfer to the lined baking tray.

Refrigerate for 10 minutes, then bake for 15 minutes until golden.

To assemble, first preheat grill (broiler) to high heat. Place the ramekins on a baking tray and sprinkle the custards with sugar to coat the entire surface. Place under the hot grill (broiler) until the sugar caramelises and begins to turn dark. Carefully remove the ramekins, top with a dollop of blackberry compote and serve with shortbread.

CHEF'S NOTE

Originally burnt with an iron kept on the kitchen fire for this exclusive purpose, the burning of sugar for crème brûlée can be done using a blowtorch or even a hot grill (broiler).

TRUE TO THE PLACE

KATHERINE WEBSTER

KITTIWAKE SOLUTIONS

• •

A quick glance at her curriculum vitae might lead one to think that Limerick woman Katherine had no training for the food business. That's because many of the experiences that shaped her youth and early professional years wouldn't be on that CV. You would read about European economic studies, work in the airline industry, expatriate assignments in Sweden, France, the Netherlands, London and Russia, with technical project management positions on a global scale.

You wouldn't read about childhood camping trips to France where she'd accompany her mother to local markets, Katherine insistent on tasting anything she hadn't tried before. Absent as well would be summer employment in Paris and Marseille as au pair to the children of a French pâté magnate. There would be no mention of the ethnic restaurants and takeaways she sought out to experience ingredients and dishes simply unavailable in her native Ireland. Nowhere is recorded her burgeoning grasp on how food defines place as place defines food. But that was in the portfolio she brought with her when she returned to the west of Ireland in 2005.

Katherine had always wanted to return to the county of her childhood summers. In fact, she'd dreamed of living in a small cottage where she could smell the sea and hear the waves crashing against the cliffs on stormy nights.

When a friend saw a new position as general manager of the Cliffs of Moher Centre Ltd advertised in the *Clare Champion*, she sent Katherine the clipping. Three months later Katherine took the job and two years after that the new Cliffs of Moher Visitor Experience opened to the public to great fanfare and acclaim during the busiest tourist season in Ireland's history.

In that first year of operation, 940,000 visitors experienced the cliffs, as well as shopping and eating at the centre. It was a banner year in the Banner County. But it didn't last.

Between flight cuts from London to Shannon and dark economic spectres on the horizon, attendance dropped by nearly a quarter of a million people in just three years. Few businesses can absorb such a customer implosion and so it was for the local gastropub that was providing visitors from around the world with a little taste of Clare.

Not wanting to tender a contract at the lowest point of the recession, Katherine convinced her bosses at Clare County Council to allow her to chance her arm at switching from landlord of the busy café to running it herself – right down to making sandwiches and serving diners – and this is when we see why Katherine is a true champion of the Burren food scene.

She supported the newly formed Burren Food Trail by insisting that as much Burren artisan produce as practicable be used in the café. From St Tola cheese to Burren Smokehouse salmon, and on to local beef, seafood, baked goods and even seaweed salads, hundreds of thousands of international guests now tasted ingredients flavoured by the soil upon which they stood, the sea they admired and the Atlantic-washed air they breathed.

It was no easy task – opening a new concept food outlet in a still-busy visitor centre in the depths of an international economic crisis – but skill, seasoned with passion, made for a pretty special outcome.

SHE'D DREAMED OF LIVING IN A SMALL COTTAGE WHERE SHE COULD SMELL THE SEA AND HEAR THE WAVES CRASHING AGAINST THE CLIFFS

The venue and local produce were sought after for special events on behalf of the European Commission, Clare County Council, even book launches and international tourism showcases, while making sure not to cannibalise local trade for evening meals and entertainment.

It wasn't just local foods in Katherine's sights. Reducing overall food waste from the kitchens, growing their own herbs in a ragged hollow in a hill behind the cliffs and expanding dietary-specific menus to accommodate a growing number of food allergies and intolerances became important parts of her remit, all while growing guest numbers beyond the 1.5 million mark.

In 2017 she left her job at the cliffs and started a multidimensional tourism consultancy, Kittiwake Solutions, specialising in attractions, the Wild Atlantic Way and, as you might have guessed, food tourism. With luck, we will see her fingerprints on many other successful ventures in the coming years.

Katherine spends as many afternoons as she can in and around the Burren with her puppy, Pickle, hiking, foraging and, at least for Pickle, generally sniffing around the place. At the end of the day, however, she curls up on the sofa in front of a fire in that idyllic seaside cottage she'd always hoped to live in, with the sound of the waves outside the window, the crackle of the fire in the grate and the sighs of a worn-out puppy right beside her.

MAKE-AHEAD FEAST

· ·

Now that she has a bit of free time, Katherine loves to walk and forage about the Burren. This make-ahead menu is perfect for those days when you want to play with friends before you sit down to a meal. After making it, you'll always have Don's treacle bread in the freezer. It's great toasted in the morning with Eva Hegarty's rhubarb and rose-petal subh (page 208).

STARTER
Smoked mackerel and goat cheese pâté
Don's treacle bread
MAIN
Lamb shanks in spiced blackberries and port
SIDE
Tian of summer vegetables
DESSERT
Blackberry and apple compote with honeysuckle-lavender yogurt

SMOKED MACKEREL AND GOAT CHEESE PÂTÉ

Serves 6

450 g/1 lb smoked mackerel fillets

75 g/2½ oz St Tola Divine goat cheese (or whipped soft chèvre)

75 g/2½ oz Greek-style yogurt

2 cloves garlic, crushed (or 10 cloves wild crow garlic with flowers to garnish)

2 limes, juiced, plus 1 lime, cut into wedges, to garnish

Sea salt and freshly ground black pepper to taste (see Chef's Note)

Remove the skin and any bones from the mackerel fillets and flake the flesh loosely into a bowl. Add the goat cheese, yogurt, garlic and lime juice, and mix with a fork until roughly combined. Season to taste.

Serve spread on thinly sliced and toasted treacle bread (page 51) and garnish with a lime wedge and wild garlic flowers, if using.

CHEF'S NOTE

Katherine forages sugar kelp, dries it and powders it in a spice grinder to use in lieu of salt – if you can find it, use it!

DON'S TREACLE BREAD

Makes 4 x 2 lb loaves

(can be halved)

680 g/1½ lb/4½ cups stoneground
   wholemeal flour

340 g/12 oz/3½ cups pinhead oatmeal

170 g/6 oz/1¼ cups plain (all-purpose)
   flour

125 g/4½ oz/1 cup oat bran

125 g/4½ oz/1 cup wheatgerm

125 g/4½ oz/1 cup porridge oats (or rolled
   oats pulsed in a food processor)

4 heaped tsp bread soda (baking soda)

1½ tsp salt

1½ tsp dark muscovado (brown) sugar

2 tbsp treacle

1.5 litres/2½ pints/6 cups buttermilk

2 tbsp olive oil

Preheat oven to 180°C/350°F/Gas Mark 4. Line 4 x 2 lb loaf tins with non-stick liners or greaseproof paper.

Mix all the dry ingredients thoroughly in a large bowl. Heat the treacle in a microwaveable jug in the microwave for 30 seconds. Stir a third of the buttermilk and all of the olive oil into the warm treacle, then pour this mixture into the dry ingredients with the remaining buttermilk and stir until thoroughly mixed.

Divide the batter equally between the 4 tins and place on a baking tray. Bake on the middle rack of the oven for 15 minutes. Reduce the temperature to 160°C/320°F/Gas Mark 3 and continue baking for a further 50 minutes. Remove the loaves to a cooling rack for 10 minutes, then tip them out of their tins and wrap each one in a towel for an hour to keep the crust from hardening.

LAMB SHANKS IN SPICED BLACKBERRIES AND PORT

. . . .

Serves 6

6 medium-sized lamb shanks (Gleninagh
    lamb, if possible)

Seasoning rub made up of equal parts sea
    salt, freshly ground black pepper and
    Chinese 5-spice

Olive oil, for browning

4 cloves garlic, crushed

1 large carrot, diced

1 large onion, diced

2 stalks celery, diced

180 ml/6 fl oz/¾ cup ruby port

1 litre/1¾ pints/4 cups vegetable stock

1 whole clove

6 whole black peppercorns

1 star anise

Sea salt

350 g/12 oz/2 cups blackberries

Preheat oven to 120°C/250°F/Gas Mark ½.

Rub the exterior of each lamb shank with the spice rub. Heat olive oil in a casserole (Dutch oven) until smoking. Sear the shanks on all sides to a deep brown and remove. Add the garlic, carrot, onion and celery. Cook, stirring, for 2 to 3 minutes. Add port, stock, clove, peppercorns, star anise and sea salt and stir. Return the shanks to the pot and bring to a simmer. Cover and transfer to preheated oven for 4 hours (Katherine uses a slow cooker set on low for 6½ hours).

In a blender, blitz all but 24 blackberries. Strain the liquid to remove the seeds and set aside.

Carefully remove the lamb shanks to a heated platter and cover. Strain the cooking liquid from the casserole or slow cooker into a saucepan and defat. Bring to the boil and boil for 5 minutes. Reduce heat to a simmer and add the blackberry juice. Simmer for another 5 minutes. Strain into a heated jug.

Garnish the shanks with the reserved blackberries and serve with the sauce and some of the tian of summer vegetables (see page 54).

TIAN OF SUMMER VEGETABLES

Serves 6

1 tbsp olive oil

1 medium onion, finely diced

1 clove garlic, minced

6 medium tomatoes, thinly sliced

6 small potatoes, thinly sliced

1 courgette (zucchini), thinly sliced

1 tsp dried thyme

Sea salt and pepper

100 g/3½ oz/1 cup Parmesan, grated

Preheat oven to 200°C/400°F/Gas Mark 6.

In a sauté pan over medium heat, add the olive oil, onion and garlic. Sweat until soft. Spread the onion and garlic mixture on the bottom of a baking dish and arrange the sliced vegetables in a shingled pattern on top, alternating the vegetables so that the colours contrast attractively. Sprinkle with thyme and season to taste.

Cover the dish with foil and bake for 30 minutes. Remove the foil and sprinkle the vegetables with the Parmesan cheese. Bake for a further 10 minutes until the cheese is browned.

CHEF'S NOTE

Cow's milk Parmesan is not the only hard Italian cheese that will work well with this dish. Try the tangy sheep's milk Pecorino Romano or rich Asiago d'allevo. Each will accent the vegetables a little differently.

BLACKBERRY AND APPLE COMPOTE WITH HONEYSUCKLE-LAVENDER YOGURT

· ·

Serves 6

2 Bramley apples, peeled, cored and sliced

350 g/12 oz/2 cups blackberries

Juice of ½ lemon

75 g/2½ oz/⅓ cup demerara (raw) sugar

1 stick cinnamon

3 whole cloves

60 ml/2 fl oz/¼ cup honeysuckle-lavender syrup (see Chef's Note)

300 ml/½ pint/1¼ cups Greek-style yogurt

Lavender flowers for garnish

In a saucepan over low heat, add the apples, blackberries, lemon juice and sugar. Stir until the sugar is dissolved. Add the cinnamon stick and cloves. Simmer for 15 minutes. Remove the cinnamon stick and cloves. Transfer the cooked fruit to a bowl and cool to room temperature, then cover and refrigerate until needed.

Stir the syrup into the yogurt.

Serve the compote topped with a dollop of yogurt and sprinkled with the lavender flowers.

CHEF'S NOTE

During the summer, Katherine makes syrups from hedgerow and garden blossoms. One of her favourites is honeysuckle and lavender. Dissolve 450 g/1 lb/2¼ cups sugar in 400 ml/14 fl oz/1⅔ cups water over high heat. Remove from heat and add a 1 litre measure (4 cups) of flowers. Let this cool to room temperature, cover and leave overnight. Strain into a clean bottle and place in the fridge, where it will keep for several weeks.

THE CHEFS

The background, training and experience of the chefs who call the Burren their home are as diverse as the flora of the landscape. Growing up in families of farmers and labourers, artists and gardaí, managers and soldiers, some took a direct path into the kitchen while others took a more circuitous journey. Some came from 'the business'; some fell into it. Regardless of whence they came, however, the passion with which they dispatch their duties aligns them as a cadre of professionals worthy of group as well as individual praise.

Each establishment in which they work is also unique. In pubs, restaurants, hotels, B & Bs, cafés and castles, these talented men and women receive the bounty of the Burren and turn it into a unique dining experience. Most don't, however, work alone. They assemble, train and manage a staff of talented individuals – sometimes young people still in school; other times people quite senior to them in age – in order to meet increasing demand. It's seldom easy and makes for a long and exhausting season.

A chef's time is a commodity always running short in their larder. For that reason, many of the meals offered here by the chefs are either simple, comforting suppers or meals they love to spend a few extra hours on during the quieter times of the year. Some even went back to their mothers' or grandmothers' recipes to recreate food memories of their youth.

Even for the more elaborate meals, there is an economy of time and components that readers will appreciate. On their rare days off, chefs don't want to search out speciality ingredients or spend unnecessary time in the kitchen.

With that, I give you the chefs of the Burren.

ISLAND LIFE

LOIC TRUFFAUT

HYLANDS BURREN HOTEL

• •

French, but with grandparents from Italy, France, Belgium and Croatia, Loic Truffaut had an upbringing few would consider conventional. His parents were part of a professional theatre company based in Limoges.

Travelling with the family to French-speaking islands in the Indian, Arabian and Caribbean Seas gave young Loic and his sister experiences few of his classmates at school could have imagined and exposed him to ingredients from around the world, influenced by French cooks and chefs, enjoyed at table with people whose minds were open and hearts full of laughter, which are his fondest memories of childhood.

He felt a draw toward the food business because it was a way to make people happy. Without training, his first jobs were in the front of the house: bussing tables, back-waitering and eventually waiting tables himself.

It was in the kitchens where the real magic was happening, but Loic couldn't seem to break into the closed society of the French back-of-house. After three years of banging his head on the swinging door, he left the business and studied to be a mechanic at a local technical school.

His first job offer came from an American company, but he knew his English wasn't good enough to make a proper go of it. At eighteen, he deferred his employment for three months and decided to travel to Ireland to better his grasp of the language. An advertisement for a kitchen porter job at The Wineport Lodge in Athlone caught his eye so he moved to the midlands to improve his command of English with the added bonus of finally being in the kitchen.

Two weeks into his washing-up duties he was approached by the head chef, who had travelled to London when he was Loic's age. While doing the same kitchen porter duties, he had been taken on by the restaurant's chef and trained in the business and management side of the kitchen. Now, years later and well accomplished himself, the head chef presented that same opportunity to Loic: to be at his apron strings for a year and learn ordering, finance, management, scheduling and all the other non-cooking aspects of being a chef.

At the end of that year Loic moved on to a newly opened hotel in Athlone and then for a short stint in Scotland (shortened by two random acts of violence against his person), after which he made the decision to move back to Athlone rather than France. A conscious move with life-long consequences.

The next few years saw him 'culinarily mobile', we'll call it. Never afraid to take a step down in rank to work at larger and better-known restaurants and hotels, he was head chef here, chef de partie there, sous-chef at another place and so on, all the while collecting new tools for his kit and new relationships, both professional and personal. The most important of those was with a young woman from Dublin called Sinéad, who was waiting tables at a hotel where he was sous-chef.

HE FELT A DRAW TOWARD THE FOOD BUSINESS BECAUSE IT WAS A WAY TO MAKE PEOPLE HAPPY

The two fell in love and moved to Galway then to Connemara, before Sinéad decided that it was her turn to immerse herself in a language and culture as Loic had years before. So the couple moved to the French Alps for a year before island life called to Loic again. Sinéad had a firm grasp on the French language and when a job at the best restaurant on Martinique, under one of the most demanding chefs on the island, presented itself, the couple were off to the Caribbean.

After two years of living and working together in the same restaurant, the couple decided to marry. Owners, however, would not allow them to take holidays at the same time for a wedding, so they left, opened a small pub with French/Caribbean/Irish-inspired bar food – Loic head of the kitchen and Sinéad attending to guests – and threw themselves an island-style wedding in their own place, catered by chef friends, and invited their families from France and Ireland to meet for the first time.

Four years was where the couple drew a line in the sand and moved to another French-speaking island, this time St Pierre and Miquelon, a small island of six thousand people off the Newfoundland coast. With only four restaurants just an easy ferry trip away from the bustling city of St John's and visiting cruise ships making port weekly, it made for a very busy three years – 80 to 90 kg of lobster per weekend busy.

Then our island called the couple back and they moved yet again, first to Ennistymon and eventually up the Burren to Ballyvaughan, where Loic now helms the kitchen for breakfast, lunch and dinner at Hylands Burren Hotel. The couple have a son, Lohan, and the Burren is home because, as Loic told me, 'for all the places we have lived, there is none more beautiful than this'.

A CHEF AT PLAY

Little is more fun for a serious foodie than to experience a talented chef at play. Your guests will be surprised by each and every bite of this inspired menu. This isn't a throw-together weeknight supper, rather a planned-for event with special friends who will enjoy the experience. Loic has spent a lifetime amassing these flavour combinations, so take some time and savour his efforts with friends who will appreciate them. Roy Bermingham's savoury scone (page 290) might be a fun accompaniment to this menu.

STARTER
Carpaccio of smoked haddock and kumquat
MAIN
Duck sausages with puy lentils
DESSERT
Szechuan pepper chocolate fondant with eucalyptus cream

CARPACCIO OF SMOKED HADDOCK AND KUMQUAT

Serves 6

165 ml/5¼ fl oz/⅔ cup sour cream

1 combava (kaffir lime), zested

5 sprigs dill, minced

White pepper

1 x 550 g/18 oz fillet smoked haddock

2 kumquats, thinly sliced

60 ml/2 fl oz/¼ cup walnut oil

Flaked sea salt

Mix the sour cream, lime zest and dill together. Season with white pepper and set aside.

Slice the haddock very thinly and arrange on a platter. Dollop sour cream around the platter and garnish with kumquats. Drizzle walnut oil over the dish and sprinkle lightly with the salt.

CHEF'S NOTE

Only naturally smoked haddock of the highest quality will do for this recipe. It isn't uncommon to find haddock that has been injected or 'painted' with artificial smoke flavourings and colours. Fresh fish, a little bit of salt, real wood smoke from a distant fire so not as to cook the fish: that's what real smoked haddock is about.

DUCK SAUSAGES WITH PUY LENTILS

Serves 6

For the sausages

1 duck, approximately 2 kg/4½ lb

300 g/10½ oz pork belly (without skin)

1 leek, white and light green, washed well
    and sliced

3 cloves garlic

2 tsp caraway seed

5 fresh sage leaves

300 ml/½ pint/1¼ cups Guinness

Sea salt and freshly ground black pepper

Sausage casings (ask your butcher)

For the stock

1 onion, peeled and diced

1 carrot, peeled and diced

1 stalk celery, peeled and diced

1 bay leaf

6 whole peppercorns

250 ml/8 fl oz/1 cup white wine

For the lentils

450 g/1 lb lardons (smoked bacon), cut
    into matchsticks

1 onion, diced

2 carrots, peeled and diced

3 cloves garlic, minced

500 g/18 oz puy lentils

1 sprig rosemary

To make the sausages, first bone the duck (or ask your butcher to do it for you). Keep the bones for the stock. Dice the duck, skin and all, and pork belly. Mix the duck, pork, leek, garlic, caraway and sage in a bowl. Grind the mixture through a mincer once. Wet with the Guinness and season. Stir to mix and refrigerate for 1–2 hours. Chill the grinding equipment as well. Grind the sausage mixture a second time. Fill into sausage casings, making 15–20 cm (6–8-inch) sausages, and chill.

To make the stock, preheat oven to 200°C/400°F/Gas Mark 6. Place the duck bones on a baking tray along with the vegetables and roast for 30–40 minutes until dark brown. Put the bones in a stockpot with enough water to cover. Add the bay leaf and peppercorns. Deglaze the roasting tin with wine, then add drippings to the stockpot. Bring to a simmer over a high heat, reduce heat to medium and simmer for 3–4 hours. Strain stock, defat, chill and reserve.

For the lentils, place a casserole (Dutch oven) over medium–high heat. First sauté the lardons with the onion, carrot and garlic for 5 minutes. Add the lentils and stir in 1.5 litres/2½ pints/6 cups of reserved duck stock and the rosemary. Bring to a boil then simmer for 30 minutes. Preheat the oven to 180°C/350°F/Gas Mark 4.

While the lentils are simmering, brown the sausages in a non-stick sauté pan. Arrange the sausages on top of the lentils once they are cooked. Place the casserole with lentils and sausages into the preheated oven for 15 minutes or until the sausages reach 70°C/160°F and then serve.

SZECHUAN PEPPER CHOCOLATE FONDANT WITH EUCALYPTUS CREAM

- -

Serves 6

For the coeur coulant

200 g/7 oz dark chocolate, chopped

10 g/ ⅓ oz/½ tsp Szechuan pepper, ground

For the fondant

200 g/7 oz dark chocolate, chopped

200 g/7 oz/¾ cup + 3 tbsp butter

40 g/1½ oz/¼ cup + 1 tsp plain (all-purpose) flour

5 eggs

100 g/3½ oz/½ cup caster (superfine) sugar

For the eucalyptus cream

250 ml/8 fl oz/1 cup double (heavy) cream

20 g/¾ oz/2 tbsp icing (powdered) sugar

Organic eucalyptus oil

CHEF'S NOTE

Szechuan pepper isn't related to the black, green or white (all from the same plant) that we all know. Of the same family of trees and shrubs, Szechuan pepper is more closely related to oranges and lemons than to black pepper.

To make the coeur coulant, melt the chocolate in a bowl set over a few inches of simmering (not boiling) water. The bowl must not touch the water. Sprinkle in half the pepper and taste. Adjust with more to your liking. Cool the chocolate until it is malleable. Form into 6 balls and freeze.

For the fondant, first preheat oven to 180°C/350°F/Gas Mark 4.

Melt the chocolate with the butter in the same manner as for the coeur coulant, and cool slightly. Mix the flour, eggs and sugar in a separate bowl until combined. Fold the chocolate into the egg mixture.

Put 6 fondant moulds (or large ramekins) on a baking tray and divide the mixture evenly between them. Drop one ball of coeur coulant into the centre of each fondant. Bake for 7 minutes.

Meanwhile, in a clean, cold bowl, whisk the cream to soft peaks. Add the icing sugar and 2 drops of eucalyptus oil, and whisk to firm peaks. Taste and adjust by stirring in more eucalyptus oil to taste.

To serve, first carefully run a thin knife around the edge of each mould to loosen the fondants. Turn them out onto plates and serve immediately with a dollop of eucalyptus cream.

COMING UP IN THE KITCHEN

LESLEY McSWEENEY

HAZELWOOD LODGE

• •

Chefs of the Burren hail from many places, near and far, but some who come from relatively near, like Lesley McSweeney from Crecora in County Limerick, travelled far and wide to get here.

Unlike many Irish chefs who travel to the continent, Australia or Southeast Asia to hone their cookery chops, Lesley headed to South Africa, Egypt, Namibia, Mozambique, Madagascar, Jamaica and the like – not working, per se, but always travelling with a culinary eye out for flavours, techniques, equipment and experiences. You can hear the passion for those travels in her voice and you can taste them in her cooking.

She, like her older brother and sister, grew up with their parents managing various hotels and catering operations around the west of Ireland. Unlike her siblings, however, she didn't run from the business but, rather, embraced it at an early age. It wasn't uncommon for her to be brought along to the hotels when she was not in school, and hotel kitchens and corridors became her childhood playgrounds.

By thirteen, she was washing up in the kitchen of a hotel her father managed in Shannon. The head chef was keen to share the basic skills with young Lesley and she graduated to making sandwiches and simple salads. So enamoured with the hustle and bustle of kitchen life was she that, at sixteen, when it came time to decide what to do after school, she decided on professional catering college at Limerick IT.

Love of food and cooking led to love of a romantic sort when she met her partner, Darren, while both were working in the kitchen of Wild Honey in Lisdoonvarna. It was with Darren that she took some of her most memorable culinary travel adventures.

Living in a beachside hut in Madagascar stands out boldly in our conversation. Buying herbs and fresh spices from women on the streets, local fishermen bringing their catch from which to choose, purchasing only what you would cook for your next meal as there was no refrigeration or storage. It sounds like a chef's dream … and for the young couple it was.

A bit more moving around jobs in Ireland and Lesley was pregnant with the couple's first daughter, Liv. It was about then that her parents, Victor and Geraldine, decided to stop managing other people's properties and purchase a guesthouse in Clare. The timing seemed right, the opportunity was on point and, well, let's just say that she felt she could work for her potential new bosses.

SHE DIDN'T RUN FROM THE BUSINESS BUT, RATHER, EMBRACED IT AT AN EARLY AGE

Desiring to infuse the international flavours she'd come to love into produce as locally sourced as possible, a large kitchen garden and polytunnels were constructed on the property and relationships with local purveyors and artisan producers were established. Respecting the fact that many of the guests they anticipated would be health-conscious walkers, hikers and artists from the Burren College of Art, the family team made the decision to emphasise, though omnivores themselves, a vegetarian menu for both breakfast and the occasional group dinner they offer to tour groups. Lesley even cultured wild yeast starter for the sourdough breads she bakes daily.

With their second daughter, Rye, joining the family in 2018, the fact that the couple live just across the garden from her kitchen and that Darren works nights at a local seafood restaurant while she works days at the lodge keeps the growing family on an even keel during the busiest months of the year. They all love the buzz of meeting people who are travelling from all over the world to experience a place they get to see out their windows every day. That said, managing a growing family, preparing twenty-plus made-to-order breakfasts, scratch baking and a fair bit of dinner trade for tour groups, seven days a week from April to November, can wring out the strongest of young chefs.

The couple take the opportunity of the off-season to travel, to see how other chefs are cooking, how other hotels are meeting guest needs. That it makes for a bit of well-earned relaxation after a hard-fought season is a bonus to the research trips. Until the girls are older, those research trips will most likely be around Ireland. Something tells me, however, that Liv and Rye had better have extra pages in their passports.

FROM THE KITCHEN GARDEN

· ·

Some will use this vegetarian menu as parts to accompany omnivorous menus. That's fine! These recipes are strong enough to stand on their own, but do prepare the lot now and again. I keep Lesley's peperonata in the fridge at all times. And the homemade ricotta … oh, yeah! If meadowsweet for the ice cream isn't in season, replace it with Oonagh O'Dwyer's gorse-flower sorbet (page 222). You'll not go wrong.

STARTER
Homemade lemon ricotta with golden beetroot salad
MAIN
Sweet potato and courgette fritters, peperonata stew and dukkah spice
DESSERT
Roasted peaches with meadowsweet ice cream and pistachio-cranberry biscotti

HOMEMADE LEMON RICOTTA WITH GOLDEN BEETROOT SALAD

. . . .

Serves 6

For the lemon ricotta

500 ml/18 fl oz/2 cups full-fat (whole)
    milk

250 ml/8 fl oz/1 cup cream

4 lemons, juiced

1 pinch sea salt

For the salad

1 golden beetroot, peeled and grated

1 orange, zested and juiced

Coarse sea salt

100 g/3½ oz baby rocket (arugula) leaves

1 orange, cut into supreme segments
    (without skin or membrane)

60 g/2 oz/½ cup hazelnuts, toasted and
    chopped

To make the lemon ricotta, combine the milk, cream and lemon juice in a saucepan. Bring to a simmer over medium heat, stirring constantly. When the liquid breaks into curds and whey, remove from heat and season with a pinch of sea salt. Pour into a cheese bag (or double thickness of cheesecloth or muslin tied into a pouch), tie the bag to the handle of a wooden spoon set across the mouth of a deep bowl and place in the refrigerator to drain overnight.

For the salad, toss the grated beetroot with the juice and zest of the orange. Season with salt to taste. Arrange the rocket leaves and orange segments on a salad plate. Mound the beetroot on the plate, add a dollop of ricotta and garnish with toasted hazelnuts. Season with sea salt to taste.

CHEF'S NOTE

Often made from the protein-rich whey left over from making mozzarella cheese, ricotta can also be made, as in this recipe, with full-fat milk. The key to making it well is to use a low and even heat. If you have an inconsistent hob, try heating the milk in a bain-marie (double-boiler).

SWEET POTATO AND COURGETTE FRITTERS, PEPERONATA STEW AND DUKKAH SPICE

Serves 6

For the peperonata

2 red peppers, deseeded and cut in
    2 cm/¾-inch slices

2 yellow peppers, deseeded and cut in
    2 cm/¾-inch slices

2 tbsp olive oil

2 red onions, peeled and thinly sliced

2 cloves garlic, crushed

Pinch salt and pepper

4 plum tomatoes, chopped

1 tbsp pimenton smoked paprika

2 tbsp sherry vinegar

1 tsp brown sugar

225 g/8 oz baby spinach

For the fritters

200 g/7 oz sweet potato, peeled and
  grated

200 g/7 oz courgette (zucchini), grated

1 clove garlic, crushed

1 tsp Ras el Hanout spice blend

2 eggs, whisked

150 g/5¼ oz/1 cup rice flour (chickpea
flour can be substituted)

1 pinch smoked sea salt

1 pinch cracked black pepper

60 ml/2 fl oz/¼ cup olive oil

To make the peperonata, place a large saucepan over medium–low heat, then add the peppers and olive oil. Cover and cook slowly for 10 to 15 minutes until soft. Add the onions, garlic, salt and pepper. Cook, uncovered, for a further 15 minutes, stirring occasionally, until onions are softened and sweet.

Add the chopped tomatoes, smoked paprika, vinegar and sugar. Reduce heat to low and continue cooking for another 15 minutes. Fold in the spinach and cook until wilted. Season to taste. (Peperonata can be made up to 4 days in advance, without the spinach, and kept sealed in the refrigerator. Simply heat back to temperature before adding the spinach.)

To make the fritters, first preheat oven to 120°C/250°F/ Gas Mark ½.

In a large bowl, toss the sweet potato, courgette, garlic and spice together. Fold in eggs, then fold in flour until completely mixed. Season with salt and pepper.

Heat a non-stick skillet over medium–high heat. Add 2 tbsp of oil and heat until shimmering.

Scoop the desired portion of batter into pan, pat down a bit and fry until golden, which takes about 4 minutes. Flip the fritter and cook until done. Transfer to a plate lined with several layers of kitchen paper (paper towel). Put the plate in the oven to keep warm while cooking the rest of the fritters. Repeat until all fritters are done, adding more oil as needed.

For the dukkah spice

2 tbsp sunflower seeds

60 g/½ cup hazelnuts

2 tbsp sesame seeds

30 g/¼ cup almonds

1 tsp cumin

3 tbsp coriander seeds

1 tsp fennel seeds

1 tbsp pimenton smoked paprika

1 tsp smoked sea salt

To make the dukkah, place a dry sauté pan over medium–high heat, add the sunflower seeds, hazelnuts, sesame seeds and almonds. Toast for 2 to 3 minutes, shaking the pan often, until light brown and fragrant. Remove to a cool plate. Return the pan to the heat and add the cumin, coriander and fennel seeds. Toast as before and remove to plate to cool. Add the cooled nuts and seeds to a blender or in batches to a spice grinder. Pulse to grind into a coarse mixture and pour into a mixing bowl. Fold in the smoked paprika and smoked sea salt. Store in an airtight container or jar.

When ready to serve, scoop the stew into warm bowls, top with fritters and sprinkle with dukkah spice. Lovely served with thick chargrilled sourdough bread drizzled with olive oil.

ROASTED PEACHES WITH MEADOWSWEET ICE CREAM AND PISTACHIO-CRANBERRY BISCOTTI

Serves 6

For the biscotti

3 egg whites

1 pinch salt

100 g/3½ oz/½ cup caster (superfine) sugar

1 lemon, zested

100 g/3½ oz/1⅓ cups plain (all-purpose) flour

50 g/1¾ oz/¼ cup dried cranberries

50 g/1¾ oz/½ cup pistachios, coarsely chopped

For the ice cream

6 egg yolks

120 g/4 oz/⅔ cup sugar

375 ml/13 fl oz/1½ cups milk

375 ml/13 fl oz/1½ cups cream

12 meadowsweet heads, reserve 2 (or substitute with half a split vanilla pod)

For the peaches

Peach stock:

- 1 ripe peach, stoned and chopped
- 2 oranges, juiced, one zested coarsely
- 1 lemon, coarsely zested
- 2 tbsp local honey
- 1 star anise

6 ripe peaches, halved and stones removed

To make the biscotti, first preheat oven to 160°C/320°F/Gas Mark 3. In a clean bowl, whisk the egg whites to soft peaks, gradually adding salt and sugar until stiff. Fold in the lemon zest, flour, cranberries and pistachios. Spread the mixture evenly onto a baking tray lined with greaseproof paper and bake for 15 to 20 minutes. Remove and cool on a rack.

Once cool, cut into 1¼ cm (½-inch) slices and arrange cut side up on the baking tray. Return to the oven and bake until they are crisp and firm, approximately 10 more minutes. Cool completely and store in airtight container. They will keep for up to a week.

To make the ice cream, whisk the egg yolks and sugar in a bowl until the mixture thickens and is paler in colour. In a saucepan over medium–low heat, stir milk, cream and meadowsweet until you see little bubbles – do not boil. Remove from the heat and set aside to infuse for 30 minutes. Strain the liquid and slowly whisk into the egg mixture.

Pour into a large, heavy-bottomed pot and heat on low, stirring constantly, until thick enough to coat the back of a wooden spoon. Strain through a fine mesh sieve and cool completely. Cover and chill overnight for best results. The next day, churn in ice-cream maker as per the manufacturer's instructions.

For the peaches, first preheat oven to 160°C/320°F/Gas Mark 3. To make the stock, combine the chopped peach, juice, zest, honey and star anise in a saucepan with 250 ml/8 fl oz/1 cup water. Bring to a boil over high heat.

Reduce heat and simmer for 15 minutes. Strain into another saucepan and simmer until reduced to a syrup.

Place the stoned peach halves on a baking tray lined with tinfoil. Roast in preheated oven for 10 minutes or until soft and then remove from oven. Preheat grill (broiler) to high. (At this point you can peel the peaches if you like.) Glaze the peaches with syrup and place under grill (broiler) until they begin to brown and bubble.

Serve the warm peaches with the biscotti and a scoop of ice cream.

CAME FOR THE WEEKEND ...

ROBBIE McCAULEY

GREGANS CASTLE

· ·

Robbie McCauley's mother, from a large dairy farm in Barefield north of Ennis, and his father, an engineer from Edinburgh, met when they were working in London. Young Robbie and his two sisters (along with many neighbours and family friends) enjoyed the country cooking his mother brought from the Clare farm to the capital of Scotland. They also enjoyed the food on annual trips to a small Italian village during their formative years.

Although he was planning a career in engineering like his father, Robbie took a summer job at the gourmet grocery Waitrose while still at school. With the looming economic crash beginning to show itself over the horizon, however, Robbie knew that any engineering jobs he might find after graduation would probably be in the Middle East. He considered an offer from his employer to accept a fully paid apprenticeship at the Royal Academy of Culinary Arts. He found out that he was accepted to the programme the night before his first Advanced Higher exams. He tells me that his first day's results were very good. After the fact sank in that he was one of only thirty to be accepted into the prestigious culinary programme, so too did the rest of his engineering exam grades sink.

Now, as a classically trained chef myself, I cannot overstate just how impressive the Royal Academy's training programme is. In fact, of the thirty who entered the programme with Robbie, only sixteen eventually finished with qualification: just over 50 per cent.

For four annual periods of three months each, the students are drilled at an intensive residential programme. Intensive because the placements to which the young apprentices are sent are all five-star hotels and eateries – many with Michelin stars. Robbie himself was headed for the exclusive Royal Automobile Club on Pall Mall for his placement.

There he worked long hours seven days a week from the time he was sixteen until he graduated just after his twenty-first birthday. He cooked for heads of state, of industry and of society. Queen Elizabeth II was a guest of the club as were several other members of the royal family. One fund-raising dinner saw the kitchen staff augmented by a cadre of chefs who held a collective fifty Michelin stars. This kind of experience for a young apprentice – not yet eighteen years of age – is nearly unheard of in the modern age of culinary education.

Upon completion of the Royal Academy programme, Robbie returned to Edinburgh and a job at the one-star restaurant at The Balmoral, where he soon realised he wasn't seeing much of those friends who had graduated university and were now in nine-to-five jobs, Monday through Friday. After nearly five years without a holiday, he joined a small group of mates and travelled

HE COOKED FOR HEADS OF STATE, OF INDUSTRY AND OF SOCIETY

around Southeast Asia for six months. Experiencing the place with friends, but also with a classically trained palate, Robbie's trip was relaxing but his chef's brain was never fully switched off.

As the holiday wound down, along with his financial reserves, Robbie started emailing CVs from internet cafés to respectable houses around the UK. As he remembered County Clare fondly from the summers of his youth and knew the Gregans Castle reputation, he thought it worth a try to get in touch there as well.

That was 2013 – the depths of the recession – and few chefs were looking to hire new talent. Gregans, however, had an opening and offered Robbie a weekend trial once he returned from holidays. He stayed for three years.

Four months in, Robbie was the de facto sous-chef and worked closely with the head chef to bring dining at Gregans back up to the levels everyone knew the place deserved. It was exactly what both chef and restaurant needed, and exactly when they needed it. But as is oft the case in the culinary world, in order to move up, one must move on … sort of.

To the one-star restaurant Campagne, in Kilkenny, as official sous-chef was his next move. Never desiring to cut the cord with his old friends who'd given him a chance when times were difficult, Robbie spent his days off coming back to the Burren to work a couple of shifts at Gregans Castle. When the head chef position became open, Robbie was the logical fit for the job.

Working where he has, Robbie has had access to the best produce from around the world – the kind of ingredients that make most chefs green with envy. That he chooses to use the suppliers that he now does isn't simply because they are local. It's because the produce – the cheese, the game, the shellfish, the smoked salmon and so on – are some of the best in the world. And he gets to serve this food in a room that looks down the valley, across the rocks and out across the bay. He feels it a privilege to help put a new coat of polish on one of Ireland's culinary gems here in the Burren.

GAME ON!

When the chef is also a hunter, you're in for quite a meal. Robbie's menu of rustic elegance is bookended with clean flavours and honest preparation. The sides are practically a meal in themselves. Although perfect as it stands, you could exchange one of the vegetables for Cathleen Connole's minted marrowfat peas (page 241) if you wanted to lighten things a bit.

STARTER
Prawns with fresh mayonnaise and sourdough bread
MAIN
Venison Wellington with game sauce
SIDES
Bacon-roasted Brussels sprouts
Glazed parsnips
Braised red cabbage
Boulangère potatoes
DESSERT
Pear and almond tart

PRAWNS WITH FRESH MAYONNAISE AND SOURDOUGH BREAD

Serves 6

3 egg yolks

20 ml/1 tbsp + 1 tsp good white wine
vinegar

1 tsp Dijon mustard

1 lemon, zested

Salt to taste

100 ml/3½ fl oz/⅓ cup + 4 tsp olive oil

200 ml/7 fl oz/¾ cup + 4 tsp vegetable oil

24 large fresh prawns (langoustines)

1 loaf of fresh sourdough

Place the egg yolks, vinegar, mustard and lemon zest in a large bowl and whisk. Season lightly. Slowly add the oils in a thin stream while whisking vigorously, until all the oil is emulsified and the sauce is thick. Season to taste with salt.

Place a large, heavy pot of well-salted water on to boil over high heat. When boiling rapidly, add the prawns and cook for 4 minutes. Strain and serve immediately with fresh mayonnaise and thickly sliced bread.

CHEF'S NOTE

For best results when making mayonnaise, use a large, clean bowl and a wire balloon whisk to help emulsify the oil into the egg yolk evenly. Make it in small batches as the raw egg will reduce its refrigerated life to 2 days. But do make it – and make it often!

VENISON WELLINGTON WITH GAME SAUCE

Serves 6

For the pancakes

100 g/3½ oz/⅓ cups plain (all-purpose) flour

1 pinch sea salt

1 egg

250 ml/8 fl oz/1 cup milk

1 handful chives, snipped

1 handful flat-leaf parsley, minced

Drop of oil

For the venison

2 tbsp olive oil

1 kg/2 lb 4 oz venison loin, well-trimmed

2 tbsp English mustard

For the duxelles

300 g/10½ oz mixed wild mushrooms, cleaned and trimmed

Sea salt and freshly ground black pepper

150 g/5¼ oz venison liver, chopped fine

60 ml/2 fl oz/¼ cup cream

For the game sauce

1 shallot, minced

15 g/½ oz/1 tbsp butter

1 sprig thyme

300 ml/½ pint/1¼ cups port

600 ml/1 pint/2⅓ cups fresh game stock (or chicken stock)

30 g/1 oz/2 tbsp butter, cold and cut into small pieces

For assembling

6 slices prosciutto

500 g/1 lb 2 oz all-butter puff pastry (frozen is just fine)

3 egg yolks, beaten

To make the pancakes, sift the flour and salt into a large bowl. In a small bowl, whisk the egg and milk together. Gradually whisk the egg and milk mixture into the flour and stir in the herbs. In a non-stick skillet over medium–high heat, add a drop of oil and swirl to coat. Add 60 ml/2 fl oz/¼ cup of batter to the pan, tilting to cover the pan with a thin layer. Cook until the edges begin to dry and curl up just a bit. Flip and cook for another 30 to 40 seconds, then remove to a plate to cool. Repeat with remaining batter. (Pancakes can be made up to 2 days in advance, wrapped in cling film and refrigerated.)

For the venison, place a large skillet over a high heat. When the pan is hot, add a tablespoon of the oil. Sear the venison loin for 2 minutes on each side to brown. Remove the meat from the pan, brush all over with the mustard and leave to cool.

To make the duxelles, place the mushrooms in the bowl of a food processor. Pulse 3 to 4 times in two-second pulses to mince. Place the pan used to sear the venison back on high heat with the remaining tablespoon of oil. Add the mushrooms, season with sea salt and fresh black pepper. Do not stir for 3 minutes. Then stir the mushrooms and cook until the moisture has evaporated and they become a thick paste. Stir in the liver and cook for 1 minute. Add the cream, reduce heat to medium and cook until it becomes a thick, uniform paste. Season again with sea salt and pepper. Transfer to a bowl to cool.

To make the game sauce, place a saucepan over medium–high heat and sweat the shallot in butter with the thyme and a pinch of sea salt. Add the port and reduce by two-thirds. Add the stock, bring to a boil and reduce heat to medium. Simmer until reduced by two-thirds and sauce is thick. Strain into a clean saucepan and set aside (can be made up to 2 days in advance). When you're ready to serve, warm the sauce and stir in the butter, one piece at a time, to make it silky – do not boil.

Continued overleaf

To assemble the Wellington, lay 2 to 3 large sheets of cling film overlapping each other on a clean work surface. Lay the slices of prosciutto overlapping lengthways in 2 rows of 3. Spread the mushroom duxelles evenly over the prosciutto. Place the venison loin on top and roll tightly into a sausage. Refrigerate while you lay out the pancakes.

Lay 2 to 3 pieces of cling film as before. Trim 3 to 4 pancakes into squares and lay them overlapping on the cling film. Remove the cling film from the prosciutto-wrapped venison and place the meat on the pancakes. Roll tightly, again in cling film, and refrigerate while you roll out the pastry.

Roll the pastry into a large rectangle big enough to wrap the meat easily. Brush the pastry with some of the egg yolk. Remove the cling film from the pancake-wrapped venison, place on the pastry and roll to completely encase. Tuck in the ends and trim off any excess, which can be cut into shapes for decorating the Wellington if desired. Lay out more cling film and finally roll into a tight package to get an evenly thick log. Tie the ends of the cling film to keep the package tight. Refrigerate overnight or freeze for an hour.

Preheat oven to 220°C/430°F/Gas Mark 7. Remove cling film, decorate with pastry shapes if desired and brush the Wellington all over with egg yolk. Place on a baking tray lined with greaseproof paper. Bake for 50 minutes for medium rare (internal temperature of 48°C/188°F), dropping to 180°C/300°F/Gas Mark 4 if the pastry is browning too much. Remove from the oven to rest for 20 minutes (if you prefer the meat well done, turn off the oven and let it rest inside).

Trim the end of the pastry, carefully carve into slices 4 cm/1½ inches thick and serve with game sauce and Robbie's glorious side dishes.

BACON-ROASTED BRUSSELS SPROUTS

Serves 6

50g/1¾ oz /¼ cup sea salt

500 g/1 lb 2 oz Brussels sprouts, trimmed
   and halved

2 tbsp olive oil

100 g/3½ oz streaky rashers (bacon), diced

Bring a large pot of heavily salted water to a boil. Add the sprouts and cook for 2 minutes. Refresh in ice-cold water until they are cold and then dry on a tea towel.

In a skillet over medium–high heat, add oil and bacon. Cook, stirring often, until it begins to crisp. Increase heat to high and add the Brussels sprouts. Toss and cook until the sprouts are caramelised and the bacon is crisp, then transfer to a warmed serving dish.

GLAZED PARSNIPS

Serves 6

9 parsnips, peeled, topped and tailed, left
   whole

250 g/9 oz /1¼ cups butter

150 g/5¼ oz/¾ cup sugar

3 tsp salt

4 star anise

Use a clean scourer to rough the parsnips so that the glaze sticks.

In a large saucepan, combine 400 ml/14 fl oz/1⅔ cups water with the butter, sugar, salt and star anise. Bring to the boil over high heat, then reduce to medium.

Add the parsnips. Cook until the parsnips are tender (approximately 45 minutes) and liquid has reduced by half.

Remove the parsnips, increase heat to high and reduce cooking liquid to a glaze. Toss the parsnips in the glaze and serve.

BRAISED RED CABBAGE

Serves 6

1 head red cabbage, cored and sliced

1 onion, sliced

200 ml/7 fl oz/¾ cup + 4 tsp port

1 stick cinnamon

1 pinch ground cloves

2 star anise

2 tbsp brown sugar

1 tbsp red wine vinegar

4 pears, peeled and diced

Sea salt

In a large casserole (Dutch oven) over a low heat, place all the ingredients, except the pears, and cover with a tight-fitting lid. Cook for 1 hour, then stir in the diced pears. Cover and cook for an additional hour until the cabbage is quite tender. If at any point the cabbage looks dry, add a splash of water. If there is still liquid in the pan at the end, uncover and increase heat to evaporate it. Season with a little salt and serve.

BOULANGÈRE POTATOES

Serves 6

2 onions, thinly sliced

3 sprigs thyme

100 g/3½ oz/½ cup butter

1.5 kg/3⅔ lb floury potatoes, peeled and thinly sliced using a mandoline

400 ml/14 fl oz/1⅔ cups chicken stock

Preheat oven to 200°C/400°F/Gas Mark 6.

In a sauté pan over medium heat, sweat the onions and thyme with butter until softened and lightly coloured (about 5 minutes).

In a buttered 2 litre/1 quart gratin dish, shingle one layer of potatoes. Sprinkle with a third of the onion mixture. Repeat with potato and onion, finishing with potato. Pour the stock over the potatoes.

Place the dish on a baking tray and bake in the middle of the preheated oven for 50 to 60 minutes until the potatoes are fully cooked and the top is golden and crisp.

PEAR AND ALMOND TART

Serves 6

For the pastry

350 g/12¼ oz/2½ cups plain (all-purpose) flour

1 pinch salt

170 g/6 oz/¾ cup + 1 tbsp unsalted butter, cold and cut into cubes

100 g/3½ oz/1⅓ cups icing sugar

3 egg yolks

For the filling

6 ripe Comice pears, peeled, halved and cored

350 g/12 oz/1¾ cups unsalted butter, softened

350 g/12 oz/1¾ cups caster (superfine) sugar

350 g/12 oz blanched whole almonds

3 eggs

50 g/1¾ oz/½ cup flaked almonds

To make the pastry, pulse the flour, salt and butter in the bowl of a food processor until it resembles coarse breadcrumbs. Add the sugar, pulse, then add the egg yolks and pulse again. The mixture will immediately combine and leave the sides of the bowl. Remove, wrap in cling film and chill for at least an hour.

Preheat oven to 180°C/350°F/Gas Mark 4.

Using a box grater, coarsely grate the pastry dough into a 30 cm/12 inch loose-bottomed fluted tin. Press the dough evenly into the bottom and sides of the tin. Blind bake the shell for 20 minutes until very light brown. Cool for 30 minutes.

Reduce the oven temperature to 150°C/300F/Gas Mark 2. To make the filling, first arrange the pears face down in the tart shell. Then, in a stand mixer, cream the butter and sugar until pale, scraping down the sides. Pulse the almonds in a food processor to chop finely and add to the sugar and butter mixture. On medium speed, beat in the eggs one by one, scraping down in between each. Pour the mixture over the pears and sprinkle with flaked almonds. Bake for 40 minutes. Allow to cool on a rack for at least 20 minutes before serving with crème fraîche or ice cream.

CHEF'S NOTE

Whenever making shortcrust pastry, as for this recipe, double the batch size. You can then wrap and freeze half so the next time you're called upon to make a pie or tart, the first half of the recipe is already done.

A GROUNDED WANDERER

VIVIAN 'VIV' KELLY

THE BURREN STOREHOUSE

. . . .

Until he was ten years old, the family farm in Mayo upon which Vivian 'Viv' Kelly grew up with his five brothers and one sister was self-sufficient. That might sound like a stretch to some, as this was only thirty years ago, but he assures me that his grandmother bought in only sugar, flour and teabags. Beyond that, it was all raised, grown, shot, caught, foraged or bartered foods that the family ate.

This did not mean that the family ate poorly. In fact, Viv says, they 'ate like kings'. Wild salmon, lobsters, mussels, cockles, pheasant, grouse, squab, rabbit, organic vegetables, Burren lamb and beef … the list of foods with which their simple farmhouse table was laden was, indeed, the stuff Viv would one day serve in restaurants to diners coming from around the world for his cooking.

When it came time to decide what to do after secondary school, his principal helped him apply to catering college. In 1994 he began his formal training at Galway-Mayo Institute of Technology, a course he loved and at which he excelled.

Viv worked in local hotels to support himself during college. Basic hotels, he says, but good places to learn the ropes and practical applications of the theory he was being taught in the classroom. Mindful of the diversity of jobs that might be available after graduation, he took his first placement at a high-end restaurant in the busy tourist town of Dingle and his second at a large-volume wedding hotel in Donegal town.

Viv made the conscious decision that the first several years of his newly minted career would find him moving employment every nine to eighteen months. He moved from hotels to restaurants, from what he calls 'industrial' volume kitchens to smaller fine-dining restaurants owned by chefs, all the while honing his skills, keeping his eyes, ears and mind open to what was happening around him.

New York and Scotland offered experience beyond the Irish shores. In New York he found work at a busy mid-town Manhattan pub where they served as many as 350 lunches in an hour. Manhattan cooking was an eye-opening experience for the young chef: terminology, ingredients, the variety of foods offered from one kitchen. Everything about how the American kitchen worked seemed to be different but familiar, the way a sunrise and a sunset across the Atlantic that separated Viv from his Mayo home were.

The new millennium found him back in Ireland, in the Connemara capital of Clifden, at a popular seafood restaurant. Although the second youngest in the kitchen, Viv was made head chef at the

THE CREAM ALWAYS RISES TO THE TOP

tender age of just twenty-one. Agency work brought him to Ennistymon for his first job to last beyond two years. He brought dishes he'd learned from America – like red-wine-braised lamb shanks – to Clare.

As he'd been climbing from one job to the next so frequently, there hadn't been much time for long-term relationships. Two years in one place afforded him time to meet a woman and begin a family. Over the next six years, the couple had three children, Katie, Eoin and Liam – all bright and talented, and one has inherited his dad's love of cooking.

While raising their family, the couple took a lease on a property in Doolin, which they christened The Lazy Lobster, and ran it with great success. A neighbour, returned from a holiday in America, presented Viv with a travel article from *The Washington Post*. In it, Viv's restaurant and his food were given high praise. 'The cream always rises to the top' was how the writer titled the article.

Anyone who knows the restaurant business knows the time and effort it takes to be successful. The same can be said for anyone who has ever raised a family. After closing The Lazy Lobster, Viv decided that doing both was impossible for him, so he left the business and took over as head tour guide at Aillwee Cave for seven years. The regular hours – something few chefs would recognise – allowed him to spend more time raising his children.

Viv's fade from the scene became something of a legend in Clare. Why did the rising star suddenly disappear from the culinary sky? Where did he go? Would he come back?

After nearly a decade of guiding people through the subterranean Burren, Viv Kelly emerged back onto the Burren food scene, first helping chef friends, then deciding that his children were old enough for him to head back into the fray full-time.

The food world had changed while Viv was 'underground'. Diners' tastes and expectations had changed. Food fashion had changed, then changed again, only to change once more. The food Viv Kelly serves at The Burren Storehouse – as well as many of the Roadside Tavern's nightly specials he creates – reflect his culinary knowledge and training along with food memories from his gran's table. It's the kind of cooking from the soul that never goes out of fashion.

A TASTE OF GRAN'S TABLE

Viv Kelly's menu isn't what his gran would have served him as a child. It is, however, based on the love of food, frugal use of ingredients and pride of place that he learned in her kitchen. The chowder comes together in minutes and the lamb braises easily. Do take the extra time and effort to make the deep-fried cabbage – it's amazing! If it's just not your thing, try Siobhán Ní Gháirbhith's Romanian cabbage slaw (page 198) and you'll still get your cabbage for the day.

STARTER
Gran's smoked haddock and potato chowder
MAIN
Slow-roasted lamb belly with potato-sage stuffing and Madeira cream
SIDE
'Beer-pura' fried cabbage
DESSERT
Pecan and maple baked cheesecake

GRAN'S SMOKED HADDOCK AND POTATO CHOWDER

Serves 6

60 g/2 oz/4 tbsp butter, cut into chunks

2 small onions, finely diced

1 leek, sliced

4 stalks celery, sliced

1 litre/1¾ pints/4 cups fish stock (see
   Chef's Note)

720 g/1 lb 10 oz smoked haddock, cubed

480 g/17 oz/2 cups potatoes, cooked and
   diced

60 ml/2 fl oz/¼ cup cream

Sea salt and black pepper

Chives, snipped (optional)

In a heavy-bottomed casserole (Dutch oven) over medium heat, melt the butter. Add the onions and sweat until soft, about 3 to 4 minutes, stirring occasionally. Stir in leek and celery, and sweat for a further 2 minutes. Add the stock and bring to a boil. Gently fold in the haddock and return to a boil. Add the cooked potato and reduce heat to medium for 3 to 4 minutes. Pour in cream and simmer for 2 to 3 minutes, season to taste and garnish with chives if using.

CHEF'S NOTE

Fish stock is perhaps the easiest of the so-called 'bone broths' to make, and certainly the fastest: 1 kg whitefish bones, cut into 10 cm (4-inch) pieces; 1 leek, sliced; 2 stalks celery, sliced; 4–5 white mushrooms, chopped; 1 bay leaf; a few black peppercorns; 2 tbsp white wine; and cold water to cover. Bring to a hard simmer over medium–high heat, skim the foam that will rise to the top, lower heat and simmer for 20 to 30 minutes, no more. Strain, chill and there you have it. Divide into 1 litre-sized ziplock freezer bags and freeze till needed.

SLOW-ROASTED LAMB BELLY WITH POTATO-SAGE STUFFING AND MADEIRA CREAM

Serves 6

For the stuffing

60 g/2 oz/4 tbsp butter

3 small onions, roughly chopped

3 cloves garlic, crushed

50 g/1½ oz fresh sage

750 g/1 lb 4 oz potato, diced and steamed

1 lamb belly, both sides (have your butcher take out breastbone and silver skin, then split in two)

Sea salt and freshly ground black pepper

For the Madeira cream

60 g/2 oz/4 tbsp butter

2 shallots, finely chopped

1 tsp cracked black peppercorns

1 bay leaf

½ tsp dried thyme

½ glass red wine

1 glass Madeira

30 ml/1 fl oz/2 tsp cream

Sea salt and freshly ground black pepper

To make the stuffing, place a medium-sized saucepan over medium heat, melt the butter, then add onions and a pinch of salt. Sweat until soft (about 5 minutes). Add garlic and sweat until fragrant, about 1 minute. Add sage and cook for one minute. Add cooked potato and increase heat to medium–high for 3 to 4 minutes. Set aside.

Preheat oven to 130°C/270°F/Gas Mark ½.

Season both sides of each piece of lamb belly and lay on a flat work surface, lengthwise left to right. Divide the stuffing between the two bellies, placing the stuffing on the third closest to you. Fold up from the bottom and roll tightly, but not so tight as to squeeze out the stuffing. Tie with butcher's twine every 8–10 cm (3–4 inches).

Place them in a deep roasting tray and add enough water to come 2.5 cm/1 inch up the bellies. Cover with foil and place in the middle of the preheated oven. Roast for 1½ to 2 hours until tender. Remove the foil, increase heat to 180°C/350°F/Gas Mark 4 for 10 to 15 minutes to brown the meat and reduce the cooking liquid. Remove the lamb to a cooling rack over a plate to catch the juices and loosely cover with foil. Reserve the pan juices.

For the Madeira cream, place a saucepan over medium–high heat, melt the butter, then add the shallots with a pinch of salt and cook until soft. Add peppercorns, bay leaf and thyme and stir until fragrant.

Add the wine and Madeira and bring to a boil. Reduce to medium heat and simmer. Reduce the liquid by half. Add the cooking juices from the roasting tin and plate under the lamb. Reduce by a quarter. Stir in cream and season to taste. Serve in a jug alongside the lamb.

'BEER-PURA' FRIED CABBAGE

Serves 6

6 outer leaves Savoy cabbage, washed and
ribbed

For the batter

125 g/4½ oz/1 cup plain (all-purpose)
flour

½ tsp sea salt

250 ml/8 fl oz/1 cup beer or lager

100 ml/3½ fl oz/⅓ cup + 4 tsp sparkling
water

2 litres/3½ pints/8 cups oil for frying

125 g/4½ oz/1 cup plain (all-purpose)
additional flour for dredging

1 tbsp sea salt

Set a large pot of heavily salted water over a high heat to
boil. Blanch the cabbage leaves for 3 to 4 minutes, then
refresh in cold water. Drain the cabbage and set on a tea
towel.

To make the batter, whisk the flour, salt, beer and
sparkling water in a bowl until smooth.

Preheat oil in a large casserole (Dutch oven) to
180°C/350°F.

Mix the additional flour and salt together in a deep dish.
Dip the cooked cabbage leaves in flour, then into the
batter and deep fry in the hot oil for 3 to 4 minutes until
crispy. Remove to a rack or kitchen paper set in a baking
tray to drain. Season with fine sea salt.

CHEF'S NOTE

For a lighter and crispier batter for this
dish, use pastry or cake flour. If you can't
find those on your grocer's shelves, add a
tablespoon or two of cornflour (corn starch)
to plain flour to reduce the protein content
of the mixture.

PECAN AND MAPLE BAKED CHEESECAKE

. . . .

Serves 6

For the base

225 g/8 oz shortbread biscuits (packaged or use Hugh Robson's from page 27)

30 g/1 oz/2 tbsp unsalted butter plus more for greasing

For the filling

625 g/22 oz cream cheese

225 g/8 oz/1 cup + 2 tbsp light brown sugar

½ tsp salt

3 eggs

120 ml/4 fl oz/½ cup cream

2 tsp vanilla extract

For the topping

20 g/¾ oz/4 tsp butter

50 g/1¾ oz/⅓ cup pecans, roughly chopped

75 g/2 ½ oz shortbread biscuits, crumbled

25 g/¾ oz/2 tbsp light brown sugar

For the maple sauce

30 g/1 oz/2 tbsp butter

50 g/1¾ oz/¼ cup caster sugar

80 ml/3 fl oz/⅓ cup maple syrup

120 ml/4 fl oz/½ cup cream

Preheat oven to 140°C/280°F/Gas Mark 1. Butter a 23 cm/9-inch springform tin and line the bottom with greaseproof paper.

For the base, crush the shortbread into coarse crumbs, melt the butter and mix together in a bowl. Sprinkle the crumbs onto the base of the prepared tin.

To make the filling, beat the cream cheese, sugar and salt in a stand mixer until light. With the motor running on slow, beat in eggs, one at a time, scraping down in between. Fold in the cream and vanilla extract. Pour the mix over the biscuit base and smooth with the back of a spoon. Bake for 50 to 60 minutes until set.

Meanwhile, to make the topping, melt the butter in a saucepan over a low heat. Add the pecans and cook for 1 to 2 minutes until fragrant. Add the shortbread and sugar and cook for 2 to 3 minutes. Leave aside to cool.

Once the cheesecake has set, remove to a rack, cover with the topping and allow to cool.

To make the sauce, melt the butter, sugar, syrup and cream together in a saucepan over a medium–low heat. Increase heat to medium and bring to a boil. Cook until mixture has become a light caramel colour. Serve over the cheesecake.

LOCAL BEFORE LOCAL WAS A THING

JOHN SHEEDY

SHEEDY'S HOTEL

· ·

In sitting down with the chefs, producers and keepers of the Burren for this book I began each interview by asking where their parents are from. In answering that question, John Sheedy spoke volumes in one word: 'Here.'

Not just his mother and father, of course, but the room of Sheedy's Hotel where we sat was where he, his father, his grandfather, his great-grandfather and his great-great-grandfather were all from. They'd farmed the land and built a guesthouse after The Falls Hotel was built to attract visitors to the healing waters of the Lisdoonvarna spa. They'd each, along with his pedigree of hard-working grandmothers, changed the land and buildings in some way, as have John and his wife, Martina. But at its heart, this is a place of quality, tradition and hospitality going back generations.

It would be easy to paint the hard-working young John as destined for the family business. Just like any boy, however, he had his bouts of chafe and rebellion – not all of which have been completely calmed. Today, he might not break the handle of his grandmother's butter churn to get out of the laborious daily task of making butter but he is known, however, to shutter the doors of his dining room to sneak away and watch his beloved GAA football teams play on a Sunday afternoon.

It wasn't just butter from the farm that was made for guests of the original Sheedy's. Vegetables were grown, beef and lamb raised and wild berries picked. Nor was it only the produce served which was of the local *terroir*. Residents of Lisdoonvarna and its environs dined alongside international visitors as the hotel's reputation for fine food and drink in convivial surroundings grew.

Like many chefs of his generation, John had to leave the country and work in Europe – France in his case – to be taken seriously in Ireland. Upon his return, he was a highly regarded set of adept hands and worked in some of the finest Irish kitchens of the day. He spent a season or two in places like Longueville House, Gregans Castle and Patrick Guilbaud, along with many of the best, but now-shuttered, restaurants of their time.

While they all provided fond memories and a collection of skills and experiences gained, none of his jobs had the same reward as that of first chef de cuisine then head chef at Ashford Castle. One would be forgiven for thinking it was for the prestige of the place and the quality of food he produced. One would, however, be only partly right.

John met his wife, Martina, at Ashford Castle. They had started work on the same day – she in reception and he heading up one of the castle's two kitchens.

After an eight-year run, John and Martina decided to open their own restaurant in Mayo. They had identified a location and building that suited their needs and were well on their way to closing the deal when John's father rang and suggested that he 'come home for a chat' in the family hotel. That was the end of plans in Mayo, as the 'chat' was an invitation to take over from his father. Invitation might also warrant inverted commas!

John remembers their second season better than he remembers the first, and for ominous reasons. That second season was the year of the foot-and-mouth-disease outbreak. With cancellations week after week, they took advantage of a bad situation by renovating guestrooms up to the standard of the food being delivered from the kitchen.

John's food is classically influenced, locally sourced, of the highest quality and labour intensive. Those are difficult standards to uphold in the days of chef shortages, staff housing difficulties and industrial farming. Burren cuisine is based on quality ingredients coaxed into being; one hand guided by tradition, the other by respect. It's an attitude John has grown to understand over the years of cooking his food for visitors from near and far.

John and Martina have two children, Róisín and Mathew, but it's too early to know if they'll take up the family business. Fingers crossed for the next generation of tourists and locals alike that this isn't the last in five generations of Sheedys to welcome and feed us in the Burren.

AT ITS HEART, THIS IS A PLACE OF QUALITY, TRADITION AND HOSPITALITY GOING BACK GENERATIONS

A RARE EVENING OFF

John and Martina don't have much time for entertaining during the busy season. If they do welcome friends, they're likely to eat in the dining room of their lovely hotel. John isn't the only one who has taken a few plays from his restaurant's book for his menu, and we are fortunate that he shares some of them with us here. The menu could be simplified by skipping the confit lamb belly or replacing the duck starter with Peter Curtin's simple oysters au naturel (page 187).

STARTER
Slow-cooked leg of duck with celeriac salad and pickled plums

MAIN
Herb-crusted rack of lamb with confit belly

DESSERT
Lemon posset

SLOW-COOKED LEG OF DUCK WITH CELERIAC SALAD AND PICKLED PLUMS

· ·

Serves 6

For the duck

170 g/6 oz sea salt

1 tsp thyme leaves, picked

6 juniper berries, crushed

20 black peppercorns, whole

6 duck legs (female if possible)

1 litre/1¾ pints/4 cups duck fat

3 cloves garlic, crushed

3 bay leaves

4 sprigs thyme

For the celeriac

½ head celeriac, peeled and cut into very
   fine julienne

1 tsp sea salt

60 ml/2 fl oz/¼ cup mayonnaise
   (homemade if possible)

1 tsp wholegrain mustard

2 tbsp chopped flat-leaf parsley

For the plums

100 ml/3½ fl oz/⅓ cup + 4 tsp water

100 ml/3½ fl oz/⅓ cup + 4 tsp vinegar

100 g/3½ oz/½ cup caster (superfine)
   sugar

2 cloves

6 plums, stoned and quartered

To prepare the duck, mix the salt, thyme, juniper and peppercorns. Season the duck legs with the mixture, place on a wire rack over a rimmed baking tray and place in the refrigerator for 12 hours.

Preheat oven to 150°C/300°F/Gas Mark 2.

Wash the duck in plenty of cold running water and pat dry. Place into a casserole (Dutch oven) and cover with melted duck fat. Add the garlic, bay leaves and thyme. Cover and place in the centre of the preheated oven for 2–2½ hours until the duck is tender. Cool in the fat, uncovered. (It can be refrigerated and kept for weeks if the fat covers the legs.)

Mix all the ingredients for the celeriac salad together, season to taste, cover and refrigerate.

For the plums, bring the water, vinegar, sugar and cloves to a boil in a large, heavy-bottomed pot. Remove from the heat, pour over the plums and leave to cool. (This can be made up to 3 days in advance and stored in an airtight container in the refrigerator.)

To serve, first preheat oven to 180°C/350°F/Gas Mark 4. Heat an oven-proof skillet over medium–high heat. Remove the duck legs from the cooled fat, place skin-side down in the skillet and put in the oven for 8 to 10 minutes. Serve each leg skin side up with salad and plums on the side.

HERB-CRUSTED RACK OF LAMB WITH CONFIT BELLY

Serves 6

For the belly

1 lamb belly, well trimmed

Sea salt and freshly ground black pepper

2 sprigs rosemary, leaves picked

60 ml/2 fl oz/¼ cup olive oil

1 head garlic, sliced in half across the
  equator

2–3 bay leaves (fresh, if possible)

4 tbsp minced parsley

4 tbsp minced mint

For the herb crust

330 g/10½ oz brioche, torn into pieces

Small handful each parsley, rosemary and
  mint, finely chopped

160 g/5½ oz Burren Gold (or Gouda-
  style) cheese

150 g/5¼ oz/¾ cup butter, softened

3 full racks of lamb

Sea salt and black pepper to taste

Vegetable oil

80 g/3 fl oz/⅓ cup Dijon mustard

Season the lamb belly with salt and pepper, then rub the rosemary and oil evenly over it. Transfer to a dish, cover with cling film and refrigerate overnight.

Next day, preheat oven to 140°C/250°F/Gas Mark 1. Put the lamb into a casserole (Dutch oven) with the garlic and bay leaves. Cover and place in the centre of the preheated oven for about 3 hours, until tender. Remove from the oven and uncover. Allow to cool for about 20 minutes or until you can handle it. Flake the meat and mix with the parsley and mint.

Lay out a double thickness of cling film on a flat surface. Arrange the flaked meat in a log along the bottom third, nearest to you. Roll into a tight cylinder and chill for 2 hours or overnight.

To make the herb crust, place the brioche and herbs in the bowl of a food processor. Pulse 4 to 5 times to blend. Add the cheese and butter; pulse an additional 4 to 5 times. Transfer to a loaf tin, cover with cling film and refrigerate for an hour to set.

For the racks of lamb, preheat oven to 150°C/300°F/Gas Mark 2. Set a wire rack in a rimmed baking tray.

Pat the lamb racks dry with kitchen paper (paper towels) and season with salt and pepper.

Continued overleaf

Play around with the herbs you use in
this crust. The richness of brioche in the
crumb and the underlying flavour of lamb
can handle many herbaceous accents. Do,
however, consider the season and age of
the lamb. Younger spring lambs have a far
more delicate flavour than older hogget
lambs. The older the animal, the stronger
the flavour, and the more 'accenting' it can
take without being overpowered.

In a skillet over medium–high heat, add 1 tsp oil and heat until shimmering and ready to smoke. Place 1 rack into the skillet and cook until well browned, which will take about 2 to 4 minutes per side, on all sides (and ends). Transfer to the prepared wire rack. Pour off all but 1 teaspoon fat from skillet and repeat cooking with remaining 2 racks.

Brush the lamb all over with mustard. Slice 1.25 cm/ ½-inch thicknesses of herb crust from the loaf tin. Press the slices onto the lamb loin side and transfer to the wire rack, fat side up. Place in oven and roast until lamb registers 57°C/135°F for medium, about 40 to 50 minutes (add more or less time if you desire it more or less done). About 20 minutes before the lamb racks are done, remove the lamb belly from the fridge. Cut into 5 cm/2-inch slices, remove cling film from each slice, place on an ovenproof plate and place into the oven with the racks of lamb.

When the meat is cooked, remove the plate of belly slices and loosely cover to keep warm. Transfer the racks to a carving board and allow to rest for 15 minutes before cutting each one into 4 double chops, serving two per person with a slice of the lamb belly.

LEMON POSSET

. . . .

Serves 6

450 ml/15¼ fl oz/2 cups cream

125 g/4½ oz/⅔ cup caster (superfine)
   sugar

2 lemons, zested and juiced

Seasonal berries or stewed fruit and
   shortbread biscuits for serving
   (optional)

In a heavy-bottomed saucepan over medium heat, bring the cream to a boil. Add the sugar, lemon zest and juice. Boil for approximately 3 minutes, stirring often so that it doesn't boil over.

Remove from heat and allow to cool and infuse for about 15 minutes. Pour into 6 ramekins and transfer to the refrigerator to set (for at least 2 hours or, if possible, overnight).

Serve with fruit and biscuits as desired.

CHEF'S NOTE

John serves his posset with seasonal fruits – stewed rhubarb in early spring, raspberries or blackberries in summer and so on. Remember that the underlying flavour of the dessert is lemon. Any fruit that is enhanced by lemon (usually the sweeter fruits) will make a lovely garnish to this posset.

FABIOLA TOMBO

THE COPPER POT

• •

Much to the dismay of many in the area, The Copper Pot in Liscannor has shuttered. Its homely bakery goods, warm ambience and French country influences are greatly missed. But pastry chef and co-owner Fabiola Tombo's creations and influence on the region can still be tasted both literally and figuratively.

The Burgundy-born woman was told when she applied for culinary training that she could never be a pastry chef without more experience. She was placed, instead, waiting tables, which she detested. After a break from the business to have her daughter, Shaima, she made a second attempt at a pastry job. Once again – this time even more fervently, because she was a young single mother and the work was so demanding – she was repelled.

But then she was introduced to a woman who recognised Fabiola's passion and drive. It was suggested that she might, perhaps, find a way into a pastry job by studying the savoury side of the kitchen and working her way laterally rather than trying to force herself through locked doors. So it was off to an apprenticeship programme in Mâcon, where she brought her baby along to lecture classes and kept her eye on her eventual goal.

Shortly after her apprenticeship, Fabiola was accepted for a position in a one-star restaurant, where she was immersed in ingredients and techniques one only reads about at school. Next the thirsty young chef was in the famed two-star Maison Lameloise in Chagny. There she moved from demi chef de partie up to chef de partie, then to chef de tournant, which is the relief chef for all stations. It may be the most difficult of the line positions in a kitchen brigade, as the tournant must know all of the details and finesse of each station, not just one. It is often from chef de tournant that a person is promoted to sous-chef.

For those reading who know something of the Michelin Guide, you may think I made a mistake in the number of stars Lameloise had. But no. Fabiola had one of the rarest of opportunities in the restaurant world. She was on the team that took a well-respected two-star restaurant into the culinary stratosphere by earning the ultimate: three Michelin stars.

She was then given another rare opportunity: to take over a two-star restaurant kitchen for herself. Fabiola moved to Beaune to take up the reins of a respected restaurant, but soon, fed up with the rankers in the kitchen and snobbery in the dining room, she slipped the golden noose of stars and took some time to remember why she had become a chef in the first place: to make pastry.

A chef friend from school had been working in a Clare hotel for a number of years and told Fabiola of a pastry job that had just become vacant. Ignoring that her school-learnt English was more than rusty, she set off for Ireland and landed as the bottom fell from the economy. Not only did she not have the language, neither did she now have a job.

Fortune led her to Gregans Castle, which needed an extra set of skilled hands, as their new pastry chef wasn't due in from Spain for a couple of weeks. She took on the task of bridging the gap, and when the man from Spain arrived, realised how remote the Burren was and turned tail, Fabiola was offered the head pastry job.

The week she was set to return to Gregans for her fifth season, the suffering Irish economy dealt Fabiola another blow and she was left in search of work yet again. Knowing of an underused kitchen space in Doolin she decided to try opening a modest little café, making simple Irish and French baked

SIMPLE IRISH AND FRENCH BAKED GOODS WITH NO FRILLS, NO PRETENCE ... BUT LOADS OF HEART

goods with no frills, no pretence, no advertising and no real budget to speak of … but loads of heart.

Fabiola's Patisserie opened in the spring of 2012 to local acclaim. So successful was it that she was approached by a potential business partner to open an expanded café down the road.

That partnership ended after two years but in that time a third partner, Adam Caffrey, had joined the team. Adam and Fabiola not only stayed business partners, moved shop to Liscannor and changed the café's name to The Copper Pot, they also became life partners. Fabiola says she couldn't resist Adam's eyes …

The couple's shared passion for unparalleled bakery products drove them to great success. It also drove Fabiola to ill health, working eighteen-hour days six days a week and dealing with the increasing pressures of the business beyond baking. It broke their hearts to close The Copper Pot, say goodbye to their team and leave a building they'd lovingly refurbished.

What the future will hold for Fabiola and Adam's own business is up in the air for now. Until they decide where it will land, however, her loving touch can be found in the desserts of the Roadside Tavern and Burren Storehouse.

A BOHEMIAN RHAPSODY

. . . .

Each of this menu's elements could stand on its own or be blended into other meals. The risotto makes for a lovely brunch, while the smoked parsnip mash is a staple winter side in my house. If parsnips aren't up your street, replace them with Ronan Kelly's smoked garlic fondant potatoes (page 139) and you'll still get the depth of flavour to accompany the richness of pork belly and scallops.

STARTER
Buckwheat-beetroot risotto with goat cheese and duck egg
MAIN
Crispy braised pork belly with pan-seared scallops
SIDE
Smoked parsnip purée
DESSERT
Coconut panna cotta with passion fruit and mango mousse and
cocoa-ginger shortbreads

BUCKWHEAT-BEETROOT RISOTTO WITH GOAT CHEESE AND DUCK EGG

Serves 6

6 medium beetroots, washed

1 tbsp vegetable oil

Sea salt and freshly ground pepper

400 g/14 oz/2⅓ cups buckwheat

1 lemon, juiced

400 ml/14 fl oz/1⅔ cups coconut milk

For the vinaigrette

1½ tbsp lemon juice

1 tsp lemon zest

1 tbsp honey

60 ml/2 fl oz/¼ cup extra virgin olive oil

Sea salt and freshly ground pepper

2 tbsp cider vinegar

6 duck eggs

To serve

About 300g/10½ oz organic baby salad
   greens

300 g/10½ oz goat cheese

Toasted seeds (optional)

1 bunch chives, snipped

Preheat oven to 210°C/410°F/Gas Mark 6.

Rub the beetroot with vegetable oil and season with salt and pepper. Roast in preheated oven for approximately an hour until tender when pierced with a sharp knife. Remove and allow to cool.

Rinse the buckwheat in 2 to 3 changes of water. In a saucepan over high heat, add the rinsed buckwheat, 1 litre/1¾ pints/4 cups boiling water and a pinch of salt. Boil for 2 minutes, then reduce heat and simmer for 10 to 15 minutes until tender but still al dente.

Peel the beetroots and cut into pieces. Put into the bowl of a food processor with the lemon juice, coconut milk, salt and pepper. Process until smooth. Stir the beetroot cream into the buckwheat and set aside.

Make the vinaigrette by whisking the lemon juice, zest and honey together, then drizzling in the olive oil while whisking vigorously. Season with salt and pepper.

Bring a large pot of water to a boil. Add the vinegar. Crack one duck egg into a small saucer. Stir the water to create a whirlpool and slip the egg into the water. Repeat with the remaining eggs in quick succession and separating each egg from the others. Remove the pot from the heat and allow it to sit for 6 to 8 minutes, depending on how firm you desire the yolks. Using a slotted spoon, remove each egg onto a few folded pieces of kitchen paper and blot dry. To serve, warm the risotto. Dress the salad greens with vinaigrette and arrange on a plate. Crumble the goat cheese over, and sprinkle with toasted seeds, if using. Place a scoop of risotto on each plate, and top with a poached egg. Season and garnish with the snipped chives.

CRISPY BRAISED PORK BELLY WITH PAN-SEARED SCALLOPS

Serves 6

1½ kg/3lb 5oz pork belly, scored

2 tbsp fennel seeds

2 tsp cardamom pods, crushed

1 tsp black peppercorns

1 bunch thyme, leaves picked

1 tbsp sea salt

4 cloves garlic, peeled

3 tbsp olive oil

1 bulb fennel, trimmed and sliced

5 fresh bay leaves

5 star anise

400 ml/14 fl oz/1⅔ cups white wine

750 ml/27 fl oz/3 cups chicken stock

For the scallops

18 large fresh scallops

15g /½ oz/1 tbsp butter

3 tsp olive oil

Sea salt and freshly ground black pepper

1 bunch watercress, to garnish

Day 1: In a dry sauté pan over medium heat, toast fennel seeds, cardamom and peppercorns until fragrant. Transfer spices to a mortar, and pound with pestle. Add thyme, salt and 3 garlic cloves and pound into a paste. Stir in 2 tbsp of olive oil. Rub pork belly with the paste. Wrap tightly with cling film, place in container and refrigerate overnight.

Day 2: Preheat oven to 180°C/350°F/Gas Mark 4. In a casserole (Dutch oven) over medium–high heat, add 1 tbsp olive oil, the sliced fennel, bay leaves, star anise and 1 clove of crushed garlic. Cook until fragrant, about 2 minutes. Push the aromatics to one side and add the pork belly, skin-side down. Cook for about 5 minutes, until golden brown. Turn the pork skin side up and season with salt and pepper. Being careful not to get any liquid on the skin, add wine and bring to a boil. Carefully add stock and return to a boil. Transfer to the oven and braise, uncovered, for 2½ to 3 hours, until tender. Transfer pork to a warm plate to rest. Defat cooking juices and place pan over medium–high heat to reduce by half. Strain through a fine sieve into a jug and keep the sauce warm.

Pat the scallops dry with kitchen paper (paper towels). To a non-stick sauté pan over high heat, add butter and oil. Season the scallops just before going into the pan. When fat begins to smoke, gently add the scallops, making sure they do not touch one another. Sear scallops for 1½ minutes per side (they should have a golden crust but be translucent in the centre).

Serve immediately with a slice of pork belly, smoked parsnip purée (page 117) and a jug of sauce on the side. Garnish with watercress.

SMOKED PARSNIP PURÉE

Serves 6

50g/2 oz/¼ cup uncooked rice

5 sprigs rosemary

5 sprigs thyme

800 g/28 oz parsnips, washed but skin on

2 cloves garlic, minced

1 onion, minced

150 ml/5¼ fl oz/⅔ cup almond milk

60 g/2 oz/4 tbsp salted butter

Sea salt and freshly ground black pepper

CHEF'S NOTE

Try this method with potatoes as well – smoked mashed potatoes are a lovely addition to hearty meat or vegetable dishes. You can use tea leaves, herbs, spices and so on in the smoking process.

Preheat oven to 200°C/400°F/Gas Mark 6.

Completely line the inside of a heavy-bottomed casserole (Dutch oven) with two sheets of tinfoil. Set over high heat and add the rice, herbs and parsnips. When the rice and herbs begin to smoke, add 2 tablespoons of water, cover, reduce heat to medium–low and smoke for 10 minutes. Transfer to the oven for 20 minutes or until the parsnips are tender.

Strip the skin and scrape off the flesh of the parsnips into a saucepan. Add the garlic, onion and almond milk and set over medium–high heat and bring to a boil. Reduce to a simmer and mash with the back of a fork. Simmer until it has reached the desired consistency. Fold in butter, season and serve.

COCONUT PANNA COTTA WITH PASSION FRUIT AND MANGO MOUSSE AND COCOA-GINGER SHORTBREADS

Serves 6

For the mousse

125 g/4½ oz/½ cup mango purée

80 g/3 oz/⅓ cup passion fruit purée (both purées available in speciality markets)

50 g/1¾ oz/¼ cup sugar

60 g/2 oz/¼ cup egg yolk (just over 3 yolks)

80 g/3 oz/⅓ cup whole egg (about 1½ eggs)

75 g/2½ oz/5 tbsp butter, softened

1 small mango, diced

6 passion fruit

For the panna cotta

1 leaf gelatine

500 ml/18 fl oz/2 cups cream

250 ml/8 fl oz/1 cup coconut milk

100 g/3½ oz/½ cup sugar

100 g/3½ oz/¾ cup desiccated coconut

For the shortbread

150 g/5¼ oz/¾ cup salted butter

75 g/2½ oz/⅓ cup dark brown sugar

10 g/⅓ oz fresh ginger, grated

200 g/7 oz/1⅓ cups spelt flour

25 g/¾ oz/3 tbsp + 1 tsp dark cocoa powder

25 g/¾ oz/3 tbsp + 1 tsp desiccated coconut

To make the mousse, mix the mango and passion fruit purées in a saucepan, place over medium–high heat and bring to a boil.

Place the sugar, yolks and eggs into a large bowl and whisk until smooth and thick.

Once the purée has boiled, remove from the heat and slowly whisk into the egg and sugar mixture. Return the mixture to the saucepan and place over medium heat. Whisk vigorously until the mixture begins to thicken, being careful that it doesn't stick to the bottom. Bring to a boil, continuing to whisk, for 1 minute. Remove from heat and allow to cool to 45°C/110°F.

With a hand-held blender, blitz in the soft butter until the mixture is smooth and creamy. Stir in the diced mango and the pulp of 3 passion fruit. Pour into 6 glasses and put in the refrigerator to set.

For the panna cotta, put the gelatine leaf into cold water for 5 minutes to soften.

Pour the cream, coconut milk and sugar into a saucepan and set over medium heat until hot. Remove the gelatine from the water, squeeze out excess liquid and add to the hot coconut cream. Stir until dissolved, remove from heat and allow to cool, but not set.

In a sauté pan over a medium–high heat, toast the coconut until golden. Remove to a plate to cool.

Pour the cooled coconut and cream mixture over the back of a spoon into the 6 glasses containing the set mango and passion fruit mousse. Take half of the toasted coconut and sprinkle it between all six glasses. Chill for at least 3 hours or overnight.

To make the shortbread, first preheat oven to 160°C/320°F/Gas Mark 3. Line a baking tray with greaseproof paper.

In a stand mixer, cream the butter and sugar together until pale and fluffy. Stir in the grated ginger. Sift the flour and cocoa powder into the bowl. Gently fold the mixtures together until the ingredients form a dough. Flatten the dough evenly on the baking tray and sprinkle with coconut. Bake for about 20 minutes. Allow to cool slightly on the tray on a wire rack, then slice or cut into shapes as desired.

To serve, mix the remaining toasted coconut with the pulp of the remaining 3 passion fruit. Spoon on top of the panna cotta and serve with a slice of shortbread.

TAKING THE LONG WAY

DANIEL CRAUGHWELL

HOTEL DOOLIN

• •

Were Daniel Craughwell to win the Lotto, he tells me that he'd set up a small farm. With low impact on land and environment, he would raise vegetables and herbs, sheep and cattle, chickens and ducks, geese and turkeys. Hell, he'd probably even get a horse or two … and a donkey!

Not what you might think of a man who grew up in the heart of Galway city – born first child to an army mechanic and a nursing student. But his memories of summers at his mother's family farm in Roscommon are strong, they are dear and they are probably what drives his passion for food and cooking – and fantasy farming.

Those summers of saving hay, cutting turf and drinking mugs of cabbage water straight from the bacon pot are fond memories. The treacle bread Daniel offers up in his menu is a direct descendant of his grandmother's recipe.

Never, as with most family farms, making any money for his labour, Daniel was stunned when he was first paid for an evening washing up at a local restaurant. His mother worked at the busy local eatery, and when they were caught short for a kitchen porter, she rang the one house in the estate with a phone to have young Danny sent down to put on an apron and muck in. That brown envelope with £12 was something of an awakening for the thirteen-year-old and the introduction to his long and successful career.

As part of his certification, Daniel was sent to a number of busy, high-quality restaurants in the west. While on one of those placements he met the young woman who would become his wife. And not just his wife but also his eventual business partner, as he and his in-laws would soon open a high-volume modern Irish cuisine restaurant in Spain.

Serving three meals a day, seven days a week for ten years – warm Spanish sun or not – will take it out of a guy. Daniel left his wife and newborn son, Nico, with the in-laws in Spain while he moved back home to find work in Galway. Though he was highly qualified, not many gave him much of a chance at finding anything, as it was the spring of 2012 and the bottom of the Great Recession. But Daniel Craughwell isn't afraid of work and it was work he was looking to find. Two days in, he was back on the employment ladder and working his way up.

As a man who appreciates the leg-up a trade education was to him, Chef Daniel has been giving back to the system in tangible ways for years. Often taking students on placement at restaurants he ran, he would make sure to augment skills that are so very important to a young apprentice but seem to have slipped from modern culinary education in Ireland. Whether it was ordering in whole chickens or raising pigs so that students could break down whole animals at no extra cost to the school, he gave back to the well from which he'd dipped.

The family were living in the same neighbourhood he'd grown up in when the position at Hotel Doolin was offered to him. From home to work was nearly a two-hour commute each way. He could have shaved perhaps fifteen minutes from the journey had he cut straight through on the N67 but he preferred to turn his Harley-Davidson right over left in Ballyvaughan to take the coast road to Black Head and around the Burren.

He added time but avoided traffic. More importantly, the oft-unmarked townlands of Gleninagh, Carnsefin, Murroogh, Fanore, Craggagh and Gortacarnaun welcomed him with different experiences every day – one day blue-black and brooding, the next with golden sands reminiscent of a California surfing film. He lost count of the times he'd stop on his way to or from work to admire a passing pod of playful dolphins or watch a gathering storm's menacing clouds.

The Burren is a place where Danny and his family have found happiness and home, neighbours who will lend a hand without shoving their nose in one's business. It's the kind of place he's happy to raise his son. Now, if only he could raise more of those organic pigs …

HE LOST COUNT OF THE TIMES HE'D STOP ON HIS WAY TO OR FROM WORK TO ADMIRE A PASSING POD OF PLAYFUL DOLPHINS OR WATCH A GATHERING STORM'S MENACING CLOUDS

AUTUMNAL SPREAD

· ·

Everything about Daniel's menu says 'party' to me. From pans full of stuffed mussels in the fridge awaiting the grill to a massive pot of jambalaya ready for second (and third) helpings, this is a backyard-festival menu. His red pepper pickle is simple to make and stores for a good long time. If you run out, however, you could whip up some of Darra's tomato chutney (page 250) from Niall Hughes's menu.

STARTER

Wild garlic and bacon stuffed mussels

MAIN

Folk Festival jambalaya

SIDES

Dooliner brown bread

Red pepper pickle

DESSERT

Doolin bog pie

WILD GARLIC AND BACON STUFFED MUSSELS

Serves 6

1.5 kg/3 lb 5 oz live mussels

6 slices quality white bread, torn

4 slices smoked streaky rashers (bacon),
    cooked and chopped

4 tbsp finely grated Parmesan

20 g/¾ oz wild garlic leaves (or garlic
    chives), roughly chopped (or 6 cloves of
    garlic and a bunch of parsley)

200 g/7 oz/¾ cup + 3 tbsp butter, melted

3 tbsp lemon juice

Freshly ground black pepper or chilli
    flakes, to taste

CHEF'S NOTE

Three major types of wild garlic grow in
Ireland. Crow Garlic (*allium vineale*) has
pungent bulbils very much like cloves of
domesticated garlic, though they can have
a long and less-than-pleasant aftertaste;
Three-Cornered Leek (*allium triquetrum*)
has long, thin green leaves and can be seen
in hedgerows around the country; Ramsons
(*allium ursinum*), also called Creamh, grows
in mixed woodlands, near streams and in
damp, shady places. Either *triquetrum* or
ursinum can be used in this recipe, and it is
the leaves of the plant, not the bulbs, that
are called for.

Scrub the mussels, remove any beards and rinse well. Put the mussels in a large saucepan set over a high heat. Cover and cook for 2 to 3 minutes, until all the shells have steamed open. Strain and allow to cool, discarding any unopened mussels.

Put the bread into the bowl of a food processor and pulse into crumbs. Add the bacon, Parmesan and wild garlic, and pulse to blend. Add the melted butter and lemon juice, season with a pinch of ground black pepper or chilli flakes and pulse until all ingredients are blended.

Take each mussel and carefully pry off the shell without the mussel in it, discarding the empty half. Pour off the cooking liquid and reserve or freeze for stock. Place each mussel in its shell on a baking tray. Divide the bread mixture between each shell, making sure the mussel meat is fully covered. Put the tray into the refrigerator for an hour.

Preheat grill (broiler) to high. Place the baking tray on a rack set 10 cm/4 inches from the heat for 2 minutes or until the stuffing is golden. Transfer the shells to sharing plates or platters and serve hot.

FOLK FESTIVAL JAMBALAYA

Serves 6

90 g/3 oz/6 tbsp rapeseed (canola) oil

800 g/1 lb 12 oz chicken fillets (boneless, skinless breasts) diced

300 g/10½ oz fresh chorizo sausage, thickly sliced

1 large white onion, diced

2 red bell peppers, diced

3 stalks celery, chopped

3 cloves garlic, minced

2 bay leaves

2 tbsp Cajun seasoning

1 tsp dried thyme

1 tsp dried oregano

600 g/21 oz/2⅓ cups easy-cook (converted) rice, washed

800 ml/28 fl oz/3¼ cups chicken stock

2 x 400 g/14 oz tins chopped tomatoes

200 g/7 oz cooked ham, cubed

200 g/7 oz large shrimp, peeled

60 ml/2 fl oz/¼ cup Worcester sauce

Sea salt and freshly ground black pepper

Hot pepper sauce to taste (optional)

1 bunch spring onions (scallions), sliced

In a large casserole (Dutch oven) set over medium–high, heat oil until shimmering. Add the chicken and sausage and brown, stirring occasionally, for 6 to 8 minutes. Remove with a slotted spoon to a platter lined with several layers of kitchen paper (paper towels).

To the casserole, add the onion, bell peppers, celery and garlic, and cook for 2 to 3 minutes. Add the bay leaves, Cajun seasoning, thyme and oregano, and cook, stirring occasionally, until vegetables are tender. Add the rice and stir to coat with oil. Increase heat to high.

Add the chicken stock, tomatoes, ham, shrimp, browned chicken and sausage. Bring to the boil, stirring continuously. Do not allow it to stick to the bottom of the casserole. Add the Worcester sauce and season with salt and pepper. Cover and reduce heat to medium. Simmer, stirring occasionally, until rice is tender, about 15 to 20 minutes. Season with hot pepper sauce if using.

Ladle into bowls and garnish with spring onions. Serve with Dooliner brown bread (page 127) and red pepper pickle (page 128).

DOOLINER BROWN BREAD

Makes 4 x 450 g/1 lb loaves

(recipe can be halved)

250 g/9 oz/1⅔ cups plain (all-purpose)
   flour

500g/1 lb 2 oz/3⅓ cups wholemeal flour

75 g/2½ oz/⅓ cup brown demerara sugar

25 g/¾ oz/1 tbsp + 2 tsp bread soda

125 g/4½ oz/1⅓ cups porridge oats, plus
   more for dusting

60 g/2 oz/4 tbsp butter, melted

60 g/1¾ fl oz/3 tbsp black treacle (or
   molasses)

1 large egg

250 ml/8 fl oz/1 cup Dooliner Beer or
   dark ale

500 ml/18 fl oz/2 cups buttermilk

120 ml/4 fl oz/½ cup water

Preheat oven to 160°C/320°F/Gas Mark 3. Grease four
1 lb bread tins.

Stir all the dry ingredients together in a large mixing
bowl. Mix the wet ingredients together well in a medium
bowl. Mix wet into dry (don't worry if it looks a bit wet).
Three-quarters fill the tins with the batter. Sprinkle a few
oats on top and bake on the middle rack for 1 hour and
12 minutes.

Cool in the tins for 20 minutes, then turn out onto a rack
to cool completely. Can be frozen, well wrapped, for up to
3 months.

CHEF'S NOTE

Cooling bread is one of the most important
and often-overlooked steps in the process.
Directly out of the oven, starches have yet
to fully gelatinise (absorb moisture and
set the structure of the bread). It can be
very difficult to wait until fully cooled –
particularly with this rich version of brown
soda bread – but do. If you want a crisper
crust, turn the loaves out of their tins
directly from the oven. For a softer crust,
turn the loaves out after 20 minutes of
cooling in the tins and immediately wrap in
a tea towel until cooled.

RED PEPPER PICKLE

Makes about 600 ml/1 pint/2⅓ cups

2 red bell peppers, seeded and finely diced

½ white onion, finely diced

200 ml/7 fl oz/¾ cup + 4 tsp tomato ketchup

3 tbsps organic cider vinegar

1 dash hot pepper sauce

Freshly ground black pepper

Combine all ingredients and transfer to a resealable glass jar. Refrigerate overnight. Will keep for 1 week, refrigerated.

CHEF'S NOTE

When making 'quick' pickles such as this, try varying the vinegar for different flavours. Each vinegar – red wine, white wine, cider, sherry and so on – will change the final product. Just make sure that the acid content is at least 5 per cent or you won't get the desired result.

DOOLIN BOG PIE

. . . .

Serves 6

400 g/14 oz chocolate bourbon biscuits

160 g/5½ oz/¾ cup + 1 tbsp unsalted
  butter, melted

120 g/4½ oz/⅔ cup caster (superfine)
  sugar

3 tbsp cornflour (cornstarch)

½ tsp salt

4 egg yolks

500 ml/18 fl oz/2 cups full-fat (whole)
  milk

1 tbsp pure vanilla extract

250 g/9 oz 50%–60% chocolate, chopped,
  melted and cooled slightly

180 ml/6 fl oz/¾ cup double (heavy)
  cream, whipped to soft peaks and chilled

Place the biscuits in the bowl of a food processor and
pulse to coarse crumbs. Set aside 60 g of the biscuit
crumbs. In a bowl, stir together the remaining biscuit
crumbs and melted butter. Firmly press mixture into the
bottom and up the sides of a 23 cm/9-inch pie plate and
freeze for 30 minutes.

In a medium-sized bowl, whisk together the sugar,
cornflour and salt. In a stand mixer fitted with a whip,
whisk the yolks until pale and smooth. Sift in the sugar,
cornflour and salt and whisk to blend. Set aside.

In a saucepan over medium heat, combine the milk and
vanilla. Bring to a simmer and then remove from heat.
Slowly whisk the hot milk into the egg mixture. Once
fully incorporated, return to the saucepan and place on
low heat. Cook, whisking constantly, until mixture begins
to thicken, which will take about 3 minutes. Continue to
whisk and, once the mixture begins to bubble, whisk for 2
additional minutes.

Remove from heat. Whisk in the chocolate until fully
combined and pour the filling into the chilled crust. Press
cling film over the top and chill for 8 hours to set.

When ready to serve, top with whipped cream and
reserved biscuit crumbs.

RONAN KELLY

THE FALLS HOTEL

- -

Ronan Kelly looked around the iconic setting of The Falls Hotel in the spring of 2018 and said to himself, 'Sure, I could work here.' It's something he has said to himself many times in his culinary career. Sometimes it was for the job, sometimes for the place, sometimes for the people. The Falls was for all of that and more.

The hard-working Carlow man grew up in an idyllic country village of fewer than 120 people. 'You knew everyone … and everyone knew what we young fellas were doing,' he says of the place.

It was from his grandmother down the lane that, he says, he got a love for cooking. Weeks might

SURE, I COULD WORK HERE

go by in the summers without him going home. She was something of a local supplier of baked goods – pies, cakes, breads and her sought-after Christmas puddings – to families well out of reach of a proper shop. Ronan graduated from peeling the apples for pies to stirring puddings and on to assistant baker in her country kitchen by the time he was ten.

His first taste of working in a city was in Dublin while at culinary college. From there it was to London, back to Dublin and eventually to Limerick, where he spent nearly a decade heading up a busy hotel kitchen. In fact, most of the places Ronan worked were busy. So much so that, after a stint heading up a short-staffed London hotel – and getting only two half-days off in a year – he took a break from the business completely.

He spent a year laying bricks with his brother back in Carlow – exactly the break he needed until he was ready to get back into the kitchen.

He went back slowly at first: a few nights a week helping out a local friend, then on to a more full-time gig while still polishing a few stones now and again. Then it was to the west where he jumped in as sous-chef for an old mate, Peter Jackson.

Chef Ronan's ethos about food probably came from his upbringing in Carlow. When you do a job, no matter what the job, do it well and do it to the end. He likes to keep his preparations simple and pure. It's an ideal that is easy to say but difficult to deliver. You can't hide less than perfect ingredients in that kind of food. His grandmother wouldn't have put windfall apples in her pies, after all.

HE LIKES TO KEEP HIS PREPARATIONS SIMPLE AND PURE

Ronan spends as much time as he can with his teenaged daughter, Ciara, as his job will allow. While she loves spending time at the beach or walking along the river with her dad, Ronan says that, like most teens, she has one eye on university and the other checking her mobile!

WINNER, WINNER, CHICKEN DINNER

. . . .

For many chefs, the perfectly roasted chicken is both simple joy and unattainable goal. Ronan's version of the bird is quite achievable. It's simple enough for a midweek supper and fine enough for a Sunday lunch, and you'll want a tub of his sorbet in your freezer from the moment you read the recipe. To kill two birds with one stone (oh, the kitchen puns!) you could skip the fondant potatoes and the breadcrumb stuffing and fill the chickens with Viv Kelly's potato stuffing (page 98).

STARTER
Heirloom tomato and buffalo mozzarella salad with soused vegetables

MAIN
Lemon-garlic roasted chicken with lemon and thyme stuffing and Madeira jus

SIDES
Honey-roasted carrots and parsnips

Smoked-garlic fondant potatoes

DESSERT
Blackberry crème brûlée with blackberry and Cointreau sorbet

HEIRLOOM TOMATO AND BUFFALO MOZZARELLA SALAD AND SOUSED VEGETABLES

• •

Serves 6

6 large heirloom tomatoes

6 ovoline (egg-sized balls) fresh buffalo
  mozzarella

175 ml/6 fl oz/⅔ cup white wine vinegar

175 ml/6 fl oz/⅔ cup cider (hard)

75 ml/1½ fl oz/¼ cup + 1 tbsp water

150 g/5¼ oz/¾ cup sugar

2 bay leaves

½ cinnamon stick

1 red bell pepper, sliced

1 yellow bell pepper, sliced

1 red onion, sliced

1 courgette (zucchini), diced small (see
  Chef's Note)

150 g/5¼ oz rocket (arugula)

Sea salt and freshly ground black pepper

6 leaves basil, thinly sliced, to garnish

Cut the tomatoes into 6 slices each and slice the
mozzarella the same thickness as the tomatoes.

In a saucepan over medium heat, place the vinegar, cider,
water, sugar, bay leaves and cinnamon. Bring to a boil.
Add the peppers and onion and simmer for 2 minutes
then remove from heat. Add the courgettes and leave to
cool.

Arrange the tomatoes and mozzarella on a platter as
if they haven't a care. Scatter rocket leaves around and
season with sea salt and pepper. Spoon the pickled
vegetables with some of the cooking liquid over the dish.
Garnish with the basil.

CHEF'S NOTE

Keep the diced courgettes separate
from the peppers and onion. Adding the
courgettes separately will help to keep
them nice and green.

LEMON-GARLIC ROASTED CHICKEN WITH LEMON AND THYME STUFFING AND MADEIRA JUS

• •

Serves 6

3 cloves garlic, peeled

60 ml/2 fl oz/¼ cup olive oil

1 bunch rosemary

1 bunch thyme

3 lemons, zested and juiced

Sea salt and freshly ground black pepper

200 g/7 oz/¾ cup + 3 tbsp butter

1 onion, diced

720 g/25 oz/6 cups fresh breadcrumbs

150 ml/5¼ fl oz/⅔ cup chicken stock

2 x 1.5 kg/3¼ lb free-range chickens

105 g/3½ oz/7 tbsp butter (divided per method)

16g/½ oz/2 tbsp flour

500 ml/18 fl oz/2 cups chicken stock

1 small onion, finely diced

450 g/1 lb brown mushrooms, sliced

1 sprig thyme

1 bay leaf

300 ml/½ pint/1¼ cups Madeira

100 ml/3½ fl oz/⅓ cup + 4 tsp red wine

30 g/1½ oz/2 tbsp cold butter, cut into 6 pieces

Preheat oven to 170°C/340°F/Gas Mark 3.

In the bowl of a food processor, blend the garlic, olive oil and 1 sprig each of rosemary and thyme. Add the grated zest of 1 lemon and the juice of 2 of the lemons. Season with salt and pepper and set aside.

In a sauté pan over medium heat, melt the butter, add the onion and sweat for 3 to 4 minutes until soft. Finely chop the remaining thyme and add to the onions. Continue to sweat for 1 to 2 minutes longer.

Place the breadcrumbs in a mixing bowl, pour in the butter and onion mixture and gently toss to mix. Add the grated rind of the other two lemons and the juice of the third and the chicken stock. Fold to mix and adjust seasoning.

Stuff the cavities of the chickens with the bread stuffing and secure them with wooden skewers. Rub the skin of both chickens with the reserved garlic and herb mixture. Place the remaining rosemary in the bottom of a roasting tin and put the chickens on a rack over it. Roast in the middle of the preheated oven for 90 to 110 minutes, rotating the pan once, until the meat in the thigh reaches 80°C/175°F. Remove from oven and place the rack over a plate to collect the juices. Loosely tent with tinfoil and set to rest for 10 minutes. Defat the cooking juices, strain and reserve.

In a saucepan over medium heat, melt 30 g/1 oz/2 tbsp of the butter, then add the flour and stir.

Cook the roux for 4 to 5 minutes until it begins to look a bit dry. Pour in the cold chicken stock, increase heat to medium–high and bring just to a boil. Reduce heat to medium–low and simmer for 20 minutes.

In a saucepan over medium heat, melt the remaining butter, add onion and sweat for 3 to 4 minutes until soft. Add the sliced mushrooms and cook until they become tender and release their moisture. Remove the mushroom and onion mixture with a slotted spoon and reserve.

Add the thyme, bay leaf, Madeira and red wine to the saucepan and increase heat to medium–high. Add reserved cooking juices from chickens (from both pan and plate), bring to a boil and reduce heat to medium. Simmer until the liquid is reduced by half. Add the thickened chicken stock and mushrooms. Continue to reduce until the sauce coats the back of a spoon. Correct seasoning, stir in the cold butter until melted and pour into a heated jug. Remove the stuffing to a heated serving dish, carve the chickens as you like and serve with the sauce.

HONEY-ROASTED CARROTS AND PARSNIPS

Serves 6

1 kg/2 lb carrots

1 kg/2 lb parsnips

200 g/7 oz/¾ cup + 3 tbsp butter, melted

300 g/10½ oz/¾ cup + 2 tbsp local honey

1 sprig rosemary

1 sprig thyme

Preheat oven to 200°C/400°F/Gas Mark 6.

Peel the vegetables and cut into chunky wedges. Place in a large saucepan with well-salted cold water over medium–high heat and bring to a boil. Reduce heat to medium and simmer until vegetables are three-quarters cooked (about 10 minutes). Drain the vegetables and place in a large mixing bowl.

Mix together the melted butter, honey and herbs and drizzle over the vegetables. Toss to coat and spread onto a roasting tray. Place in the upper third of the oven, reduce heat to 180°C/350°F/Gas Mark 4. Roast until golden in colour, approximately 15 to 20 minutes.

CHEF'S NOTE

Local honey is one of the best ways to taste and remember a place. Find authenticated local honey wherever you travel and bring it home. Honey will last for years if stored properly and you can remember your travels every time you use it in a regional recipe.

SMOKED-GARLIC FONDANT POTATOES

Serves 6

6 large rooster potatoes, roughly the same size, peeled

300 g/10½ oz/1½ cups butter

120 ml/4 fl oz/½ cup chicken stock

3 cloves smoked garlic (available at speciality grocers')

2 bay leaves

1 sprig thyme

Trim two of the long sides of the potatoes so that they can lie flat. Melt the butter in a deep sauté pan over medium–high heat. Place the potatoes, cut-side down, in the pan and cook until well browned (5 to 6 minutes per side).

Pour the stock around the potatoes, add smoked garlic cloves, bay leaves and thyme and bring to a boil. Reduce heat to medium, cover with a tight-fitting lid and simmer until the potatoes are just cooked through (approximately 30 to 45 minutes). Carefully remove from the pan to a heated platter and cover to keep warm until serving.

CHEF'S NOTE

Smoked garlic can be found in many speciality shops now. Its slightly sweet caramel flavours are balanced by sharp tones from the smoke. You could substitute cloves of roasted garlic, but the final dish will lack the extra depth smoked garlic offers.

BLACKBERRY CRÈME BRÛLÉE WITH BLACKBERRY AND COINTREAU SORBET

Serves 6

250 g/9 oz/1¼ cups caster (superfine) sugar

2 punnets blackberries, 24 reserved for custard

80 ml/3 fl oz/⅓ cup Cointreau liqueur

300 ml/½ pint/1¼ cup rosé Champagne

2 lemons, juiced

600 ml/1 pint/2½ cups cream

1 vanilla pod, split lengthways

9 egg yolks

1 egg

190 g/6¾ oz/¾ cup + 2 tbsp caster (superfine) sugar plus additional for dusting

In a medium-sized saucepan over medium–high heat, place the sugar and 500 ml/18 fl oz/2 cups water. Bring to a boil, stirring so sugar dissolves; reduce heat to medium–low and simmer for 10 minutes. Remove from heat and allow to cool to room temperature.

Place the blackberries and Cointreau in a food processor and blend until smooth. Once the syrup has cooled, add the Champagne, lemon juice and blackberry and Cointreau mixture. Churn in an ice-cream maker according to the manufacturer's instructions or put into a container and into the freezer, stirring every 2 hours until frozen (this method should take about 6 hours).

Preheat oven to 130°C/270°F/Gas Mark ½.

In a saucepan over medium heat, add the cream and vanilla pod. Bring to a simmer, stirring often. Do not boil. Remove from the heat and scrape the seeds from the pod into the cream.

In a large bowl, mix the yolks, egg and sugar. Slowly pour the cream into this mixture, whisking constantly. Return it to the saucepan and place over low heat for a few minutes, whisking gently until thickened. Pour the mixture from the saucepan to a mixing bowl to stop it from overcooking.

Place 4 blackberries each in 6 ovenproof ramekins. Place a tea towel in a deep roasting tin and put the ramekins on the towel. Divide the custard mix evenly between the ramekins.

Set a kettle to boil. Place the roasting tin in the middle of a preheated oven. Pour enough boiling water from the kettle into the pan to come three-quarters of the way up the side of the ramekins. Bake for approximately 30 minutes until set.

Carefully remove the roasting tin from the oven. Using tongs, remove the ramekins from the water and cool on a rack. The custards can be refrigerated, covered, and kept for up to 2 days at this point.

To serve, sprinkle a little sugar over each custard. Using a blowtorch, carefully burn the sugar on top of the dish so that it caramelises and turns a deep golden-brown. Do not over-caramelise as it will become too bitter. Scoop the sorbet into champagne flutes and serve alongside the crème brûlée.

DAVID McCANN

DROMOLAND CASTLE

In so many ways, mentoring apprentice chefs is not unlike parenting. Like parents, chefs demand and advise, challenge and support, expect much but give even more in return. Comparable to the way his Garda Síochána inspector father nudged young David McCann through a 'teenage' patch, the master chef mentors with a firm but fair hand. Though maybe not quite as firm …

Chef David is known to give a leg-up to aspiring young cooks who could use a break to get into the business. While many of the staff at Dromoland Castle can trace their family's work on the grounds back generations, one or two new apprentices from around the world and around the corner train in his kitchens.

He has seen much change in the years since he came to Dromoland. He has also seen much stay nearly unchanged. It's a metaphor for his style of cooking in many ways: grounded in the classics of

WHEN HOME FROM HOME BECOMES HOME

technique and style, but willing and able to evolve with ingredients and flavours as required.

I intended to include the chef of Dromoland Castle because of the plain fact that the head of the O'Brien family – the Baron Inchiquin – whose family home was the castle, owned the Burren. Seemed like a fair enough reason. What I didn't know was that David spent most summers of his youth traversing the Burren between his grandmother's farm in south county Mayo and his aunt's home in Kilkee. His memories of food, fun and hard work on the farm connect him to the place. It's a connection he has strived to pass on to his own children.

David came to head the kitchen of Dromoland Castle in 1995 while still in his twenties: quite a feat when you consider that Dromoland had recently won a Michelin star and David was back in Ireland only two months.

The list of places at which he has worked and the names of celebrated chefs – both past and present – with whom he has worked are a veritable who's who of Michelin stars and European master chefs, household names even to those who mightn't think they know much about that stratum of the culinary world.

SIMPLE, RUSTIC, PACKED WITH FLAVOUR AND VERY LITTLE WORK

They all seemed to lay a path to the castle's door. Even beloved Irish hotelier (and now television personality) Francis Brennan had a hand in bringing the humble Drogheda man west to Clare.

David and his wife, Anne, found a family home just outside the village of Newmarket-on-Fergus to raise their three children. Whenever possible, they took the family to the ancestral farm and into the natural surroundings of the Burren. Even now David is known to take his youngest son on a run along a 5 km loop of the bogs from which he helped save turf for his grandmother. It's part of keeping connection to his family's history – a time and a place when simply surviving and raising a family to adulthood was seen as success.

Always keen to take two days off together in the week – one for family and one for himself – the cosy family meal that David offers is one he often cooks on a Sunday afternoon at home or back in Drogheda when his brothers and sisters gather with their families. It's exactly the kind of food one would think of in a chef's home: simple, rustic, packed with flavour and very little work.

NOT YOUR MOTHER'S POT ROAST

Don't get us wrong: chefs love to cook. There are days, however, where we'd like to not think too much about what we're cooking – even if we have friends coming to dinner. David gives us tried and true recipes from his home kitchen that allow for a little mental down time while still wowing with flavour and creativity. His kale salad makes for a great work-day packed lunch as well. In fact, this salad with Eva Hegarty's courgette soup with seaweed crackers (page 206) says rainy-day lunch all winter long.

STARTER
Kale and quinoa salad with feta
MAIN
Braised feather blade of beef in red wine with purée of braised vegetables
SIDES
Buttered mashed potatoes
Oven-roasted broccoli
DESSERT
Pineapple pudding

KALE AND QUINOA SALAD WITH FETA

Serves 6

100 g/3½ oz/⅔ cup quinoa, well rinsed
    under running water

Sea salt

1 small handful sultanas (golden raisins)

200 g/7 oz young kale leaves, stemmed,
    washed and torn small

100 g/3 oz feta cheese, diced

60 g/2 oz/½ cup cashews nuts, toasted

4 spring onions (scallions), peeled and
    sliced

2 pomegranates, deseeded

1 red onion, peeled and diced

2 tsp dry dillisk flakes

1 tsp chopped chervil

1 tsp chopped coriander (cilantro)

1 tsp chopped mint

For the vinaigrette

1 tsp Dijon mustard

40 ml/1½ fl oz/3 tbsp cider vinegar

20 ml/¾ fl oz/5 tsp apple juice

1 lemon, zested

1 clove garlic, crushed

120 ml/4 fl oz/½ cup extra virgin olive oil

Sea salt and freshly ground black pepper

Place the quinoa in a saucepan with double the amount of cold water and a little sea salt. Bring to a boil over high heat, reduce to medium and simmer for approximately 12 minutes. Once all the liquid is absorbed, remove from heat, fluff with a fork and stir in the sultanas. Pour out onto a baking tray to cool.

Spin the kale leaves completely dry and put into a large salad bowl. Sprinkle the remaining ingredients, including the cooled quinoa, into the bowl

To make the vinaigrette, add the mustard, vinegar, apple juice, lemon zest and garlic to a small bowl. Whisk in the olive oil in a thin stream to emulsify. Season with salt and pepper.

Toss the salad in the vinaigrette, making sure it is coated completely. Correct the seasoning and serve.

BRAISED FEATHER BLADE OF BEEF IN RED WINE WITH PURÉE OF BRAISED VEGETABLES

. . . .

Serves 6

1.5 kg/3⅓ lb beef feather blade, trimmed and tied

2 onions, peeled and quartered

3 carrots, peeled and cut into large pieces

2 stalks celery, washed and cut into large pieces

3 cloves garlic, peeled

2 bay leaves

1 sprig thyme

500 ml/18 fl oz/2 cups red wine

500 ml/18 fl oz/2 cups beef stock

Salt and freshly ground black pepper

3 tbsp sunflower oil

CHEF'S NOTE
Once you try this neglected cheaper cut of beef you'll be asking your butcher for it regularly. It comes from the shoulder of beef, so has great flavour and marbling of fat. The meat braises beautifully, and that marbling makes for a rich, luxurious red wine sauce.

Preheat oven to 160°C/320°F/Gas Mark 3.

In a large bowl, place the beef, vegetables, herbs and red wine. Cover with cling film and refrigerate overnight. Remove and drain, reserving the wine. Pat beef dry.

In a saucepan over medium–high heat, bring the wine and stock to the boil. Reduce heat to medium and simmer, skimming well. Reduce the liquid by half and reserve. Season the beef well with salt and pepper. Heat oil in a large frying pan over high heat until shimmering. Brown the beef on all sides and ends.

Place the drained vegetables into a braising tray and put the browned beef on top. Add the reduced liquid, cover with a lid or tightly with tinfoil and place into the middle of the preheated oven. Braise for 1 hour. Reduce oven to 140°C/280°F/Gas Mark 1 and continue to cook for a further 2½ hours until tender. Remove the beef to a warm plate, cover loosely with tinfoil and keep warm.

Remove the thyme and bay leaves from the tray. Strain the liquid into a saucepan over medium–high heat, bring to the boil and skim off any fat. Reduce heat to medium and simmer to reduce by a third.

Place the vegetables and reduced cooking liquid in a blender and blend to a smooth purée.

To serve, cut the beef into 6 equal pieces. Spoon a dollop of purée on each plate and spread with the back of the spoon. Place the beef on top of the purée and spoon over the rich red wine sauce. Serve with buttered mashed potatoes (page 148) and roasted broccoli (page 150).

BUTTERED MASHED POTATOES

Serves 6

12 medium potatoes, scrubbed well

100 ml/3½ fl oz/⅓ cup + 4 tsp cream

60 g/2 oz/4 tbsp butter, plus more if
   desired

Sea salt and black pepper

½ bunch scallions, sliced (optional)

Place the potatoes in a large pot of cold salted water. Bring to a boil over medium–high heat. Reduce heat to medium–low and simmer until skins begin to break and potatoes are nearly tender (about 30 minutes). Turn off heat. Drain the potatoes and return the pot to the ring that was turned off. Cover the pot with a dry tea towel to absorb steam, put the lid on top and leave for 10 minutes. In a small saucepan, heat the cream and half the butter over medium–low heat until the butter is melted and cream is hot.

Peel the potatoes, using the towel to hold them as they'll be hot. Mash by hand using a food mill or a ricer. Fold in the cream and butter mixture. Season with salt and pepper to taste, adding more butter if desired – the butterier the better! Garnish with scallions if using.

OVER-ROASTED BROCCOLI

Serves 6

2 large heads broccoli (about 1.5 kg/3 lb)

6 tbsp extra virgin olive oil

1 tsp sea salt

1 tsp caster (superfine) sugar

Freshly ground black pepper

Preheat oven to 260°C/500°F/Gas Mark 10. Adjust an oven rack to the lowest position and put a large rimmed baking tray on the rack to preheat.

Cut the broccoli at the juncture where the florets meet the stems. Remove the outer peel from the stalks and cut into 3–7 cm/2–3-inch lengths and each length into 1½ cm/½-inch thick pieces or batons. Cut the crowns into 4 to 6 wedges (4 wedges if heads are about 10 cm/4 inches in diameter or 6 wedges if larger). Place the broccoli (wedges and batons) in a large bowl, drizzle with oil and toss well until evenly coated. Sprinkle with the salt, sugar and pepper, to taste, and toss to combine.

Working quickly, remove the baking tray from the oven and transfer the broccoli to the tray. Spread into an even layer cut-side down. Return the baking tray to the oven and roast for 9 to 11 minutes, until cut sides of stalks are well browned and tender and florets are lightly browned.

CHEF'S NOTE

Contact with the preheated baking tray is of paramount importance to the success of this dish. Use as large a tray as your oven will allow, or two trays if needed. A thick aluminium tray is best as it will retain heat better than a thin one. The aim is to concentrate the broccoli's own flavour while enhancing it with the sweet–bitter balance from the caramelisation of sugars.

PINEAPPLE PUDDING

· ·

Serves 6

For the brown crumbs

40 g/1½ oz/3 tbsp rich demerara (dark brown) sugar

125 g/4½ oz/1 cup brown soda bread, crumbled (homemade, of course)

For the pineapple crisps

50 g/1¾ oz/¼ cup caster (superfine) sugar

100 ml/3½ fl oz/⅓ cup + 4 tsp water

6 slices fresh pineapple, very thin, peeled

For the pineapple filling

50 g/1¾ oz/2 tbsp + 1 tsp local honey

40 g/1½ oz/3 tbsp caster (superfine) sugar

30 ml/1 fl oz/2 tbsp water

1 stick cinnamon

1 star anise

3 cloves

3 cardamom pods

400 g/14 oz pineapple, peeled, cored and diced

30 g/1 oz/2 tbsp butter

50 ml/1¾ fl oz/2 tbsp + 1 tsp Cointreau

6 moulds, 6 cm in diameter and 6 cm high (about 2¼ inches x 2¼ inches)

Preheat oven to 160°C/320°F/Gas Mark 3.

Mix the sugar and brown breadcrumbs together. Place on a baking tray and bake until golden brown, 5 to 8 minutes, stirring occasionally. Place in a bowl and mix to break up the larger pieces.

To make the pineapple crisps, preheat oven to 100°C/200°F/Gas Mark ¼.

In a saucepan over medium–high heat, bring the sugar and water to a boil. Add the pineapple slices and simmer for 1 minute. Remove the slices of pineapple and place on an oven tray lined with greaseproof paper. Put the tray in the middle of the preheated oven and bake until crisp (approximately 1½ hours).

For the pineapple filling, melt the honey, sugar, water and spices in a saucepan over medium heat, and cook until the syrup begins to turn golden caramel in colour. Add the diced pineapple and increase heat to high. Add the butter and reduce to a simmer, cooking gently until the mixture begins to thicken. Remove from the heat and add the Cointreau. Pick out the whole spices.

Place 1 tablespoon of pineapple mixture in the bottom of each mould, then add a layer of brown breadcrumbs. Continue to repeat the layers until the moulds are filled. Press firmly and leave to rest at room temperature for 1 hour.

To serve, warm slightly in a low oven, turn out of the moulds onto individual plates and garnish with a pineapple crisp.

THE PRODUCERS

Some of the world's chefs feel it their calling to bend food to their will. Enlightened chefs know that their job, rather, is to source impeccable ingredients and do as little as possible in order to let them shine. Finding those perfect ingredients is where the food producers of the Burren scintillate. Tapping into the wonders of limestone tumbling through shale down to the sea to figuratively mine raw materials for chefs and home cooks to exploit is no less a passion than is the cooking of the ingredients created by our producers.

It is an impossible task to create something as extraordinary as Burren produce in a vacuum. Each producer has learnt how to work in concert with land, sea and weather to rear, raise, roast, forage, ferment and brew foods unique to the Burren. From harvesting wild yeast in the mountains to rearing twenty-five generations of specially bred sheep, from hand-roasted and -blended coffee to harvesting sustainably whatever the tide exposes, and more, Burren food producers are a key link in bringing the unique taste of the Burren to the chefs of north Clare as well as to the rest of the country and across the seas.

The meals they offer are a thoughtful combination of one another's ingredients and their individual tastes and experiences. They are tended with a caring touch and served with the love you'd expect from the deft hands of passionate artisans.

While the specific ingredients can, of course, be substituted if not available to you, much of the fun of recreating these menus will be sourcing a taste of the Burren because many of the producers can ship their products right to your kitchen.

INTERNATIONAL HOUSE OF OYSTERS

CIARA O'HALLORAN

THE REDBANK FOOD COMPANY

· ·

As with so many others I spoke to while researching this book, Ciara O'Halloran and her three siblings grew up living the kind of life many try to emulate today. It was a simple life in so many ways but, like many 'simple' things, difficult to recreate. From a two-teacher primary school to foraging 'mystery tours' of the Burren, a more idyllic Irish childhood is hard to imagine.

From the big country house, with extensive gardens, forestry and orchards (and admittedly a waist-high lawn at the back), a menagerie of farm animals and foods considered exotic by schoolmates, Ciara's upbringing outside of Kinvara is to be envied. She says that it was a 'mad' upbringing … but a good kind of mad.

Those exotic foods were influenced by the flow of international business contacts her father would bring to the house as a matter of course in his seafood export business. Gerry ('Hoppy' to his friends) O'Halloran is a marine scientist, who helped open the first oyster farm on the coast near Carna in Connemara. The original incarnation of Redbank was established in 1962 as an exporter of live crustaceans and shellfish by a Belgian who settled in the Burren. Hoppy and some of his scientist colleagues from that original Connemara shellfish farm took over the space in the mid-1980s and grew the business to twenty-five employees.

When times were tight, Ciara remembers meals of oysters and mussels, clams, lobsters and crabs and prawns – oh, the horrors of her youth!

With visitors from Japan, New Zealand, China, Europe, the US and the Middle East coming by the house during trips to negotiate trades with her father or to take psychodynamics training courses with her mother, Ciara and her siblings learned to see their farming village through international eyes.

Dinners at the O'Hallorans' were often a hotchpotch of influences. Now standard in Irish kitchens, the likes of pasta dishes or curries, or even homemade wines (made of anything from blackcurrants to bananas!) garnered them a reputation as the 'hippies' of Kinvara. Hoppy closed the family business in 2007.

Ciara studied outdoor education at NUI Galway after a gap year in the US. The degree opened up jobs in youth development work, which would take her to New Zealand, Kenya and Zambia. It was work she loved: creating youth leadership programmes to move the thinking of young people in

Africa toward sustainability by searching out investment rather than looking for aid. Importantly for Ciara, she also learned from the work how much can be done on a shoestring start-up budget if one thinks lean and keeps ultimate goals clearly in view.

Environmental-sustainability issues learned in Africa also weigh heavily on Ciara's mind now that she has reopened The Redbank Food Company with her dad (and the occasional help of her two brothers). With pristine Grade-A waters where their oysters are raised being paramount in not only the image but also the flavour of the shellfish, conservation of the environment is more than just a nice thing to do for future generations.

The waters that flow down through the mountain are filtered by miles of underground limestone estuaries, which lead to underwater vents, bringing nutrients to the oyster beds.

CONSERVATION OF THE ENVIRONMENT IS MORE THAN JUST A NICE THING TO DO FOR FUTURE GENERATIONS

Conservation of the Burren and continued sustainable farming and agriculture of the area is something you can taste every time you sit on the flaggy shore and open an oyster.

SHELL COTTAGE KITCHEN

· ·

When Ciara and her siblings were growing up, they begged their mother not
to serve something as *exotic* as pasta when their friends came to dinner. A
stew or roast would have been far less spoken of between classes the next day.
How times have changed! Her variation on a theme fits right into our modern
expectation of fresh Irish ingredients melding with international flavours.
Birgitta Hedin-Curtin's oyster rumaki (page 33) would really take this menu
around the world.

STARTERS
Garlic breaded clams
Grilled oysters with chorizo and Parmesan
MAIN
Shellfish linguini in white wine cream
DESSERT
Apple, berry and hazelnut crumble

GARLIC BREADED CLAMS

Serves 6

4 cloves garlic, minced

60 g/2 oz/4 tbsp butter

2 tbsp parsley, minced

1 kg/2 lb 4 oz hard-shell clams

1 healthy splash white wine

100 g/3½ oz/¾ cup dry breadcrumbs

2 tbsp Parmesan, grated

CHEF'S NOTE

Saying 'clams' is about as descriptive as saying 'potatoes'. A vast array of varieties are on the market around the world. Here in Ireland the most common clams are Palourde or 'Manila', which are wild, and the White Palourde, sometimes called 'surf clams', are the farmed version of the same variety. Both will work just fine in any recipes in this book that call for clams.

Preheat grill (broiler) to medium–high.

Mash the garlic, butter and parsley together on a small plate until well combined. Can be refrigerated, covered, overnight at this stage.

Place the clams and a good splash of wine in a large, covered pot over a high heat. Bring to a boil and steam until clams begin to open (about 5 minutes). Remove the pot from the heat and, using a slotted spoon, transfer clams to a platter to cool a bit. Reserve the liquid for the pasta dish (page 161).

In a small saucepan over medium–low heat, melt the garlic butter. Break the two halves of each clam apart and place the half with the meat on a baking tray. Sprinkle the clams with breadcrumbs, drizzle with melted garlic butter and top with a sprinkle of cheese.

Place under grill (broiler) for 4 to 5 minutes, until golden brown and hot. Serve straight from the tray or transfer to a warmed serving platter.

GRILLED OYSTERS WITH CHORIZO AND PARMESAN

Serves 6

1½ dozen small oysters

60 g/2 oz/¼ cup cured chorizo, finely
  chopped

1 shallot, finely minced

60 g/2 oz/¼ cup Parmesan, finely grated

Preheat grill (broiler) to medium–high. Line a baking tray with tinfoil. Make two lines of crumpled foil to act as beds for the oysters.

Shuck the oysters over a bowl to catch any juices, which should be reserved for the pasta dish (page 161). Press the half of the shell with the oyster onto the crumpled foil to seat. Sprinkle each oyster with a bit of chorizo, shallot and cheese. Place under preheated grill (broiler) for 4 minutes until cheese melts and chorizo is bubbling. Serve straight from the tray or transfer to a warmed serving platter.

SHELLFISH LINGUINI IN WHITE WINE CREAM

Serves 6

4 cloves garlic, minced

60 g/2 oz/4 tbsp butter, softened

2 tbsp parsley, minced

1 kg/2 lb 4 oz mussels

1 kg/2 lb 4 oz clams

About 300 ml (1¼ cups) white wine

60 ml/2 fl oz/¼ cup olive oil

5 shallots, minced

200 g/7 oz mushrooms, chopped small

500 g/1 lb 2 oz dry linguini

300 g/10½ oz cherry tomatoes, halved

400 ml/14 fl oz/1⅔ cups cream

25 g/¾ oz/½ cup parsley, minced

2 tbsp dill, minced

Ground dillisk seaweed (or sea salt) and
   freshly ground black pepper

60 g/2 oz/¼ cup Parmesan, finely grated

Mash the garlic, butter and parsley together on a small plate until well combined, then set aside.

Wash and de-beard mussels and wash clams. Set a large covered pot over medium–high heat. Add the clams, mussels, half the garlic butter and a splash of the white wine. Cover, bring to a boil and steam until shellfish have begun to open, which will take about 5 minutes. Remove from heat.

In the meantime, bring a large pot of heavily salted water to a boil for cooking the pasta.

Carefully pour the shellfish into a strainer set over a large bowl to catch the liquid and cover to keep warm. Return the pot to the heat and reduce to medium. Add in the olive oil, remaining garlic butter, shallots, mushrooms and a pinch of salt. Sweat the vegetables until the mushrooms have given off most of their liquid.

Add the reserved cooking liquid from the shellfish (if you have reserved liquids from your starter course, add here as well) and enough wine to make approximately 500ml/18 fl oz/2 cups in total. Bring to a boil, then reduce heat to medium and reduce the liquid by about a quarter.

Cook the pasta to your taste and drain.

Add the tomatoes, cream and cooked shellfish to the sauce and increase heat to high. Bring to a hard simmer, add the parsley and dill, correct the seasoning with seaweed (or sea salt) and black pepper and add the cooked pasta. Toss and serve on a large warmed platter with a sprinkling of Parmesan.

APPLE, BERRY AND HAZELNUT CRUMBLE

. . . .

Serves 6

1 kg/2 lb 4 oz apples, peeled, cored and
  sliced

1 tbsp orange zest, finely grated

50 g/1¾ oz/¼ cup demerara (raw) sugar

1 tsp ground mixed spice (see Chef's
  Note)

200 g/7 oz/1⅓ cups blackberries

Butter for greasing

For the crumble

150 g/5¼ oz/⅔ cup plain (all-purpose)
  flour

50 g/1¾ oz/¼ cup demerara (raw) sugar

90 g/3 oz/6 tbsp butter, cold

100 g/3½ oz/1 cup hazelnuts, roughly
  chopped

1 tsp ground mixed spice

Preheat oven to 180°C/350°F/Gas Mark 4. Grease an ovenproof baking dish with butter.

In a large bowl, toss together the apples, zest, sugar and spice until coated. Gently fold in the blackberries and pour into the prepared baking dish.

To make the crumble, sift the flour into a large bowl and then mix in the sugar. Rub in the butter until the mix resembles fine breadcrumbs. Fold in the chopped hazelnuts and spice. Spoon the crumble topping over the fruit.

Place the dish on a baking tray in the middle of a preheated oven for 40 minutes. Remove and cool on a rack for at least 20 minutes. Serve with ice cream.

CHEF'S NOTE

Mixed spice can be made if not available in your local shop. Here is a typical recipe using ground spices: 1 tbsp allspice, 1 tbsp cinnamon, 1 tbsp nutmeg, 2 tsp mace, 1 tsp cloves, 1 tsp coriander, 1 tsp ginger. Blend all the spices together and store in a sealed jar away from light for up to 6 months (1 year if you grind the spices fresh).

ACRES OF DIAMONDS

DONAL MONAGHAN

GLENINAGH BURREN LAMB

• •

Donal Monaghan is from Claregalway and his wife, Neasa, from Gleninagh, about halfway between Ballyvaughan and Black Head. Their farm lies at the foot of mountains and on the edge of Galway Bay, on the land of her family's home place. It is in their sitting room, with their daughter, Yasmin, playing on the floor, that we find we know some of the same people in Seattle, Washington in the US. Only in Ireland.

Donal is a carpenter by training and had a full-time business designing and contracting kitchen refits while still helping his father on the family sheep farm north-east of Galway city. This wasn't just any sheep farm. For nearly three decades, the flocks that are now Gleninagh Burren Lamb have been vaccine-free and no worse the wear for it. In fact, the customers who specially order their lamb will say that it's the best lamb in the west – even the whole of the country.

Donal and Neasa met at a wedding and eventually moved to Gleninagh in 1996. Ten years later they had assembled enough land to move the flock to Clare.

The people who come up with such things have deemed the way many people in the world now work to be the 'gig economy', meaning that few people have one job from graduation to retirement anymore and many have a number of 'gigs' that they work at any one time. Many Irish farmers laugh at the idea, as they've been 'gigging' for generations.

It's probably what brought Gleninagh Burren Lamb to the forefront of the Burren food scene before many other farmer–producers. It was a perfect fit, as far as Donal the farmer and Neasa – a trained chef – were concerned. When a friend who sold wine started to tell people they should try their lamb, the couple began marketing directly to the customers, who hadn't known they could buy directly from the farmer.

'Farming has changed,' Donal told me, 'and not always for the better.' He feels that many have forgotten they are raising food. Farming has become big business to them, which is something Donal tries very hard to avoid.

It is difficult for a small farmer with around a hundred breeding ewes, along with the ancillary stock required to maintain that sized farm. Rather than growing the flock, however, Donal also raises grass seed for his own wholesale business as well as for a large distributor. He is very active in the

Burren Food Trail, offering speciality cuts to chefs during promotional events that showcase the area and its produce to people from around the globe.

It's not an easy life, but it is one the family relish. They spend more time outside than inside. During the lambing season, that includes the overnight hours. Even in their little bit of spare time they're either cycling, swimming or climbing. Donal is currently spending a bit more time on the mountain because he is training for a trek to Everest Base Camp. As one does …

Like many zealous converts, Donal is fiercely protective of the physical and spiritual space of the Burren he now calls home. It's like the farmer, he says, who sold his land to go off in search of wealth in the gold rush, only to hear that the man he'd sold to had ploughed up acres of diamonds. 'There's no place like it,' he says of their little strip of green, dotted with white sheep, in between the grey of Gleninagh Mountain and the blue of Galway Bay. And he's right.

CUSTOMERS WHO SPECIALLY ORDER THEIR LAMB WILL SAY THAT IT'S THE BEST LAMB IN THE WEST

FARMHOUSE POSH

· ·

The love with which Donal and Neasa Monaghan tend their land comes through in the preparation of this meal. It's another of our make-ahead wonders as well. The 'ravioli' can be waiting in the refrigerator and the stew slowly braising while you take a cycle, hike or even a kip after a long morning in the gardens. A drop of the craythur in the cupcakes sets this dessert on the 'make them again' list. Hugh Robson's chutney-stuffed baked apples (page 25) might make a bright side to the rich and hearty stew.

STARTER
Smoked salmon and shrimp 'ravioli'
MAIN
Farmhouse lamb and barley stew
SIDE
Cheese scones
DESSERT
Irish coffee cupcakes

SMOKED SALMON AND SHRIMP 'RAVIOLI'

Serves 6

For the filling

225 g/8 oz small shrimp

500 ml/18 fl oz/2 cups quality beer or ale, very cold

225 g/8 oz cream cheese, softened

1 tbsp tomato purée (paste)

½ tsp black pepper, freshly ground

¼ tsp sea salt

1 pinch red (cayenne) pepper, to taste

1 shallot, minced

1 stalk celery, peeled and minced

120 ml/4 fl oz/½ cup mayonnaise

1 tbsp Worcester sauce

For the vinaigrette

1 tsp Dijon mustard

40 ml/1½ fl oz/3 tbsp cider vinegar

20 ml/¾ fl oz/4 tsp apple juice

1 lemon, zested

120 ml/4 fl oz/½ cup extra virgin olive oil

Sea salt and freshly ground black pepper

To assemble

12 thin slices (about 250 g/9 oz) cold-smoked salmon

1 bunch watercress, washed

1 lemon, cut into 6 wedges

3 tbsp dill, minced

In a medium pot of heavily salted boiling water, place the shrimp and cook for 4 minutes. Drain, place the shrimp in a bowl and pour the cold beer over to chill and flavour. Once cooled, drain the beer and discard. Peel and finely chop the shrimp and set aside.

In a bowl, mix the cream cheese, tomato purée, seasoning and vegetables with a fork to blend. Whisk in the mayonnaise and Worcester sauce. Fold in the cooked shrimp, correct the seasoning, cover and chill.

To make the vinaigrette, add the mustard, vinegar, apple juice and lemon zest to a small bowl. Whisk in the olive oil in a thin stream to emulsify. Season with salt and pepper, and set aside.

To assemble, place a piece of greaseproof paper on a flat work surface. Lay out 6 thin slices of smoked salmon on top. Onto the widest part of the slices, spoon a dollop of the shrimp mousse. Lay another slice over the first (it may take more to cover) and press around the mousse. You may leave it as is or use a cutter to make the 'ravioli' into a shape. Repeat till all the ravioli are finished.

Transfer each one to a chilled plate and drizzle vinaigrette around it. Garnish with watercress drizzled with a bit of vinaigrette as well. Dip lemon wedges into minced dill and place one on each plate.

FARMHOUSE LAMB AND BARLEY STEW

Serves 6

1.5 kg/3½ lb stewing lamb, diced

60 ml/2 fl oz/¼ cup olive oil

2 tsp ground turmeric

2 cloves garlic, peeled and crushed

Sea salt and freshly ground black pepper

60 ml/2 fl oz/¼ cup rapeseed (canola) oil

6 small onions, peeled and quartered

6 carrots, peeled

2 parsnips, peeled

2 red bell peppers, deseeded and cut into
large pieces

150 g/5¼ fl oz/⅔ cup barley

60 ml/2 fl oz/¼ cup Ballymaloe tomato
relish, or tomato purée (paste) mixed
with 1 tbsp sugar

CHEF'S NOTE

Neasa leaves most of the vegetables whole in this stew. As it will braise for a very long time, this makes sense. The shorter the cooking time of a dish, the smaller the pieces must be cut, not only for the cooking of the vegetables, but also for flavouring the dish as a whole.

In a large bowl, toss the lamb with the oil, turmeric, garlic, sea salt and black pepper. Cover with cling film, pressing down on the meat, and refrigerate overnight

Preheat oven to 180°C/350°F/Gas Mark 4.

In a casserole (Dutch oven) over medium–high heat, add 1 tsp of oil and heat until shimmering. Add 1 handful of the marinated lamb, spreading it evenly, and do not stir for 4 minutes to brown. Stir the lamb to brown on all sides for an additional 4 to 5 minutes. Remove to a colander set over a bowl to capture the juices. Repeat, one handful at a time. It is important to not crowd the lamb, or it will steam rather than brown.

Once all the lamb has been browned, add a quarter cup of the reserved cooking juices to the casserole to deglaze, scraping well. Add onions, carrots, parsnips and peppers to the casserole. Pour the rest of the cooking juices into a measuring jug and top with water to make 1 litre/1¾ pints/4 cups. Add to the pot and bring to a boil. Stir in the barley, reduce heat to medium and simmer for 10 minutes. Stir in the relish and add the lamb – the liquid should just cover the lamb, so remove or add as needed. Cover and place in the middle of a preheated oven for 2 hours. After 2 hours, remove lid, turn off oven and leave for an additional hour. Correct seasoning and serve.

CHEESE SCONES

Serves 6

225 g/8 oz/2½ cups self-raising (self-rising) white flour

2 tsp caster (superfine) sugar

60 g/2 oz/4 tbsp butter, room temperature

2 spring onions (scallions), sliced

60 g/2 oz/¼ cup flavoured Gouda-style cheese, grated (see Chef's Note)

1 pinch salt

100 ml/3½ fl oz/⅓ cup + 4 tsp milk

Preheat oven to 180°C/350°F/Gas Mark 4.

In a bowl, mix together the flour and sugar. Rub the butter into the flour and fold in the spring onions, cheese and salt. Fold in a bit of milk to bind (you might not need it all). Turn onto a floured work surface and pat flat to 1.25 cm/½ inch.

Cut as desired and place on a baking tray lined with greaseproof paper. Bake in the middle of the preheated oven for 20 minutes, until golden on top. Cool on a wire rack and serve with butter – loads of butter!

CHEF'S NOTE
Garlic and nettle or black pepper flavours are preferred for the cheese, but unflavoured will work too.

IRISH COFFEE CUPCAKES

Makes 12

110 g/4 oz/1 stick butter, room
    temperature

120 g/4½ oz/⅔ cup brown sugar

2 eggs

160 g/5½ oz/1¼ cups self-raising (self-
    rising) flour

30 ml/1 fl oz/2 tbsp milk

1 tbsp strong brewed coffee

For the icing

110 g/4 oz/1 stick butter, room
    temperature

225 g/8 oz/2½ cups icing (powdered)
    sugar

1 tbsp strong brewed coffee

30 ml/1 fl oz/2 tbsp Irish whiskey, or more
    to taste

Preheat oven to 180°C/350°F/Gas Mark 4. Line muffin tin with 12 paper cases.

In the bowl of a stand mixer, cream the butter and brown sugar until light and fluffy. Mix in one egg at a time, scraping down in between, and mix on high speed until very light. Reduce speed and fold in the flour, then add the milk and coffee and fold in gently.

Divide the batter between the paper cases. Bake in the middle of the preheated oven for 20 to 25 minutes, until a toothpick comes out clean. Remove to a cooling rack, cool in the tins for 10 minutes, then remove and cool completely.

To make the icing, cream the butter and icing sugar on high speed. Mix the coffee and whiskey together and slowly stir into the icing. Spread onto the cooled cupcakes and serve.

YOU CAN'T RUN IN THE BURREN

BRIAN O'BRIAIN

ANAM COFFEE

. . . .

If you were to put a pin in a copy of *The Burren: A Map of the Uplands of North-West County Clare*, the topographical map made by cartographer Tim Robinson, at the spot where Brian O'Briain's Anam Coffee roastery sits nestled on a wooded slope at the forked meeting of boreens, you'd be forgiven for thinking it the back of beyond. Geographically very near the centre of the Burren, Brian and his husband Alan are figuratively at the centre of a community the novice eye might miss.

The buildings on the land include but are not limited to their update of an 1860 cottage, a former Gouda-style cheese dairy and the former automobile garage that now houses two small but industrial coffee roasters. That building also serves as corporate headquarters, packaging facility, marketing centre and upcycling centre for many by-products of Anam's business.

It's not a large space, but it's a space in which every detail has been considered. As with their busy lives in London, which Brian left and to which Allan still commutes weekly, time and space in the roastery have been thought out, planned and then executed with the utmost care.

From a Dublin family, Brian grew up in the Shannon area and emigrated to London where he eventually landed a high-powered job in the airline industry. When that position allowed no time for his personal needs around his father's ailing health, Brian knew that it was time to move on, but to what was the question. Leaving that position was an uncharacteristic decision but one that eventually led to a pastoral life and the creation of some amazing coffee.

Not so uncharacteristically, his next moves were deliberate, calculated and, though he wasn't exactly sure of the final career destination, precise.

He was accepted onto a Bord Bia master's degree programme where he worked on marketing Irish products throughout Scandinavia from his base in Stockholm. He acted as a consultant to a Donegal seafood company. He travelled extensively, and everywhere he visited, he noted the number of people seeking out great coffee.

Once it was agreed between the couple, local enterprise boards, banks and potential customers that Clare could support its own artisanal coffee roastery, the job was only part done. Roasting schools, tasting courses, visits to an international array of coffee-bean farmers and understanding the intricacies of flavour science all had to be completed.

Where they would establish the place was all but decided before he even began. The couple had for years used the Burren as a retreat from their high-stress life in England. The number of reasons it was here they would come to unplug are vast, but at the end of the day it comes down to something they still experience when Alan flies home on Friday evenings. It's about pace.

'No matter the strength of your boots, the sturdiness of your stick or the pressing of the world around you,' Brian says, 'you can't run in the Burren.'

You mightn't know that when you see how far and how often Brian traverses the area every week to deliver to, train and advise his coffee customers. The pace of the man was obviously conditioned. It's not an easy business to run from a place like the townland of Kilcorney. Nothing, however, slows him down like a walk in the Burren with Alan and their dog, Charlie. Nothing, perhaps, save a good cup of Anam (which means 'soul' in Irish, by the way) coffee, or perhaps the other passion he also likes to share: cooking for friends.

NO MATTER THE STRENGTH OF YOUR BOOTS, THE STURDINESS OF YOUR STICK OR THE PRESSING OF THE WORLD AROUND YOU, YOU CAN'T RUN IN THE BURREN

THAT'S ENTERTAINMENT!

. . . .

Was there ever a more perfect pairing than steak and chips? This menu does everything it says on the tin. Meat on a fire is older than the Muintir Nemid and as Burren as a dolmen, and this menu will have them coming from every hill and valley around. The sauces Brian offers are easy and tasty. If they seem too much work, make a double batch of Peter Jackson's horseradish crème fraîche from his grilled mackerel starter (page 41) and serve it in their place. It's a party, after all – no harm, no foul.

STARTER
Mackerel salad with beetroot and dill crème fraîche
MAIN
Grilled rib-eye steaks with duck-fat chips
Trio of steak sauces: Argentine chimichurri, spicy tomato, whiskey-peppercorn
DESSERT
Blackberry, almond and cardamom cake with black fruits

MACKEREL SALAD WITH BEETROOT AND DILL CRÈME FRAÎCHE

Serves 6

6 smoked mackerel fillets

2 beetroots, washed, peeled and finely grated

¼ head red cabbage, cored and very finely sliced

1 small red onion, peeled and French sliced (see note)

2 tbsp balsamic vinegar

60 ml/2 fl oz/¼ cup extra virgin olive oil

2 tbsp extra-fine capers

Sea salt and freshly ground black pepper

200 ml/7 fl oz/¾ cup + 4 tsp organic crème fraîche

2 bunches dill or chervil, leaves picked

Carefully skin the mackerel fillets and set aside.

In a large bowl, toss the beetroot, cabbage and onion to mix.

In a small bowl, whisk the vinegar and add the oil in a thin stream to emulsify. Add the capers. Season with sea salt and pepper. Dress the salad with vinaigrette and mound on 6 cold plates. Place a mackerel fillet against the salad on each plate and put a dollop of crème fraîche alongside the salad. Nestle the herbs in small bunches to garnish.

CHEF'S NOTE

To French-slice an onion, top, peel and cut in half from pole to pole. Using a chef's knife, cut off the root end at a 45° angle to release it from connecting the leaves. Now slice the onion from top to bottom, thus creating thin strips, which are milder than cross-cut slices.

GRILLED RIB-EYE STEAKS WITH DUCK-FAT CHIPS

Serves 6

6 large (5 cm/2-inch thick) bone-in rib-
eye steaks

Sea salt and freshly ground black pepper

60 ml/2 fl oz/¼ cup olive oil

6 large floury potatoes (Maris Piper,
Rooster or Russet)

2 litres/3½ pints/6 cups duck fat, melted
(or vegetable oil seasoned with as much
duck fat as you have)

Coarse sea salt

Season the steaks well and rub with olive oil. Cover and refrigerate for 4 hours or overnight (even better).

Wash and dry the potatoes, but leave the skin on. Slice into desired-sized chips and place in a bowl of lightly salted cold water.

Preheat fat in a large, heavy-bottomed casserole (Dutch oven) over a high heat to 150°C/300°F.

Drain a handful of chips at a time and pat dry on a tea towel. Gently slip the chips into the hot oil and blanch until they are very light brown and stop bubbling. Remove with a slotted spoon to a rack set over a rimmed baking tray to cool. (This can be done up to a day in advance, with the chips then sealed in an airtight container and refrigerated.) Remove the steaks 2 to 3 hours before cooking to come to room temperature. Preheat oven to 120°C/250°F/Gas Mark ½.

Heat a griddle pan over high heat until smoking, or preheat a barbecue. At the same time, reheat the fat to 190°C/375°F. Fry the chips (in 2 to 3 batches) until golden brown and crisp. Remove with a slotted spoon to a large mixing bowl lined with several layers of kitchen paper (paper towel). Blot off excess fat, season well with sea salt and place on a baking tray in the oven to keep warm. Repeat in batches, always returning the fat to temperature. While the chips are frying, place the steaks on the hot pan or barbecue and do not move them for 3 minutes. Turn the steaks over and cook for an additional 3 minutes for medium rare, longer for better done. Remove the steaks to a warm platter to rest for at least 10 minutes. Serve the steaks with chips and sauces (page 181) for passing around.

TRIO OF STEAK SAUCES

Argentine Chimichurri sauce

1 large bunch parsley, leaves only

4 cloves garlic, peeled and smashed

¼ cup, packed, oregano leaves, fresh

60 ml/2 fl oz/ ¼ cup red wine vinegar

½ tsp red pepper flakes

½ tsp sea salt

¼ tsp freshly ground black pepper

250 ml/8 fl oz/1 cup extra virgin olive oil

Into the bowl of a food processor, place the parsley, garlic, oregano, vinegar, red pepper flakes, salt and pepper. Process until finely chopped, which will take about 1 minute, scraping down with a rubber spatula as needed. With the motor running, drizzle the oil in a thin stream. Scrape down the bowl and pulse a few times to combine. Transfer to an airtight container and refrigerate for at least 2 hours or up to 1 day to allow the flavours to blend. Before serving, stir and correct seasoning. Will keep in the refrigerator for up to 1 week.

Spicy tomato sauce

60 ml/2 fl oz/¼ cup olive oil

1 small onion, minced

Sea salt

1 clove garlic, finely sliced

1 tbsp cumin seeds

1 heaped tsp hot paprika

2 bay leaves, fresh if possible

800 g/1 lb 12 oz fresh tomatoes, peeled and finely chopped

Black pepper, freshly ground

1 tbsp sherry vinegar

In a saucepan over medium heat, add the olive oil, onion and a pinch of salt, and sweat for 5 minutes. Add the garlic, cumin, paprika and bay leaves; stir and continue sweating for 3 more minutes. Add the tomatoes and season with salt and black pepper. Increase heat to medium–high and bring to a boil, then reduce heat to medium–low and simmer, stirring occasionally, for 30 minutes – add a bit of water if needed. Remove from heat and stir in the vinegar. Will keep, covered, in the refrigerator for up to 1 week.

Whiskey-peppercorn sauce

400 ml/14 fl oz/1⅔ cups beef stock

1 tbsp peppercorns (green or black, or a mixture), cracked

60 ml/2 fl oz/¼ cup Irish whiskey

250 ml/8 fl oz/1 cup double (heavy) cream

Sea salt

In a small saucepan over medium heat, combine the beef stock and cracked peppercorns. Simmer until reduced by nearly half, stirring frequently. Add the whiskey and simmer for 1 minute. Add the cream and continue simmering without boiling until the sauce is reduced to about a third. Correct seasoning with sea salt and serve warm.

BLACKBERRY, ALMOND AND CARDAMOM CAKE WITH BLACK FRUITS

• •

Serves 6

125 g/4½ oz/½ cup + 1 tbsp butter, room temperature

200 g/7 oz/1 cup golden caster (raw) sugar

1 tsp pure vanilla extract

3 medium eggs, free range if possible

250 g/9 oz/1½ cups ground almonds

2 tsp gluten-free baking powder

1 tsp cardamom, ground

¼ tsp salt

200 g/7 oz fresh blackberries

200 g/7 oz summer berries for garnish (black plums and mission figs are beautiful as well)

Crème fraîche, to serve

Preheat oven to 160°C/320°F/Gas Mark 3. Lightly oil a 23 cm/9-inch round cake tin.

In a stand mixer, cream the butter, sugar and vanilla until pale and fluffy. Add the eggs one at a time along with a spoonful of ground almonds to stop the mix from splitting (breaking). Scrape down in between.

In a large mixing bowl, combine the remaining ground almonds with the baking powder, ground cardamom and salt. Fold the dry ingredients into the butter mixture.

Stir until just blended and add the blackberries, stirring a couple of more times to incorporate.

Pour the batter into the prepared cake tin and bake in the middle of the preheated oven for 40 to 50 minutes or until the cake has risen, looks golden brown and feels firm to the touch. Remove and cool completely on a wire rack before turning out. Decorate with summer berries and serve with crème fraîche.

CHEF'S NOTE

This cake is gluten-free by happenstance rather than by design. Almond flour has been used in Mediterranean baking in place of wheat flour for centuries. Make an extra one of these and keep it in the freezer for when friends with gluten issues come to tea.

PETER CURTIN

BURREN BREWERY

Onomatologists – those versed in the history of names – tell us that the Curtins, descended from an *ollamh*, or leading scholar to the ancient kings, have always been defined by the times in which they have lived.

Peter Curtin's father was born on the day of the Easter Rising in 1916. His life was, therefore, defined by the time in which he lived. Peter says that he himself was born in the 'Dorothea Lange' period of Irish life – a black-and-white time – and that his own life has been defined by the journey Ireland has made since he was born in the very place we sat for a conversation: a pub since his parents' time, a bread bakery in his grandfather's time, now the anchor for a chain of Lisdoonvarna businesses that includes a pub, restaurant, multi-use event centre, visitor centre and smokehouse.

OLLAMH OF THE BURREN

While still an attraction for its mineral spa, the Lisdoonvarna of Peter's youth was home to only three cars and one tractor.

Peter described his life to me using the metaphor of a snail meandering across a pane of glass on a dewy evening. With no apparent target or intention, the snail will make his way across and over, up and down and around, to eventually reach no place in particular. It really is all about the journey and not the destination for the snail, and so too for Peter.

Drawn from the rocky place that is the Burren, Peter spent part of his life as a merchant mariner and fisherman. The requirement for focus and presence was one of the joys of life at sea for him. While his conscious brain was occupied by the constant flood of variables with which one must contend to remain safe while days from the nearest land, his unconscious was freed up to explore far beyond the moment. It may be an experience he tries to recapture on his Sunday walks through the Burren where one must concentrate on every step to remain safe in a place that urges the mind to wander and to wonder.

Now an avid and talented brewmaster as well as a beloved publican, Peter is lauded for his beers by experts and neophytes alike. For one of his beers, a gruit beer called Euphoria, he harvested wild yeast from the Hill of the Fairies, and he works with a local herbalist to blend native herbs to create its unique flavour. He says it has a 100 per cent strike rate with everyone – even those who don't tend toward beer.

Through yeast in his brewing and ovens used to smoke fishes in the smokehouse, Peter has kept connected to his historic link to the baking of bread. His next joint venture with pastry chef Fabiola Tombo is to create a sourdough starter using his patented live yeast and lees from his brewing process, which can be turned into bread.

PETER IS LAUDED FOR HIS BEERS BY EXPERTS AND NEOPHYTES ALIKE

Though it has been over a century since The Roadside Tavern supplied bread to the town of Lisdoonvarna, Peter Curtin is closing the loop back upon itself after a sinuous meandering of generations. It's not unlike the path of his snail on that window or the pleasant conversation we shared over a cuppa one fine morning in The Roadside Tavern.

A FEW OF HIS FAVOURITE THINGS

Hands on. That's how Peter brews, and that's how he wants to eat this menu. He's a grand man for the pan. This is roll up your sleeves, grab a roll of kitchen paper and don't get your hands too close to your neighbour's mouth kind of food. Your guests will be slurping oysters, sucking shellfish and slopping garlic butter everywhere. A mess will be made, and joy will ensue. If the trifle is a bit too seasonal for you, replace it with John Sheedy's lemon posset (page 110) for nearly the same effect.

STARTER
Pouldoody Bay oysters au naturel
MAIN
Shellfish boil with garlic butter
DESSERT
Irish whiskey and sherry trifle

POULDOODY BAY OYSTERS AU NATUREL

Serves 6

2 dozen native Atlantic oysters
   (Pouldoody Bay, if you are lucky
   enough)

6 lemons, cut in half along the equator

1 tbsp sugar

1 bunch curly parsley, leaves only, chopped

Shuck the oysters over a bowl to catch their juices and place them – in the deepest half of the shell – on a serving platter. Divide the captured juices evenly between them. Heat a large non-stick skillet over high heat. Sprinkle the cut sides of the lemons with a bit of sugar. Press the lemon halves onto the hot pan to burn the sugar for about 30 to 40 seconds. Dip the lemon halves in chopped parsley and serve alongside the oysters for squeezing.

CHEF'S NOTE

Burning the sugar on the surface of the lemon halves in this dish will change your experience with the oyster in ways you've never imagined. More than just an acidic foil to the oyster's rich saltiness, it will have you considering other ways in which to use burnt lemon in your repertoire.

SHELLFISH BOIL WITH GARLIC BUTTER

Serves 6

450 g/1 lb salted butter

60 ml/2 fl oz/¼ cup extra virgin olive oil

6 cloves garlic, 3 crushed, 3 thinly sliced

1 pinch chilli pepper flakes

1 lemon, zested

1 bunch curly parsley, leaves only, minced

6 Atlantic lobsters (600 g/1½ lb each)

Sea salt

500 ml/18 fl oz/2 cups dry white wine

1 lemon, sliced

2 kg/4½ lb mixed shellfish, scrubbed and
    rinsed – clams, cockles, mussels, prawns,
    shrimp, etc.

Sourdough bread, to serve

In a large saucepan over medium–low heat, melt the butter with the olive oil, garlic and chilli flakes. Remove from heat and whisk well. Set aside to cool for 30 minutes.

Stir in the lemon zest and parsley and transfer to a bowl and place in refrigerator. Stir every 10 minutes as the butter cools so that it stays incorporated. Will keep, covered and refrigerated, for up to 2 days.

In a large stockpot, cover the lobsters with lukewarm sea water (if you cannot use sea water, use 170 g/6 oz of fine sea salt for every 1.8 litres/half gallon of fresh water – it will be very salty, like the sea). Put the pot over medium heat and slowly bring to a hard simmer. The lobsters will die at about 45°C (112°F). By the time the water comes to a simmer, the lobsters will be ready for further cooking with the other shellfish.

Melt the garlic butter in a medium-sized saucepan over medium–low heat.

In a very large stockpot or shellfish steamer set over high heat, add wine, lemon slices and 500 ml/18 fl oz/2 cups of the lobster cooking water. Cover and bring to a boil.

Add shellfish in the order of time it will take them to cook:

- Par-cooked lobsters – 5 to 7 minutes
- Prawns (langoustines) – 5 to 6 minutes
- Clams – 4 to 5 minutes
- Mussels – 4 to 5 minutes
- Shrimp – 4 to 5 minutes
- Cockles – 3 to 4 minutes

Transfer the cooked shellfish to platters or trays. Serve hot with melted garlic butter and thick slices of your local artisan baker's sourdough bread – chargrilled is nice!

IRISH WHISKEY AND SHERRY TRIFLE

• •

Serves 6

For the sponge cake

1 tbsp vegetable oil, for greasing

3 eggs

85 g/3 oz/⅓ cup + 2 tbsp caster (superfine) sugar

85 g/3 oz/¾ cup plain (all-purpose) flour

For the custard

6 egg yolks

150 g/5¼ oz/¾ cup caster (superfine) sugar

40 g/1½ oz/¼ cup + 2 tsp plain (all-purpose) flour

1 pinch salt

1.1 litres/2 pints/4½ cups milk

90 g/3 oz/6 tbsp unsalted butter

1 tbsp + 1 tsp vanilla extract

To assemble

120 g/4 fl oz/½ cup gooseberry jam

60 ml/2 fl oz/¼ cup sherry-cask-aged Irish whiskey

60 ml/2 fl oz/¼ cup dry sherry

60 ml/2 fl oz/¼ cup simple syrup (equal parts sugar and water brought to a boil and cooled)

250 ml/8 fl oz/1 cup cream, whipped

Preheat oven to 180°C/350°F/Gas Mark 4. Grease two 33 cm x 23 cm (13 inch x 9 inch) baking trays with the tablespoon of vegetable oil.

To make the sponge, whip the eggs and sugar until they reach the ribbon stage. Sift flour over the egg mixture and gently fold together. Divide the batter between the greased baking trays. Bake for 30 to 40 minutes, until springy and lightly browned. Cool completely before using.

To make the custard, in a medium bowl, beat yolks and sugar until well mixed. Sift the flour and salt together. Stir into the eggs. Add 60 ml (¼ cup) of milk and mix well. In a small saucepan, heat the remaining milk and the butter over medium heat until the butter is melted and the mixture begins to steam – do not boil. Remove from heat and temper into egg mixture by adding 60 ml (¼ cup) at a time, stirring the eggs very well so that they do not scramble. Place the mixture in the saucepan and return to heat, stirring constantly. Cook until 70°C/160°F and thickened. Remove from the heat and pass through a fine-mesh sieve into a clean bowl. Stir in the vanilla. Use while still warm and pourable.

To assemble, cut the sponge into 5 cm x 8 cm (2 x 3 inch) rectangles and prick with a fork. Spread the sponge pieces with jam and sandwich together. Set aside. Add the whiskey and sherry to the syrup. Place one-quarter of the sponge pieces into a glass bowl. Sprinkle with one-quarter of the fortified syrup. Pour one-quarter of the custard onto cake. Spread to cover. Repeat in layers until you cover with the final quarter of custard. Chill for 4 hours or overnight. Top with whipped cream.

SIOBHÁN NÍ GHÁIRBHITH

ST TOLA IRISH GOAT CHEESE

· ·

To say that Siobhán Ní Gháirbhith comes from a family who valued education may be the understatement of this text. Her grandparents were teachers. Her granddad moved to the parish of Inagh from East Clare, met his wife and settled in a home provided by the community, as was customary at the time. They had eight children – one of whom is Siobhán's father – and seven of the eight became teachers. Siobhán and her elder sister were trained as teachers. Siobhán's partner in life and business, John, is also a trained teacher. It remains to be seen if their two children, Caoilte and Luisne, will take up the profession, but teaching runs strong in their family.

Siobhán's grandfather began acquiring land around their home in the 1920s to lease out to farmers to graze their herds and flocks, and by the time she was growing up on the farm there were 70-odd acres on which she and her five siblings could roam as only farm children know how. She developed a love for the land, which would see her moving back to the farm after leaving teaching and pursuing a degree and career in promoting locally sourced and produced foods in the Shannon region.

Not what she calls 'the greatest quality of land', being 10 kilometres from the sea and in the

STILL TEACHING

shadow of Slievecallan, it wasn't much use for conventional farming. As luck and timing would have it, however, the neighbours who had been making fresh, soft goat cheese, under the moniker of St Tola, were looking to exit the business after over a decade in their second career.

In 1998 Siobhán moved home and began to learn the trade of goat farming and cheesemaking while building the sheds and facilities required to house the goats and make cheese on their own land. The next year they had moved the flock and milked them in their new home but were still bringing milk to the other farm for cheesemaking. Much had changed in regulations since the original St Tola cheese house was built. Within the next year, however, the whole operation – local microbial flora and all – was in place and modern St Tola had begun.

The market for the types of cheeses Siobhán and her international crew now can't outpace was not then what it is today. She had to figuratively put on her teaching robes and educate potential customers about raw milk cheese. In a way, she feels that she couldn't have been successful in the business had it not been for two factors: her teaching skills and the business skills of her partner, John, the owner–operator of successful shellfish farms in south Kerry.

She and John met in a well-known 'ballroom of romance' one June bank holiday weekend in Dingle. It was he who really encouraged Siobhán to take on the challenge of the cheesemaking business. The couple and their children live between the two farms, one in Inagh and the other in Templenoe on the Kerry coast.

Pride of place and knowing whence one comes has been instilled in Siobhán by her parents. She's an Inagh, County Clare woman, and John is from Kerry. While Caoilte already identifies as a Templenoe man and plays forward for the local GAA football club, where Luisne will call her home is still up in the air.

Siobhán feels that her family extends well beyond her parents (who still live in the farmhouse on the land) and her two children. The herdsman, farmhands and cheesemakers all make up the extended family at St Tola. Not only Irish hands tend the goats on the farm, but staff from the western Eurasian steppes and eastern Europe all pitch in to make their cheese sought-after by chefs and discerning cheese lovers alike.

THE HERDSMAN, FARMHANDS AND CHEESEMAKERS ALL MAKE UP THE EXTENDED FAMILY AT ST TOLA

BURREN BARBECUE

The team at St Tola come from a broad swathe of European countries. Siobhán's menu reflects flavours from here and from far afield. Romanian slaw, Polish potato salad, Greek goat and Middle Eastern aubergine all show up to this United Nations of Flavour. If periwinkles are hard to come by, try Fiona Haugh's tomato soup (page 255) hot or cold (without the cream). Lay this buffet on the table and *fág a' bealach*. Your guests will come running!

STARTER
Foraged periwinkles with chilli-lime butter
MAIN
Yogurt-marinated kid goat kebabs with roasted aubergine dip
SIDES
Romanian cabbage slaw
Potato salad
DESSERT
Chocolate cheesecake

FORAGED PERIWINKLES WITH CHILLI-LIME BUTTER

Serves 6

225 g/8 oz/2 sticks salted butter

2 tbsp Thai sweet chilli sauce

1 lime, juiced and zested

1 kg/2 lb 4 oz periwinkles, well rinsed

Sea water or sea salt

In a saucepan over medium–low heat, melt the butter with the chilli sauce. When melted, stir in the lime juice and zest, reduce heat to low and keep warm.

In a stockpot over high heat, bring 1 litre/1¾ pints/ 4 cups sea water or heavily salted water to a boil. Add the periwinkles and cook for 4 to 5 minutes until firm. Drain and serve on a platter, with pins to extract, with chilli-lime butter for dipping and fresh brown bread.

YOGURT-MARINATED KID GOAT KEBABS WITH ROASTED AUBERGINE DIP

• •

Serves 6

300 ml/½ pint/1¼ cups natural Greek-
style yogurt

2 tbsp prepared mint sauce

2 tsp ground cumin

1 tbsp sea salt

800 g/1 lb 12 oz lean kid meat (can
substitute lamb), diced

For the roasted aubergine dip

2 large aubergines (eggplant)

2 tbsp mayonnaise

1 tbsp lemon juice

1 tsp English mustard

Sea salt and freshly ground black pepper

1 onion, cut into large chunks

Wooden skewers

6 large pittas

225 g/8 oz mixed salad leaves

In a bowl, mix the yogurt and mint sauce together, then divide the mixture in half. Stir the cumin and salt into one half of the yogurt mix and pour this into a large ziplock bag. Add the goat to the bag, seal and massage to coat the meat. Place in the refrigerator for at least 4 hours or overnight, if possible.

For the dip, first preheat oven to 200°C/400°F/Gas Mark 6.

Place the aubergine in a roasting dish and roast for 20 minutes, turning 4 times during cooking.

Remove and cool for 10 minutes or until you can handle it. Peel off the skin, chop the flesh and put into a colander set over a bowl to drain for 20 minutes.

In a bowl, mash the aubergine pulp with the mayonnaise, lemon juice and mustard. Season to taste with salt and freshly ground black pepper. Will keep, covered, in the refrigerator for 2 days.

Heat the grill (broiler) to medium or preheat a barbecue. Thread the kid meat onto 6 skewers, alternating with pieces of onion. Arrange the skewers on the wire rack of a grilling tray and grill for 3 to 4 minutes on each side.

Warm the pittas in a toaster or on the barbecue for 1 to 2 minutes and split open. Fill each pitta with kid, onion, leaves and a bit of the reserved yogurt. Serve with the smoked aubergine dip.

ROMANIAN CABBAGE SLAW

Serves 6

500 g/1 lb 2 oz white cabbage, cored and
    thinly sliced

½ tsp fine sea salt

2 tbsp sunflower oil (more to taste)

2 tbsp white wine vinegar

1 tsp caster (superfine) sugar

Freshly ground black pepper

2 tbsp parsley, minced

Place the cabbage in a colander set over a large bowl and toss with salt. Leave for 30 minutes to draw out moisture. Take handfuls of the cabbage and squeeze them to release the extra liquid.

Place the squeezed cabbage into a large mixing bowl. Add the oil, vinegar, sugar and freshly ground black pepper to taste. Toss well and adjust seasoning. Fold in the parsley.

CHEF'S NOTE

Cabbage leaves are crisp, to the point of being hard, because of the amount of water held within the cell walls. That water will be released when dressed. Salting the raw sliced cabbage allows for some water to be released before you dress the salad, thus keeping the flavours concentrated rather than watered-down.

POTATO SALAD

. . . .

Serves 6

10 medium waxy potatoes, peeled and cut
into 3–4 cm/1–1½-inch cubes

4 medium eggs, free range, hard-boiled,
peeled and sliced

20 small pickled gherkins, thinly sliced
lengthwise

2 roasted red peppers, sliced into strips
(jarred are fine)

1 white onion, peeled and minced

Black olives (optional)

1–3 tbsp mayonnaise, preferably
homemade, to taste

Sea salt and pepper to taste

Place the potatoes in a large pot, cover with cold, salted water and set over high heat. Bring to a boil, reduce heat to medium and simmer until tender, which will take about 6 minutes. Drain the potatoes and lay them out on a baking tray to cool completely.

In a large bowl, toss together the potatoes, eggs, gherkins, peppers, onions and olives if using. Fold in the mayonnaise to coat, then season to taste and serve.

CHEF'S NOTE

When boiling potatoes, always begin in cold water. This allows the potatoes to come up to temperature with the water and not cook from the outside in so that the outside falls apart while the centre is still raw.

CHOCOLATE CHEESECAKE

Serves 6

For the base

400 g/14 oz chocolate chip biscuits

1 tbsp cocoa powder

45 g/1½ oz/3 tbsp unsalted butter, melted
(more for greasing)

For the cheesecake

800 g/1 lb 12 oz St Tola curd goat cheese
(or cream cheese)

200 g/7 oz/1 cup granulated sugar

1 tsp vanilla extract

100 ml/3½ fl oz/⅓ cup + 4 tsp double
(heavy) cream

150 ml/5¼ fl oz/⅔ cup sour cream

4 eggs

200 g/7 oz dark (70%) chocolate, roughly
chopped

Raspberries, to serve

Line the base of a 23 cm/9-inch springform tin with greaseproof paper. Butter the paper and sides.

In the bowl of a food processor, pulse the biscuits with the cocoa powder until finely ground. With the motor running, slowly pour the melted butter into the processor. Pour out into the prepared springform pan. Press evenly and refrigerate for 1 hour.

Preheat oven to 150°C/300°F/Gas Mark 2.

In the bowl of a stand mixer fitted with a paddle, place the cheese, sugar, vanilla extract, cream and sour cream. Beat together until very smooth. With the motor running, add one egg at a time, scraping down between additions. Increase the speed and mix until just smooth and creamy. Be careful not to over-mix.

In a bowl set over a saucepan with a few inches of simmering water (do not let the bowl touch the water) add the chocolate and stir until melted. Remove from heat and stir a spoon of the cream and cheese mixture into the melted chocolate. Continue to stir the cheese into the chocolate to combine the lot.

Spoon the mixture onto the cold base. Place the springform tin on a baking tray and bake in the middle of the preheated oven for 50 to 60 minutes. The cheesecake should still be wobbly in the middle when tapped. Turn off the oven and let the cake cool inside with the oven door propped open for 2 hours (if possible). Cool on a rack for an additional 2 hours. Refrigerate overnight before serving with fresh raspberries.

EVA HEGARTY

BURREN FREE RANGE PORK FARM

Eva Hegarty is from a mainly Swedish-speaking minority in Jakobstad, on Finland's Bothnian coast, and has always loved the study of languages. From primary school through to university, she studied Swedish, Finnish, French, English and German, and now she has a bit of Irish under her belt. She lived in Sweden and France to perfect her skills. Languages being a skill that could take her in many directions, she followed a dual career track in hospitality and human resources for a number of years.

Travelling was a passion for Eva in her youth, and she and her friends followed their love of traditional Celtic music to Ireland – first to Dublin and then a second trip to the west of the country. She liked Ireland so much that her friend in the Irish embassy in Stockholm kept faxing her job openings in the country.

FOUND IN TRANSLATION

In 1999 she moved to Cork city for a HR job and surrounded herself with musician and artist friends. They would travel the country looking for good music.

One Friday night in Ennis found her and a group of friends invited to a céilí at Cois na hAbhna. While dancing and enjoying the music, she met Stephen, a young farmer from Kilfenora – home of the celebrated Kilfenora Céilí Band. Their mutual love of trad music and dancing kept them in contact at long distance and they eventually married.

The couple built their home on the Hegarty farm – a fragmented 30 acres at the edge of the Burren proper where both shale and limestone meet. Stephen's family had been able to make a living from the land, but things had changed by the turn of the new millennium. A couple of cows for milking, hens and ducks for eggs and a vegetable plot would do little more than feed a family. They searched out ways to make a living while staying true to the traditional farming lifestyle. Just as importantly, if the land of the Burren isn't farmed and tended, the whole of the place would be overrun with blackberries and wild hazel trees.

Eva came upon the idea of free-range pork as no one else seemed to be doing it. Many of their neighbours remembered the day when every farmyard had a *cráin* (sow) and remember the flavour of that 'real' pork. Eva is told that her pigs are the closest thing anyone has found to the taste of that farm-raised pork of decades gone by.

The couple keep two Saddleback sows, which used to have a litter each but now, to keep to a low-intensity ethos on the farm, only have a litter every other year. It's not enough to supply local restaurants or hotels, though Eva is known to do the odd Long Table with the Burren Food Trail. Most of the pork they produce goes to in-the-know customers, who order in advance or through their website.

On the occasional weekend, Eva and Stephen still might be found in Kilfenora at the dance. But with also managing the glamping facility that they've added to their farm, it's hard to get away, even for an evening.

HER PIGS ARE THE CLOSEST THING TO THE TASTE OF THAT FARM-RAISED PORK OF DECADES GONE BY

CROSS-CULTURE COMFORT FOOD

· ·

This hearty Hegarty lunch is often served to guests and glampers coming to visit Eva and Stephen's free-range pig farm after a tour of the Burren. Nothing satisfies after a windy hike on the cliffs or up the mountains like a bowl of warm soup and crispy pork belly. If you haven't any rhubarb handy for the subh, or if you forgot to gather ye rosebuds while ye may, the pork will be equally served by a sprinkle of Fiona Haugh's rocket gremolata (page 256).

STARTER

Courgette soup with seaweed crackers

MAIN

Confit of pork belly with rhubarb and rose-petal subh

SIDE

Hasselback potatoes

DESSERT

Goat cheese panna cotta with bacon syrup and toasted hazelnuts

COURGETTE SOUP WITH SEAWEED CRACKERS

Serves 6

For the seaweed crackers

250 g/9 oz/1⅔ cups flour, plain (all-purpose) or ½ plain plus ½ wholemeal

1 tsp sea salt

40 g/1½ oz/⅓ cup mixed seeds (sesame, chia, fennel, flax, etc.), plus more for dusting

40 g/1½ oz/⅔ cup seaweed (dillisk, sea lettuce, nori, etc.), dried and ground

60 ml/2 fl oz/¼ cup olive oil

120 ml/4 fl oz/½ cup cold water

1 tsp golden syrup

For the soup

700 g/1 lb 8 oz courgettes (zucchini), washed

30 ml/1 fl oz/2 tbsp olive oil

1 onion, minced

1 pinch sea salt

2 tbsp porridge oats

1 tsp dried thyme

600 ml/1 pint/2½ cups water

3 tbsp vegetable stock

80 ml/3 fl oz/⅓ cup coconut milk

1 lemon, zested and juiced

1½ tsp curry powder

2 tbsp balsamic vinegar

80 ml/3 fl oz/⅓ cup Greek-style yogurt

Parsley, minced

To make the seaweed crackers, first preheat oven to 180°C/350°F/Gas Mark 5.

In a large mixing bowl, combine the flour, salt, seeds and seaweed. Stir in the oil, water and syrup until the dough comes together, adding more water as needed. Cover and refrigerate for 2 hours.

Turn onto a lightly floured work surface, roll the dough thinly and sprinkle with more seeds, pressing them in. Cut to the desired size and shape with a cookie cutter and place on a baking tray lined with greaseproof paper. Bake in the middle of the preheated oven for 10 to 15 minutes, until light golden. Cool on a wire rack. Can be stored in an airtight container at room temperature for up to 1 week.

To make the soup, coarsely grate 600 g/1 lb 4 oz courgettes and finely grate the remainder. In a large saucepan over medium heat, add the oil, onion and salt and sweat until soft. Add the oats and stir until lightly coloured and fragrant. Add the coarsely grated courgettes, thyme, water and stock and bring to a simmer for 5 minutes.

Remove from heat and purée with a hand-held blender until smooth. Return to heat and stir in the coconut milk, 2 tsp lemon zest and 2 tbsp lemon juice. Season to taste with curry powder and the vinegar. Add the finely grated courgette, stir it in, correct the seasoning and serve with a dollop of yogurt, a sprinkle of parsley and seaweed crackers.

CONFIT OF PORK BELLY WITH RHUBARB AND ROSE-PETAL SUBH

• •

Serves 6

For the subh

1 kg/2 lb 4 oz rhubarb, young and tender

2 lemons, juiced

1 kg/2 lb 4 oz/5 cups sugar

2 handfuls fresh red rose petals

6–8 jam jars with lids

For the confit

4 cloves garlic

½ tsp white pepper, ground

½ tsp black peppercorns, whole

½ tsp smoked paprika

100 g/3½ oz/½ cup sea salt

120 ml/4 fl oz/½ cup local honey

1 litre/1¾ pints/4 cups water

1 kg/2 lb 4 oz free-range pork belly, rind on

Lard or olive oil

Sugar for caramelising

To make the subh, first wash the rhubarb and cut into small pieces. Place in a large, heavy-bottomed saucepan. Sprinkle with the juice of the lemons and cover with the sugar. Cover and leave to stand overnight.

The next day, stir in the rose petals and bring to a boil over medium–high heat. Do not reduce the heat but boil rapidly, stirring regularly, until the setting point is reached (test this by spooning a bit of the subh onto a cold plate to see if it jells when cooled). Remove from heat, cool slightly and pour into sterilised jars and seal. Keeps for several months in the fridge.

Day 1: In a large saucepan over medium–high heat, combine all the ingredients for the confit except for the pork belly and the fat or oil. Bring to a simmer and stir until the salt has completely dissolved. Remove from heat, cool to room temperature and refrigerate until cold. Place the pork belly in a large ziplock bag, pour in the cooled brine, remove all the air and seal the bag. Place in a deep baking dish and refrigerate for 4 to 5 hours or overnight, turning occasionally.

Day 2: Preheat oven to 110°C/230°F/Gas Mark ¼. Remove the pork from the brine and pat dry with kitchen paper (paper towel). Place the pork skin-side down in an oven-proof dish that is just big enough to hold it and deep enough to allow 4 cm/1½ inches of room above (the better the fit, the less fat you'll need). In a saucepan over medium heat, melt or warm (not too hot) enough lard or oil to cover the pork belly by at least 2 cm/¾ inch. Place the dish on a rimmed baking tray and pour the lard/oil into the dish and cover with tinfoil. Place in preheated oven for 4 hours until easily pierced with a fork.

Carefully remove the pork from the dish with 2 spatulas, being careful not to break the skin or meat. Set the pork on a chopping board, skin-side up. Strain and reserve the fat. Using a Chap Zai (pricking tool) or a handful of wooden skewers wrapped together with tape, pierce the skin all over, without breaking through the fat layer to the meat, while still warm. Place the pork skin-side down in a clean dish. Cover with cling film and put a flat plate, or another same-sized dish, on top. Weight the top with about 1 kg/2 lb 4 oz and refrigerate for at least 12 hours.

Day 3: Unwrap the pork and place it on a chopping board, skin-side down. Trim edges to make clean, perfectly straight sides. In a large non-stick skillet over medium–high heat, melt 2 tbsp of the reserved fat. Carefully lay the pork skin-side down on the pan and reduce heat to low. Cover the pan with a piece of greaseproof paper to avoid splatters, leaving a gap away from you.

Leave the skin to crisp up over low heat for 15 to 20 minutes, then remove the parchment paper. Cook for an additional 5 minutes. Check the skin and see that it is thoroughly blistered. If not, increase heat to medium–low and continue cooking for another 5 minutes. Once the skin is blistered to your satisfaction, turn the pork over (reducing heat back to low if you had increased it) and heat the meat side slightly, for just 1 to 2 minutes.

Remove the pork to a chopping board, skin-side up. Cover the skin with an even layer of granulated sugar – it should be thick enough that you don't see the skin underneath. Caramelise the sugar with a blowtorch until completely melted and browned. Let the caramel harden. Invert the pork so that the brûlée side is facing down. Using a large, very sharp knife, cut through the meat layer and, once the knife hits the skin layer, press hard until you hear a crackle and feel that the knife has cut through the skin.

Serve slices with rhubarb and rose-petal subh and Hasselback potatoes (page 210).

HASSELBACK POTATOES

Serves 6

2.5 kg/3½ lb medium-sized floury potatoes, scrubbed (Roosters, Maris Piper, Russet, etc.)

150 g/5¼ oz/4½ tbsp butter

120 ml/4 fl oz/½ cup olive oil

2 lemons, zested in strips with a vegetable peeler

Coarse sea salt and freshly ground black pepper

Preheat oven to 200°C/400°F/Gas Mark 6.

Cut across the length of each potato at 3mm/⅛-inch intervals but do not cut through all the way (cutting the potato while it rests on a kitchen spoon may help keep you from slicing too far).

In a large roasting tin over medium–high heat, melt the butter and oil until sizzling. Add the potatoes and the lemon zest and toss to coat well with fat. Season well. Roast on the bottom shelf of a preheated oven, basting occasionally, for 1 hour to 1 hour 15 minutes until the potatoes are golden brown and tender. Discard the lemon peel and season with more salt and pepper to taste.

CHEF'S NOTE

Two things are key to great Hasselback potatoes: 1) the slicing, so do this job with a thin knife and be careful not to slice too far through, and 2) the basting. You can't get enough butter into those slices, but remember that every time you open the oven to baste, you release heat. Take the pan out of the oven, close the door, baste and return the pan to the hot oven.

GOAT CHEESE PANNA COTTA WITH BACON SYRUP AND TOASTED HAZELNUTS

Serves 6

750 ml/27 fl oz/3 cups cream

250 ml/8 fl oz/1 cup goat milk

3 gelatine leaves, soaked in cold water

200 g/7 oz soft goat cheese

450 g/1 lb free-range streaky rashers (bacon), cut into lardons

60 ml/2 fl oz/¼ cup organic maple syrup

250 ml/8 fl oz/1 cup water

2 tbsp hazelnuts, toasted and crushed

Rocket (arugula) leaves, to garnish

In a saucepan over medium–low heat, add the cream and milk, stirring regularly. When hot, whisk in softened gelatine and stir until melted. Whisk in the goat cheese until the mixture is smooth and pour into small ramekins or glasses. Cool to room temperature and refrigerate for at least 4 hours or overnight.

In a skillet over medium–high heat, cook the bacon until crisp. Deglaze the pan with the maple syrup and water and reduce by half. Strain, discarding the bacon, and pour the syrup into a small saucepan. Whisk over high heat for 3 to 4 minutes, until the syrup thickens. Remove from heat and allow to cool, whisking occasionally so that it does not separate. Cover and refrigerate. Bring to room temperature 30 minutes before serving.

Remove the panna cottas from the fridge onto a plate and drizzle with the bacon syrup. Sprinkle with hazelnuts and garnish with small rocket leaves.

HOME IS A BEAUTIFUL WORD

OONAGH O'DWYER

WILD KITCHEN

· ·

Born in England, raised in Tipperary and tempered in London, before following her parents to the west of Ireland, Oonagh O'Dwyer has several places which she has called home. Now settled in Lahinch on the steps of the Burren, she has found the place where she knows she is, indeed, home.

While she has snippets of memory from her early years in England, it was back in Tipp where the family ran a nursing home at their house that Oonagh's first full memories formed – singing to residents with her father, reciting the evening rosary with them, the time the parish priest stopped in the kitchen after offering communion to his aged flock so that he could bless the Christmas cakes Oonagh was making with her mother.

Then they moved into Ballyglass House, a gracious country estate near the Glen of Aherlow that had once allegedly changed hands in a poker game. Her parents worked very hard (her mother as a nurse, spending six to eight weeks away in London to help pay for the refurbishment of the old house). It was here that Oonagh began what we'll call 'foraging with training wheels' in the orchards and gardens of the estate, which had long since gone wild. This led to further trips into the forestry and mountains around the home where the stabilisers came off; her life-long passion for wild foods has flourished since.

Oonagh loved this time in her life. So much did she love it that her heart was broken when the family decided to sell and move to the west of Ireland. Oonagh left the country in a huff and moved to London in protest.

Time heals all wounds, and by the time she visited the family for Christmas, all was forgiven and her mended heart became smitten with Clare where her parents were now running a pub. She returned to London long enough to tie up loose ends and came once again to help out in the family business. First it was the pub in Lahinch, where she discovered the wonderful world of seaweeds, then at the guesthouse in Ennistymon. Oonagh ran the guesthouse when her father became ill and wasn't able to keep up the pace of the busy rooms, bar and restaurant that the property offered to guests and locals alike.

Oonagh studied at the Organic College in Limerick and went on to teach Level 5 Organic Horticulture until the Wild Atlantic Way tourist trail was launched and someone said to her that she might be able to make a few euro taking people on the seaweed-foraging walks she had become known for around the coast. And so began Wild Kitchen. To where it will evolve is wonderfully unknown.

HER LIFE-LONG
PASSION FOR WILD FOODS
HAS FLOURISHED

TAKE A MEAL ON THE WILD SIDE

A walk on the coast or in the fields with Oonagh O'Dwyer is a trip to the supermarket. The fruits of a keen eye and nimble hands can be seen throughout this menu. You needn't go lamping *coiníní*, as many butchers and speciality grocers now carry rabbit. You will, however, have to spend a bit of time outdoors to create this menu. If nettles are out of season, regular colcannon will do, or even Paul Haugh's scallion mash (page 231). It won't be quite as wild, but it'll be a good reminder to freeze more nettles next spring.

STARTERS
Wild crudités of beetroot carpaccio, samphire salsa verde and radishes with seaweed butter and dandelion oil

Railway cake

MAIN COURSE
Bacon-roasted rabbits with sloe-gin giblet gravy

SIDE
Nettle colcannon

DESSERT
Blackberry bread and butter pudding with gorse-flower sorbet

WILD CRUDITÉS OF BEETROOT CARPACCIO, SAMPHIRE SALSA VERDE AND RADISHES WITH SEAWEED BUTTER AND DANDELION OIL

Serves 6

For the dandelion oil

2 handfuls dandelion flowers

120 ml/4 fl oz/½ cup extra virgin olive oil
(or enough to cover)

For the seaweed butter

225 g/8 oz/2 sticks goat butter, softened

1 tbsp dillisk seaweed, dried and flaked

1 tsp smoked sea salt

For the salsa

1 handful foraged rock samphire

1 tbsp mint leaves

1 tbsp parsley

1 tsp capers

3 pickled gherkins, sliced lengthwise

1 tsp organic cider vinegar

1 tbsp olive oil

½ tsp sea salt

5 medium organic beetroots (mix the
colours), scrubbed

18 organic baby radishes scrubbed,
stalks on

Additional veg such as baby carrots and
pickled gherkins (optional)

1 handful foraged leaves (rocket,
dandelion, sorrel, etc.)

Make the dandelion oil in spring or early summer. Shake the dandelion flowers to remove any creatures, place in a jar and cover with olive oil. Tap the jar on the counter to remove any air bubbles. Cover with a piece of cloth held with a rubber band and place in a sunny spot for 1 week. Strain the oil into a clean bottle and use for dressing.

To make the seaweed butter, place the softened butter into a small bowl and mash with the back of a fork. Add the dillisk and a pinch of smoked salt and mix well. Cover and refrigerate for 1 hour or overnight. Scoop into small balls using a melon baller or small ice-cream scoop. Refrigerate until ready to serve.

For the salsa, place the samphire in a bowl and cover with boiling water from a kettle for 1 minute. Drain and refresh in ice water for a minute or two. Drain. Place the blanched samphire, herbs, capers and gherkins on a chopping board and coarsely chop together. Scrape into a small bowl and stir in the vinegar, oil and salt.

Place a medium saucepan with lightly salted water over medium–high heat and add the beetroot. Bring to a boil and reduce heat to medium. Simmer for approximately 30 minutes, until tender. Remove from heat, strain and allow to cool until you can handle the beetroot. Peel and then cover, allowing it to cool completely (can be refrigerated overnight at this point). Slice very thinly with a mandoline.

Attractively arrange crudité ingredients on a large platter and scatter with torn leaves. Drizzle with dandelion oil. Place samphire salsa verde and seaweed butter in small bowls or pots alongside. Serve with toasted slices of railway cake (page 219).

RAILWAY CAKE

• •

Makes 1 round loaf

450 g/1 lb plain (all-purpose) flour, plus
   more for dusting

1 tsp bread (baking) soda

1 tsp salt

2 tsp sugar

1 handful currants or sultanas

1 egg

350 ml/12 fl oz/1½ cups buttermilk or
   sour milk

Preheat oven to 220°C/430°F/Gas Mark 8.

Into a large bowl, sift the flour and bread soda, then stir in the salt, sugar and dried fruit. Mix well. Into a mixing jug, add the egg and buttermilk and whisk to blend well.

Make a well in the flour mixture and add most of the milk and egg mixture. Bring together with your fingers, being careful not to over-mix, and add more milk if needed.

Flour your hands, then gather the dough together to form a round 5 cm/2 inches high. Place on a floured baking tray, dust lightly with flour and cut a cross on top with a sharp knife.

Bake in the middle of the preheated oven for 10 minutes, then reduce heat to 200°C/400°F/Gas Mark 6 for 30 to 35 additional minutes. Tap the underside of the loaf: when it sounds hollow, it's done. Cool on a wire rack.

CHEF'S NOTE

I loved Oonagh's story of how railway cake got its name. It comes from a time when currants were dear, so a small handful might be all that could be afforded for non-special occasions. The loaves are slashed with a cross, creating four quarters or 'stations'. There might be only a currant at every station.

BACON-ROASTED RABBITS WITH SLOE-GIN GIBLET GRAVY

· ·

Serves 6

2 rabbits, cleaned and dried, giblets and
    trimmings reserved

6 leaves fresh sage

2 tsp thyme leaves, chopped

Sea salt and freshly ground black pepper

2 tbsp olive oil

12 slices good-quality streaky rashers
    (bacon)

For the gravy

Giblets, without the liver (use that for
    something else)

1 leek, white and light green only, washed
    and sliced

2 carrots, peeled and chopped

2 stalks celery, chopped

3 sprigs parsley

3 sprigs thyme

6 black peppercorns

60 g/2 oz/4 tbsp butter

1 shallot, minced

60 g/2 oz/¼ cup plain (all-purpose) flour

2 tbsp sloe gin

Sea salt and freshly ground black pepper

Preheat oven to 180°C/350°F/Gas Mark 4.

Season the rabbits, inside and out, with the herbs, salt and pepper, and rub with oil. Wrap each rabbit well with 6 rashers. Place in a covered roasting tin and into the preheated oven. Roast for 1 hour, then remove the cover and continue to roast for a further 10 to 15 minutes. Remove to a rack set over a platter to collect any juices. Strain the cooking juices from the roasting tin, defat and reserve for gravy.

To make the gravy, place the giblets and trimmings into a large saucepan with 2 litres/3½ pints/3 quarts of cold water. Place over medium–high heat and bring to a hard simmer; skim and reduce heat to medium. Add the vegetables, herbs and peppercorns, then simmer, uncovered, for 2 hours. Strain and cool.

In a saucepan over medium–low heat, melt the butter and sweat the shallot with a pinch of salt for 2 minutes. Stir in the flour and cook until it appears a bit dry, which takes about 5 minutes. Whisk in the cooled rabbit stock in a thin stream so that it does not clump. Simmer, stirring occasionally, for 15 minutes. Stir in the sloe gin, strain into a serving jug and season to taste.

Place each rabbit onto a chopping board and, with a large chef's knife, cut into serving pieces. Serve on a warm platter with gravy on the side and a big bowl of nettle colcannon (page 221).

NETTLE COLCANNON

· ·

Serves 6

1 colander-ful of young nettle tops (see
   Chef's Note)

1 kg/2 lb 4 oz floury potatoes, equal sized,
   scrubbed (Queens, Golden Wonders,
   Russets, etc.)

200 ml/7 fl oz/¾ cup milk

3 spring onions (scallions), sliced

Butter, to taste

Sea salt and freshly ground black pepper

CHEF'S NOTE

Pick nettle tops in the spring. Use gloves
and sharp scissors and wear long sleeves.
The cooking water from nettles can be used
as a restorative tea.

Wash the nettles and spin dry. Bring a large pot of water
to a boil over high heat, add the nettles and reduce heat to
medium. Simmer for 10 minutes, uncovered, strain and, if
you like, reserve the water (see Chef's Note). If the leaves
are large, you can roughly chop the blanched nettles.
Place the potatoes in a metal colander or steamer over a
saucepan of boiling water and cover. Reduce heat so that
the water is heavily simmering and steam the potatoes
until tender. In a small saucepan over low heat, warm the
milk and spring onions together.

Using a tea towel and a sharp paring knife, peel the
potatoes and mash thoroughly. Add the milk and onions
and stir well. Fold in the blanched nettles with as much
butter as you like and season to taste.

Serve with an extra lump of butter in the middle.

BLACKBERRY BREAD AND BUTTER PUDDING WITH GORSE-FLOWER SORBET

· ·

Serves 6

For the sorbet

500 ml/18 fl oz/2 cups water

½ cup gorse flowers (see Chef's Note)

300 g/10½ oz/1½ cups caster (superfine) sugar

1 lemon, juiced

1 sprig lemon balm

For the pudding

12 slices stale bread (white, brioche, etc.)

Butter for greasing

2 eggs

285 ml/9½ fl oz/1¼ cups milk

Large pinch of ground nutmeg

25 g/¾ oz/2 tbsp caster (superfine) sugar

1 handful sultanas (golden raisins)

250 g/9 oz blackberries

30 g/1 oz/2 tbsp butter, cut into 8 pieces

25 g/¾ oz/¼ cup flaked almonds (optional)

CHEF'S NOTE

You wouldn't want to eat too many gorse flowers or have them on a regular basis due to slightly toxic alkaloids. Don't let that deter you from having them now and again, though. They are delicious!

To make the sorbet, simmer the water, flowers and sugar in a large saucepan over low heat, stirring until sugar is dissolved. Increase to high heat and bring to a boil for 1 minute, then remove from heat and allow to cool. Add the juice of the lemon and the lemon balm, and refrigerate until cold. Remove the lemon balm leaves, but leave the gorse flowers for effect.

Churn in an ice-cream maker to manufacturer's instructions, or put into a container and into the freezer, stirring every 2 hours until frozen (this method should take about 6 hours). Place in a sealed container and freeze until needed (will keep for 2 weeks).

To make the pudding, preheat oven to 180°C/350°F/Gas Mark 4.

Cut the slices of bread into triangles and layer in a buttered baking dish. In a mixing bowl, whisk together the eggs, milk, nutmeg and sugar. Pour half the egg mixture over the bread and allow it to absorb for 5 minutes. Add the remaining liquid. Scatter the sultanas and arrange the blackberries over the soaked bread and dot with butter.

Bake in the middle of a preheated oven for 15 minutes. Sprinkle with the almonds, if using, and bake for a further 10 minutes. Remove to a rack to cool. Serve with the gorse-flower sorbet.

THE KEEPERS

Innkeepers and shopkeepers are an integral part of the food story in a place as remote as the Burren. Without their willingness to share their intimate knowledge of the place and its unique culinary offerings, many visitors would miss out on this important facet of a trip to the area.

A good innkeeper can read what experiences a guest might be looking for, even if their charges are unaware themselves. An extensive collection of local produce in a shop can introduce visitors to flavours they'd not known they'd been missing all their lives. Being a good keeper isn't about handing out maps or stocking only the expected – the keepers in this section are just as fervent in their pursuit of a memorable experience for their customers and guests. Their own love of food is evident in the broad selections they offer in their establishments.

Not everyone has the personality for the kind of interaction with the public required of a keeper. Chefs often joke about there being a reason that they work *behind* a swinging door. The keepers profiled here have the innate ability to turn a stay into a memory, a transaction into a friendship.

Each has their own complex connection to the Burren. They convey that connection to the place, the people and the food as ambassadors – sometimes in broken sentences of a foreign tongue or exaggerated sign language. Whatever it takes to meet the needs and exceed the expectations of people who bring them their custom, the keepers will do it.

So, if you ever have occasion to welcome someone into your home for a meal, the menus curated by our keepers will make them feel as comfortable as international visitors to the Burren have felt for decades.

PAUL HAUGH

THE WILD ATLANTIC LODGE

When you sit down with someone you've never met before and you end up talking about how he nearly mucked up his proposal of marriage, you know you're in for a good chat. That was just one of the funny stories Paul Haugh, owner of The Wild Atlantic Lodge in Ballyvaughan, shared with me in the comfortable surroundings of the snug at his hotel.

Others included how a former army mechanic, whose father was a butcher-turned-publican, might end up owning grocery shops, butcheries, a pub and now a three-star hotel and restaurant. Each was its own story. Each wove into the other. Every one of them included twists and turns of fate that afforded opportunities that Paul and his wife, Mary, were willing to take.

Paul spent most of his youth in the southwest of Clare. He was born and raised in Kilkee and, though his father had a successful butcher's there, by the time Paul would have been old enough to

IT'S A FUNNY STORY

learn the trade, the shop and abattoir had
been taken over by Paul's uncle. His father
had moved on to running a pub at that point
so Paul worked under a master butcher in
Galway to learn the business.

By 1999 he had opened a modern
butcher's in the market town of Ennistymon,
which was soon expanded into a full grocery
shop. Then, along with his brother Sean, he
expanded the butcher–grocery business into
a second shop in County Limerick. It was a

HE HAS FINALLY FOUND THE BUSINESS HE SHOULD HAVE BEEN IN THE WHOLE TIME

good working life. It was busy, for sure, but Paul's shops kept many families employed in both Clare
and Limerick, a fact of which he is rightfully proud.

Phone calls play a role in some of Paul's 'funnier' business stories – both funny ha-ha and funny
peculiar. Like the one he received one winter's day from his mother's first cousin asking him to come
up to Ballyvaughan from Ennistymon straight away for a chat. He swapped his butcher's coat for a
heavy coat and made his way through the weather to the woman's home above her pub. It was this
phone call that led to him eventually being bequeathed the licensed premises.

Or the phone call he had from home one evening with an employee back at the shop. He says
that, although he remembers the evening like it was yesterday, he can't remember the exact content of
the conversation other than it had to do with the general trend of business. He hung up the phone,
stood in his kitchen for a couple of minutes, then called the regional director of the supermarket
chain for which he had been a successful franchisee and offered the two shops up for sale. It was that
phone call that eventually brought Paul and his family to live in Spain for eighteen months of early
retirement.

Paul says that he has now finally found the business he should have been in the whole time:
running a hotel that has a small bar, a comfortable restaurant and nicely appointed guest rooms. His
commute from Lahinch to Ballyvaughan allows for distance between work and home that some of
his former endeavours did not. The reliability of his core staff allows him to be away when he's away.
And every interaction with every guest is an opportunity to make their day in Ballyvaughan or their
stay in Ireland just a little bit better.

Paul Haugh is a businessman. He would probably be successful in a myriad of business situations.
Helping people to enjoy the Burren just a little bit more than they might have otherwise is success
beyond what can be reviewed.

FOR A COLD, DARK NIGHT

Here is a menu that speaks of home as well as of travels. It shouts Playa Blanco as loudly as it does the Burren. Don't be afraid to spice up the shrimp if your guests can handle a bit of heat – the avocado will keep things cool. Mary's celebration cake will be on everyone's birthday wish list after you serve it once. Odd as it might seem for a braised dish rather than a roast, Neil Hawes's Yorkshire puddings (page 282) won't be long for the table if served alongside this meal.

STARTER

Chilli shrimp with guacamole salad

MAIN

Beef cheeks in red wine

SIDE

Scallion mashed potatoes

DESSERT

Mary's ultimate chocolate celebration cake

CHILLI SHRIMP WITH GUACAMOLE SALAD

Serves 6

18 large shrimp, shell on

1 tbsp mild chilli powder

1 pinch (or to taste) chilli flakes

2 tbsp olive oil

4 avocados, ripe Haas if available

1 lemon, juiced

1 lime, juiced

6 sprigs parsley, leaves minced

6 sprigs dill, minced

1 red onion, minced

1 tsp mild chilli powder

Sea salt

120 ml/4 fl oz/½ cup lager

Organic salad leaves

1 lemon, cut into 6 wedges

In a bowl, toss the shrimp with the chilli powder, flakes and oil. Marinate in the refrigerator for 1 to 2 hours.

In a large bowl, mash the avocados to the desired consistency. Add the juice of the lemon and lime, the herbs, onion and chilli powder. Mix thoroughly and season to taste with salt. Cover and refrigerate.

Heat a non-stick skillet over medium–high heat. Add the shrimp and cook for 2 minutes each side, turning with tongs. Remove the shrimp to a cold plate to cool, add lager to the pan, swirl and pour into a bowl. When the shrimp are cool enough to handle, peel and place in the bowl with the lager and toss.

To serve, place a mound of guacamole on a chilled plate, top with 3 shrimp and arrange a few leaves around. Drizzle the seasoned beer over the leaves and shrimp. Garnish with lemon wedges.

CHEF'S NOTE

Cooking shrimp with the shell on is like cooking meat bone-in. The flavour is far superior, and the shell keeps moisture in. Peeled and deveined shrimp can be used in this dish, but the end result is well worth the extra step of peeling the cooked shrimp.

BEEF CHEEKS IN RED WINE

Serves 6

6 beef cheeks, fat and membrane removed
  (ask your butcher to do this for you)

Sea salt and freshly ground black pepper

60 ml/2 fl oz/¼ cup rapeseed (canola) oil

4 white onions, diced

2 courgettes (zucchini), diced

2 red pepper, diced

2 green pepper, diced

2 yellow pepper, diced

2 carrots, diced

4 cloves garlic, smashed

450 g/1 lb butter

1 tbsp paprika (smoked for extra flavour)

1½ bottles earthy red wine, such as Cahors
  or Gigondas

2 x 400g/14 oz tins chopped tomatoes

1 litre/1¾ pints/4 cups beef stock

1 sprig rosemary

Preheat oven to 180°C/350°F/Gas Mark 4.

Season the beef cheeks well with salt and pepper and rub with oil. Heat a casserole (Dutch oven) over high heat and sear the cheeks on all sides, then remove to a plate. Add the vegetables and garlic with half the butter. Stir until the butter is melted. Season with salt, pepper and paprika and allow to cook for 2 minutes. Add the wine and bring to a boil. Reduce heat to medium and simmer for 5 minutes. Add tomatoes, stock, rosemary, cheeks and any accumulated liquid from the plate, bring to a simmer, cover and place in preheated oven. Braise for 3 hours until soft and very tender.

Remove the cheeks to a warm platter, stir the remaining butter into the sauce and correct the seasoning. Serve the cheeks on scallion mashed potatoes (page 231) with sauce and vegetables generously ladled on top.

CHEF'S NOTE

The flavour of any muscle meat increases in direct proportion to how much the muscle is used. Few muscles are used in ruminants (like cattle, sheep and goats) as much as their cheek muscles, due to their near-constant chewing. Muscles used that much, however, need long cooking in low temperatures with moisture, so they don't dry out, and acid (wine, in this case) to turn the firm muscle moist and tender.

SCALLION MASHED POTATOES

· ·

Serves 6

12 medium potatoes, scrubbed well

100 ml/3½ fl oz/⅓ cup + 4 tsp cream

60 g/2 oz/4 tbsp butter, plus more if
   desired

Sea salt and black pepper

6 spring onions (scallions), thinly sliced

Place the potatoes in a large pot of salted cold water. Bring to a boil over medium–high heat. Reduce heat to medium–low and simmer until skins begin to break and the potatoes are nearly tender (about 30 minutes). Turn off the heat. Drain and return to the pot to the ring that was turned off. Cover the pot with a dry tea towel to absorb steam, place the lid on top and leave for 10 minutes.

In a small saucepan, heat the cream and half the butter over medium–low heat until the butter is melted and the cream is hot. Peel the potatoes, using the towel to hold them as they'll be hot. Mash them by hand, using a food mill or a ricer. Fold in the cream and butter mixture and season with salt and pepper to taste, adding more butter if desired. Fold in the sliced scallions and serve.

MARY'S ULTIMATE CHOCOLATE CELEBRATION CAKE

Serves 6

For the cake

115 g/4 oz/1 stick unsalted butter, plus
    more for greasing

115 g/4 oz/½ cup plain (all-purpose) flour,
    plus more for dusting

55 g/2 oz/½ cup cocoa powder

1 tsp baking powder

⅛ tsp salt

6 eggs

225 g/8 oz/1 cup + 3 tbsp caster
    (superfine) sugar

2 tsp vanilla essence

For the icing

225 g/8 oz chocolate, chopped

85 g/3 oz/6 tbsp unsalted butter

3 eggs, separated

250 ml/8 fl oz/1 cup whipping cream

3 tbsp caster (superfine) sugar

Preheat oven to 180°C/350°F/Gas Mark 4. Line the bottoms of three 20 x 3 cm/8 x 1-inch round cake tins with greaseproof paper. Butter the paper and sides of the tins. Dust each tin evenly with flour.

For the cake, place a small saucepan over low heat and melt the butter, spooning off the foam from the surface, then set aside. Into a large mixing bowl, sift the flour, cocoa, baking powder and salt together 3 times, then set aside.

In a heatproof bowl set over a pan of hot water, whip the eggs and sugar until doubled in volume and ribbons trail from the whisk, which takes about 10 minutes (an electric mixer can be used). Add the vanilla.

Sift a third of the dry ingredients over the eggs and fold; repeat two more times. Fold in the melted butter. Divide the batter between the prepared tins and bake for 25 minutes, until the cakes pull away from the sides of the tins. Transfer to a rack to cool.

To make the icing, add the chopped chocolate to a bowl set over a pot of simmering (not boiling) water (do not let the bowl touch the water) and melt. Remove from heat and stir in the butter and egg yolks. Return to over the pan of water and stir until thick. Remove from heat and set aside.

In a large bowl, whip the cream until firm, then set aside. In another bowl, whip the egg whites until stiff, then add the sugar and whip until glossy. Fold the cream into the chocolate mixture, then carefully fold in the egg whites. Refrigerate for 20 minutes to thicken.

Assemble by sandwiching the cakes with about a third of the icing, stacking carefully. Spread the remaining icing on the top and sides of the cake.

CATHLEEN CONNOLE

BURREN FINE WINE AND FOOD

. . . .

Cathleen Connole grew up on a 150-acre farm in Glenfort, Croagh North, about halfway between Ballyvaughan and the Corkscrew Hill. It's land that her father worked as a mixed farm of beef and dairy cattle, sheep, tillage and a garden for family use. His father farmed that same land the same way. While Cathleen's sister now farms only dry stock of beef cattle, it's still in the family.

Cathleen, a banker who worked most of her thirty-year career in Dublin, returned to Clare to be closer to the land she missed. It was a calculated move to be nearer to where she'd planned to return from the time she'd left to study at university in Limerick.

Ready for an early retirement from banking, Cathleen took over a building on the family land, which her brother – a winemaker and importer himself – had used as a small wine shop and wholesale facility.

BELONGING TOGETHER

SHE AND THE BURREN JUST BELONG TOGETHER

As these things will, and with the nudging of trusted friends, the wine shop added coffee, seating, then Cathleen's famous scones, then a few other home-baked goods.

Whether or not she knew it at the time, Cathleen was emulating a space and style of experience she'd always loved about the region of France where the family have an apartment from which to transact wine business. That the Burren Food Trail was getting started around the same time as Burren Fine Wine and Food was taking on this new dimension is another example of the way things seem to work in this part of Clare.

The same way she enjoys collecting a slice of quiche, a wedge of cheese, a baguette or a pastry in the central square of the town of Canaules-et-Argentières (which she tells me is pronounced almost identically to her surname), she has created a place for tourists and local customers alike to come and be looked after while they review or plan their day. A slice of brown bread with butter, a scone with cream and homemade jam, her renowned Burren Béilini Plate – something of an Irish version of a tapas plate, using locally sourced products – in the cosy stone surroundings of the former coach house of the property make for a memorable experience.

She believes that it is important for people to slow down in their lives. Growing up and now working on the Corkscrew Hill Road, Cathleen has seen her share of tour coaches and hired cars passing at speed as they go from one tourist destination to the next. Now her daughter invites those same tourists to saddle up on a bicycle and take a morning spin around the area to smell it as it wakes in the morning. Then they get to smell the hot scones and coffee her mother has prepared while they were out cycling.

Cathleen cycles herself. She also enjoys walking the farm, taking in the pastoral scenes as she forages for nettles or simply sitting on a stone wall overlooking both the fairy fort and church ruin that represent two periods of history experienced on her family's land in the Burren.

She left for university. She left for work. She leaves for her annual wine-buying trips to the Languedoc. She has always enjoyed those ventures away. But at the end of it all, for Cathleen, it's the Burren she returns to. It is to the land of her family that she feels closest. She says that she and the Burren just belong together.

Truer words were never spoken!

A PROPER SUNDAY ROAST

· ·

There is a time and a place for 'modern' Irish cookery, just as there is for a proper Sunday roast. Cathleen's meal is required fare when her son is scheduled to return to the home place. It speaks of the land and the sea that make the Burren a special place for food and for family. The herbs used on the lamb mesh perfectly with the rosemary of the roast potatoes. If you're looking for a nice transition from surf to turf, Sinéad Ní Gháirbhith's tomato and blood orange sorbet (page 270) might be just the ticket.

STARTER
Crab and smoked salmon salad
MAIN
Roast leg of lamb with vegetable gravy
SIDES
Minted marrowfat peas
Rosemary-roasted potatoes
DESSERT
Rhubarb crumble

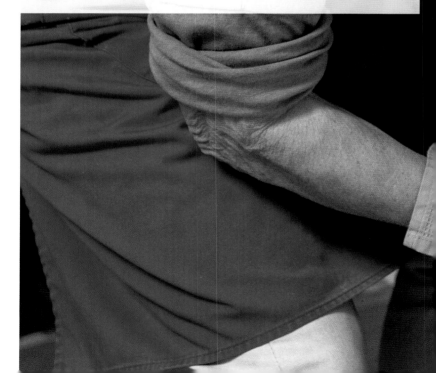

CRAB AND SMOKED SALMON SALAD

Serves 6

3 crabs, cooked and cleaned (both white and brown meat)

60 ml/2 fl oz/¼ cup mayonnaise

60 ml/2 fl oz/¼ cup vinaigrette of your liking (Fabiola's on page 115 would be lovely)

Sea salt and freshly ground black pepper

Salad leaves

6 slices smoked salmon

1 pinch cayenne pepper

1 lemon, cut into 6 wedges

In a bowl, fold the white crabmeat with mayonnaise to taste, season and set aside.

In another bowl, fold the brown meat together with 2 tbsp vinaigrette, season and set aside.

In a third bowl, dress the salad leaves with the remaining vinaigrette.

Divide the leaves between 6 plates, and overlay each with one slice of salmon. Add a dollop each of white and brown crab onto the plates. Garnish with cayenne and a lemon wedge.

ROAST LEG OF LAMB WITH VEGETABLE GRAVY

Serves 6

1 x 2½–3 kg/5½–6½ lb leg of lamb

10 sprigs thyme, more for garnish

3 cloves garlic, peeled and cut in half

Sea salt and freshly ground black pepper

1 onion, peeled and minced

1 red pepper, deseeded and minced

250 g/9 oz mushrooms, sliced

15 g/½ oz/2 tbsp plain (all-purpose) flour

250 ml/8 fl oz/1 cup vegetable stock, cold

CHEF'S NOTE

The number of holes to make in the lamb will depend on how much flavour you want to add, but 10 cm/4 inches apart is a good guideline. For younger spring lamb, Cathleen recommends using less garlic and fewer herbs.

Preheat oven to 200°C/400°F/Gas Mark 6.

Using a very sharp paring knife, make deep holes the width of the knife blade (just large enough to stuff with garlic and a sprig of herb) all over the leg (see Chef's Note). Stuff the holes with sprigs of thyme and garlic halves. Refrigerate for up to 2 hours.

Place the lamb on a rack in a roasting tin in the middle of the preheated oven. After 20 minutes, reduce heat to 180°C/350°F/Gas Mark 4. Cook 1 hour for rare, 1½ hours for medium and 2 hours for well done. Remove the lamb from the roasting tin and place on a rack over a platter to collect the juices. Tent loosely with tinfoil and allow to rest while you make the sauce.

For the sauce, strain the cooking liquid through a fine sieve. Leave to settle. Discard all but 2 tbsp of the fat and reserve the cooking liquid. Add the 2 tbsp of fat to the roasting tin. Place the roasting tin over medium heat and add the onion with a pinch of salt. Stir for 4 minutes. Add the pepper and mushrooms and sweat until soft (about 5 minutes).

Move the vegetables to the sides and sprinkle in the flour. Stir to make a pan roux and cook for about 3 minutes. Whisk the cold vegetable stock into the roux, then whisk in the reserved cooking liquid. Stir the vegetables into the thickening sauce. Simmer for 10 to 15 minutes, add the accumulated juices from beneath the lamb, season and pour into a heated jug for serving.

Remove any obvious thyme sprigs from the lamb and carve. Arrange on a platter and top with some of the sauce. Garnish with sprigs of thyme and serve with a jug of the sauce for passing around.

MINTED MARROWFAT PEAS

. . . .

Serves 6

2 tbsp olive oil

1 bunch spring onions (scallions) sliced

Sea salt

1 tbsp fresh mint, minced, plus whole
   leaves to garnish

500 g/18 oz frozen Marrowfat peas,
   thawed and rinsed (garden peas can be
   substituted)

45 g/1½ oz/3 tbsp butter

Freshly ground black pepper

In a large skillet over medium–high heat, add the olive
oil, spring onions and a pinch of salt. Sweat together for 1
minute, then add the minced mint and peas. Cook for an
additional 3 to 4 minutes until heated through.

Remove from heat and mash with a potato masher and
fold in the butter. Season and garnish with fresh mint.
Serve in a heated bowl.

ROSEMARY-ROASTED POTATOES

Serves 6

1 kg/2 lb 4 oz small potatoes

6 cloves garlic, skin on but smashed

30 ml/1 fl oz/2 tbsp extra virgin olive oil, or more to coat potatoes

2 tbsp fresh rosemary leaves

Coarse sea salt and freshly ground black pepper

Preheat oven to 220°C/450°F/Gas Mark 8.

Halve the potatoes and place in a large mixing bowl with the garlic, olive oil and rosemary. Toss to mix. Season well with salt and pepper. Scatter evenly on a baking tray. Roast in the upper third of the preheated oven for 20 minutes or until tender. Correct seasoning and serve.

CHEF'S NOTE

If your family is willing to experiment a bit with the Christmas dinner (and not all families are), try serving these herb-touched roasties alongside your turkey.

RHUBARB CRUMBLE

Serves 6

12 stalks rhubarb, washed and cut into
   1–2 cm/½–¾ inch pieces
100 g/3 oz/½ cup sugar

For the crumble
150 g/5¼ oz/1 cup plain (all-purpose)
   flour
75 g/2 oz/⅓ cup caster (superfine) sugar
75 g/2½ oz/5 tbsp butter, cold and cut
   into bits, plus more for greasing

Preheat oven to 180°C/350°F/Gas Mark 4. Butter an ovenproof dish.

In a saucepan with a couple of tablespoons of water over medium heat, add the rhubarb and sugar. Simmer until the sugar is dissolved and the rhubarb is soft but still holds its shape. Remove from heat to cool slightly.

For the crumble, in a bowl, mix the flour, sugar and butter with your fingers until it resembles coarse crumbs.

Pour the cooled rhubarb into the prepared dish and cover with the crumble topping. Bake in the middle of a preheated oven for 30 minutes or until bubbly and nicely browned. Serve with custard, cream or ice cream as desired.

NIALL HUGHES

SEAVIEW HOUSE

· ·

A former diving instructor, Niall Hughes describes the physical and spiritual sensation of swimming out of the many freshwater caves which dot the coast of the Burren. It begins when you turn around at the head of a cave and see all black save a pencil point of light. Then the point becomes a brightening blue circle, and the circle grows to envelop the diver.

'Where the cold water meets the warmer, the fresh meets the salt … there is a curtain of shimmer.' It's called a thermocline, but Niall describes the dreamlike change in gravity, of buoyancy, as 'a wave, a vortex … like moving from one world to another'.

It's an appropriate way of describing it for a man who grew up in a lakeside community north-west of Nenagh in Tipperary. From Garrykennedy and a rural life of game fishing with pals, sailing on the lake and shooting with his father, a garda, Niall studied electronic engineering in Galway, worked in Limerick and took on something of a city persona. Now, however, he is back in the countryside of Doolin and can't see himself ever leaving.

FROM ONE WORLD TO ANOTHER

Part of the reason for that is Darra, his wife. It is here on her family land where the couple built their lovingly appointed boutique bed and breakfast. It's in Doolin where the couple met. It is from this place that Niall rides out on his 17-hand mare, Misty, every Tuesday. Doolin and the Burren aren't just home for now: they're home for good.

Niall's journey through an electronic engineering career wouldn't have happened if his parents had let him pursue the first career path he considered in his youth. He wanted to attend Cert training to become a chef. They felt him too clever and gently guided him – in the way a sergeant of An Garda Síochána gently guides his son – toward the leaving certification exams rather than the vocational programme.

Ticking off boxes of what he didn't want to do in life rather than what he wanted to do, he was left with engineering, and electrical engineering seemed to be where the jobs were. He says it was that career which got them the mortgage to build their dream home and B & B. 'It served its purpose,' he says. His experience in self-employment side jobs also helped with the hospitality aspect in ways he never would have expected.

From developing web pages to the novel business of renting out pre-paid mobile phones to visiting tourists, he tucked every lesson he learned along the way into his experience portfolio, which has served him and his visitors well.

But he never lost his budding passion for cooking. Be it flavours he experiences on the family's travels through Asia, or the richness of a hen's egg from the garden below his window, Niall Hughes is passionate about food in a way many trained chefs are not. He's also passionate about the origins of the food he cooks and serves.

When he first tasted St Tola goat cheese, the tomatoes from his late father-in-law's polytunnel and those eggs from the neighbour's hens, he knew that they should somehow be linked. This was the genesis of the signature dish of the house that he shares in his menu. It was also the incipience of the 'food miles' campaign, which lets his guests know how far the ingredients for each dish travelled to their plate.

'They can have French toast with local Burren honey – 60 food miles – or with real maple syrup that travelled 1,100 miles to the table. Their call.' But it's then an informed call.

Local food is fresher, it has a smaller carbon footprint, it encourages local employment and it tastes of whence it came – the same place those people came to visit.

It's just another way of moving from one world to another.

THE 'FOOD MILES' CAMPAIGN LETS HIS GUESTS KNOW HOW FAR THE INGREDIENTS FOR EACH DISH TRAVELLED TO THEIR PLATE

BRUNCH OR LUNCH OR TEA, OH MY!

Not every dinner party has to be at dinnertime. Even if you do serve this in the evening, there's something a bit anarchistic and fun about breakfast for dinner. If you have a large enough pan, you could even make the frittata for 6 rather than individual versions. The trick to this menu is using what you have around. Sure, it's perfect just the way it is, but don't be afraid to experiment a bit as well. Oonagh O'Dwyer's railway cake (page 219) would make a lovely addition if you've the time and inclination.

STARTER
Apple fritters with spiced orange syrup
MAIN
Niall's goat cheese frittata
SIDE
Darra's tomato chutney
DESSERT
Spiced figs with marmalade ice cream

APPLE FRITTERS WITH SPICED ORANGE SYRUP

Serves 6

For the syrup

10 navel oranges (about 1.4 kg/3 lb), washed

1.4 kg/3 lb (approximately) jam sugar

250 ml/8 fl oz/1 cup cold water

3 cardamom pods, crushed

1 cinnamon stick, broken

4 cloves

1 used vanilla pod (optional)

For the fritters

2 eggs

125 g/4½ oz/⅔ cup dark brown sugar

100 g/3½ oz/½ cup caster (superfine) sugar

500 ml/18 fl oz/2 cups milk

1 tsp vanilla extract

120 ml/4 fl oz/½ cup sunflower oil

160 g/5½ oz/1¼ cups wholemeal plain flour

300 g/10½ oz plain flour

25 g/¾ oz/¼ cup bran (oat or wheat bran will work)

2 tsp bread (baking) soda

½ tsp salt

110 g/3½ oz/½ cup raisins

5 cooking apples, peeled and diced

2 tsp ground cinnamon

1 handful sultanas

Butter and oil for frying

To make the syrup, thinly slice all 10 oranges, remove pips and weigh the slices. To a large heavy-bottomed pot, add the oranges, the same weight of jam sugar and the water. Place the spices in a muslin spice bag and add to the pot. Bring to a simmer over low heat, stirring often, until the sugar is fully dissolved. Increase heat to medium and simmer until syrup reaches 105°C/221°F on a digital thermometer. Strain, discarding the muslin bag, and pour into sterilised jars. Makes about 750 ml/1¼ pints/3 cups and will keep, refrigerated, for several weeks.

To make the fritters, first preheat oven to 110°C/230°F/ Gas Mark ¼.

In a large mixing bowl, whisk the eggs and sugars together, then add the milk and vanilla. Mix well. Whisk in the sunflower oil.

In another bowl, stir the flours, bran, soda and salt together. Stir the dry ingredients into the wet and add the raisins. Cover tightly and refrigerate until needed. (The batter will last for up to a week in the refrigerator.)

In a large bowl, mix the apples with the cinnamon. Fold in the sultanas and stir in enough of the batter to coat the apples. Heat a non-stick skillet over medium heat and add a knob of butter with a little vegetable oil. Drop rounded tablespoons of the apple batter into the pan and fry for 2 to 3 minutes per side until golden brown. Remove to a warm plate and keep warm in the oven while you fry the remaining fritters.

To serve, drizzle with spiced orange syrup.

NIALL'S GOAT CHEESE FRITTATA

Serves 6

For the caramelised onions

2 tbsp olive oil

3 large red onions, peeled and thinly
sliced

Sea salt

For the frittatas

Butter and oil, for frying

6 tbsp caramelised red onions (see above)

12 cherry tomatoes diced

18 mushrooms, diced

12 large eggs, free range if possible

90 ml/3 fl oz/6 tbsp milk

2 tbsp tarragon (or any herb you like),
torn/minced

90 g/3 oz/6 tbsp soft goat cheese,
crumbled

Sea salt and freshly ground black pepper

CHEF'S NOTE

Niall is quite adept at turning out these individual frittatas. However, if you have a 30 cm/12-inch skillet, you could make one large frittata for the whole party. The cooking method is the same, if a bit longer, for the eggs to set. Once finished, turn out onto a board and cut into wedges.

To make the caramelised onions, place a large, heavy-bottomed sauté pan over low heat and add the oil. Once warm, add the onions and a good pinch of salt. Stir to coat. Cook very slowly for 15 to 25 minutes, stirring occasionally to prevent sticking. If the onions begin to stick, add a little water, scrape well and keep stirring until the onions are sticky and caramelised (a further 5 to 10 minutes). Remove from heat.

Either use straight away or place single tablespoon-sized scoops into a muffin tray, cover in cling film and freeze. Once frozen, remove from the tray, place in a ziplock bag and store in freezer until needed.

For each individual frittata (see note), first preheat grill (broiler) on high.

To a 12–15 cm/5–6-inch cast iron or non-stick skillet over medium–high heat add a knob of butter and 1 teaspoonful of oil. Once the butter is melted, add 1 tablespoon of the caramelised onions, 2 tomatoes and 3 mushrooms. Sauté until the mushrooms are soft.

In a small bowl, whisk 2 eggs, 1 tbsp milk and 1 tsp tarragon (or your chosen herb). Season with a bit of salt and pepper. Add to the skillet and stir. Reduce the heat to medium.

Once the egg mixture begins to set, dot with the crumbled goat cheese. Place the skillet under a hot grill until it has puffed up and is golden on top. Pierce the top of the frittata to ensure it is cooked through. If not, another minute under the grill should finish it off. Keep warm in a low oven while making the other frittatas.

Serve hot with Darra's tomato chutney (page 250).

DARRA'S TOMATO CHUTNEY

Makes 4–6 jars

1 kg/2 lb 4 oz ripe tomatoes, chopped

200 g/7 oz/1 cup light brown sugar

150 ml/5¼ fl oz/⅔ cup cider vinegar

1 onion, diced

4 cardamom pods

3 cloves garlic, crushed

1 tsp sea salt

½ tsp chilli flakes

¼ tsp mixed spice

To a large heavy-bottomed pan over medium–high heat add all the ingredients and stir well. Bring to a boil, then reduce heat to medium. Simmer, stirring occasionally, until reduced by about half (about 30 minutes) Ladle into sterilised jars, cover and refrigerate. Will keep for months.

CHEF'S NOTE

If you have a hard time finding mixed spice in the shops, see the note in Ciara O'Halloran's apple, berry and hazelnut crumble (pag 162) for a home-made version.

SPICED FIGS WITH MARMALADE ICE CREAM

. . . .

Serves 6

For the marmalade ice cream

1 litre/1¾ pints/4 cups milk

375 g/13 oz/1¾ cups + 2 tbsp caster
   (superfine) sugar

5 egg yolks

500 ml/18 fl oz/2 cups cream

2 tbsp prepared orange marmalade

For the spiced figs

2 oranges

1 star anise

5 black peppercorns

1 cardamom pod, crushed

12 dried figs (about 250 g/9 oz)

2 tsp brown sugar

To make the marmalade ice cream, add the milk to a heavy-bottomed pot and bring almost to a boil – the froth stage, just before it comes up the side of the pot. Whisk the sugar and egg yolks until they double in volume. Temper the milk into the egg mixture by adding 60 ml/ 2 fl oz/¼ cup at a time, stirring the eggs very well so that they do not scramble. Return to a clean pot.

Simmer gently on a low heat while stirring, until it coats the back of a spoon. Remove from heat and transfer to a clean bowl and allow to cool to room temperature. Stir in the cream, then add the marmalade. Transfer to an ice-cream maker, churn and freeze according to manufacturer's instructions. Place in an airtight container and keep in the freezer.

To make the spiced figs, first use a small sharp knife to cut 2 strips of rind, about 2 cm/¾ inch wide and 7 cm/2¾ inches long from the oranges. Remove the white pith from the rind and discard. Julienne the zest into strips. Squeeze the oranges into a measuring jug and add enough water to measure 375 ml/13 fl oz/1½ cups. Place the star anise, peppercorns and cardamom into a spice bag.

In a saucepan over medium heat, combine the orange juice mixture, orange rind, figs and spice bag. Cover and bring to the boil, then reduce heat to low and simmer, covered, for 20 minutes or until the figs are tender. Using a slotted spoon, transfer the figs and orange rind to serving bowls. Remove the spice bag from the syrup and discard. Add the sugar and bring to the boil over medium heat. Cook, uncovered, for 3 to 4 minutes or until the sugar dissolves and the syrup thickens slightly. Serve with marmalade ice cream and a drizzle of spiced syrup.

FIONA HAUGH

THE MARKET HOUSE

· ·

The old Clare market town of Ennistymon is quickly becoming the new market town of the county. Playing no small part in the revitalisation is Fiona Haugh and her Market House food hall. What had been a place everyone drove through – to get to the beach or the cliffs or the Burren – she envisaged as a place that people wouldn't just come *through* but come *to*.

'You have to go where the people are, Trevis,' she told me. Perhaps it's something she learned from her father and the way he grew his businesses. They moved from the family farm in Kilkee when she was three years old to Miltown Malbay where her dad took over a small butcher's shop with attached abattoir. On day one there was a queue out the door – even in the difficult times in the mid-1980s when he opened.

GO WHERE THE PEOPLE ARE

Fiona worked in her uncle's busy shop in Ennistymon. The family business expanded with a large supermarket in Rathkeale, which she managed for a number of years after leaving Cork Institute of Technology where she studied business and tourism.

These were the days of the Celtic Tiger and one day she just had enough. She found her replacement, sold her house and headed off on a one-year working holiday, which took her two years to complete.

After four months touring Thailand, Laos, Cambodia and Vietnam – where, on a boat travelling down the Mekong Delta, she says she felt truly relaxed for the first time in years – she spent three months in Australia, then went to New Zealand. After a year and a half working in Queenstown on Lake Wakatipu and then Nelson on the east coast of Tasman Bay, home called and she returned to find Ireland in the grip of the Great Recession.

The next two years found her working at a musicians' pub in Kinvara while she finished her degree in business and marketing at Galway-Mayo Institute of Technology. Then she moved to Galway and immersed herself in the world of international commerce as a buyer for one of Europe's largest toy-store chains. She was on the fast track for senior management when her dad called with an opportunity neither of them could let pass by.

Converting a listed 1870s butter-market building – which had since seen life as a gymnasium, a furniture store and an Italian restaurant, as well as several stints as a derelict shell – into a food hall with butcher shop, delicatessen and café seemed like an interesting challenge. It turned out to be more interesting than the two had expected, and more challenging than Fiona cares to remember.

It's often said that opening one's own business is the most expensive master's degree possible. The pair made their fair share of mistakes along the way. One example Fiona gives is that she had never so much as baked a scone in her life but had every intention of making all the home-baked goods for the café.

There may have been stumbles along the way, but the evolution of the Market House has been a real gem in the renaissance of the market town and an estimable addition to the food scene of the Burren.

SHE ENVISAGED IT AS A PLACE THAT PEOPLE WOULDN'T JUST COME THROUGH BUT COME TO

A BUTCHER'S KITCHEN

Fiona's menu blends Irish produce with dishes from France and Italy into a warm culinary hug. Deep, rich flavours are offset with bright sparkles from tomatoes, olives and strawberries. Keep her olivada on hand as an accompaniment to cheese or as a spread for sourdough bread. You'll be glad you did. If you feel the need for a vegetable but can't think of one that will stand up to the bold flavours of the beef, try David McCann's roasted broccoli (page 150). It will shy away from no main.

STARTER
Fresh tomato soup
MAIN
Braised shin of beef with rocket gremolata
SIDE
Olivada mash
DESSERT
Farm-fresh strawberry meringue

FRESH TOMATO SOUP

Serves 6

2 tbsp olive oil

1 medium onion, peeled and diced

1 carrot, peeled and diced

1 stalk celery, diced

Sea salt and freshly ground black pepper

2 tsp tomato purée (paste)

1 kg/2 lb 4 oz ripe tomatoes, quartered

1 tsp sugar

2 bay leaves, torn

1.2 litres/2¼ pints/5 cups vegetable stock

80 ml/30z/⅓ cup cream, to garnish

CHEF'S NOTE

The beauty of this soup is that, while it uses a good quantity of fresh tomatoes, they needn't be the prettiest of the bunch. The lumpy, split, scarred tomatoes that you can get at a discount from your local farmers' market work perfectly for this soup. In fact, I often get a basketful of those in August and September when the tomatoes are plentiful and freeze them whole for dishes just like this.

In a large, heavy-bottomed stockpot over medium–low heat, add olive oil and heat until hot. Add onion, carrot and celery with a pinch of salt and sweat, stirring occasionally, until soft and beginning to colour (10 to 15 minutes). Add tomato purée and stir to incorporate. Add quartered tomatoes, sugar and a bit of black pepper. Add torn bay leaves, cover and simmer for 10 minutes, shaking the pot occasionally.

In a saucepan over medium–high heat, bring the vegetable stock to a simmer. Stir the stock into the soup, increase heat to high and bring to a boil. Reduce heat to low, then cover and simmer for 20 to 25 minutes, stirring occasionally.

Remove from heat, uncover and allow to cool for a few minutes. Remove the bay-leaf pieces and discard. Using a hand-held blender, blitz until the soup is very smooth. Rewarm the soup over medium heat until it begins to bubble. Season to taste.

Ladle into warm bowls and garnish with a swirl of cream.

BRAISED SHIN OF BEEF WITH ROCKET GREMOLATA

Serves 6

200 g/7 oz pork skin, with no fat

60 g/2 oz duck fat

3 kg/6 lb 12 oz shin of beef on the bone, crosscut into 4–5 cm/1–1½-inch slices

750 ml/27 fl oz/3 cups red wine

100 ml/3½ fl oz/⅓ cup + 4 tsp cognac or brandy

500 ml/18 fl oz/2 cups veal stock

4 onions, peeled and diced

4 carrots, peeled and sliced

250 g/9 oz smoked bacon, cut into lardons

4 cloves garlic, sliced

4 shallots, peeled and sliced

1 bouquet garni of:

- 2 sprigs thyme
- 4 sprigs parsley
- 1 sprig sage
- 1 sprig rosemary
- 2 bay leaves, all tied with kitchen twine

¼ tsp quatre épices (French four spice)

Sea salt and freshly ground black pepper

150 g/5¼ oz/1 cup plain (all-purpose) flour for paste

100 g/4 oz rocket (arugula), finely minced

2 lemons, zested

1 anchovy fillet, minced (optional)

Preheat oven to 150°C/300°F/Gas Mark 2.

Bring a saucepan of water to the boil, add the pork skin and blanch for 8 minutes. Drain and rinse under cold running water, pat dry and cut into 2 cm/½-inch squares and set aside.

In a large, high-sided sauté pan set over medium heat, melt the duck fat until very hot. Working in batches of 3 to 4 pieces of beef at a time so as not to crowd the pan, brown well. Remove to a rack set over a plate to catch the juices. Repeat until all the beef is browned, then season.

In a saucepan over medium–low, heat the wine and cognac. In another saucepan over medium–low, heat the stock.

Add onions to the pan in which you browned the beef and sweat until softened and beginning to colour, then set aside.

In a large ovenproof casserole (Dutch oven), layer half of each as follows: pork skin, beef, carrot, onion, lardons, garlic, shallots. Add bouquet garni, quatre épices, salt and pepper. Repeat layers and season again. Pour the hot wine over. Add enough stock to come to the level of the top layer, but not cover it. Place over medium–high heat and bring to a boil.

Place the flour in a small bowl and mix in enough water to make a thick, gluey paste. Smear the paste around the rim of casserole lid and firmly press in place on top of the casserole. Transfer to the bottom shelf of the preheated oven and cook for 3½ hours until tender. Remove and uncover, skimming any fat from the surface.

To make the gremolata, mix the minced rocket (arugula), lemon zest and the anchovy, if using, in a small bowl. Stir together with a fork to mix well.

To serve, sprinkle a small handful of gremolata on top of the beef and place the remainder in a dish to pass around the table. Have the olivada mash (page 257) on the side.

OLIVADA MASH

Serves 6

For the olivada

225 g/8 oz mixed olives, pitted and
    coarsely chopped

30 ml/1 fl oz/2 tbsp extra virgin olive oil,
    more to taste

1 tbsp flat-leaf parsley, minced

2 tsp thyme leaves, minced

2 tsp rosemary leaves, minced

1 orange, zested

1 lemon, zested

1 pinch red pepper flakes

1 anchovy fillet, finely minced

Freshly ground black pepper

1 kg/2 lb 4 oz floury potatoes, peeled and
    cut into quarters (Roosters, Maris Piper,
    Russet, Golden Wonder, etc.)

500 ml/18 fl oz/2 cups chicken stock

Coarse sea salt and freshly ground black
    pepper

80 ml/3 fl oz/⅓ cup extra virgin olive oil,
    more to taste

To make the olivada, mix all the ingredients well in a large bowl at least 1 hour before using so that the flavours blend. You can refrigerate it at this stage, but remove it at least 30 minutes before use (it will keep for 4 days).

For the mash, combine the potatoes, chicken stock and a good pinch of salt in a large, heavy-bottomed pot. Add enough cold water to cover the potatoes by at least 2.5 cm/1 inch. Place over medium–high heat and bring to a boil. Reduce heat to medium and partly cover, simmering until the potatoes are very tender. Drain, but reserve 500 ml/18 fl oz/2 cups of the cooking liquid.

Return the potatoes to the pot and place over medium–low heat to dry. Shake the pot and stir with a wooden spoon for about 1 minute. Reduce heat to very low. Mash with a hand masher (this dish is best if the potatoes are a little bit lumpy). With a wooden spoon, beat in the olive oil. Beating vigorously with the spoon, drizzle in 80 ml/3 fl oz/⅓ cup of the cooking liquid at a time, adding as much liquid as you like for your desired texture.

Fold in 120–170 ml/4–6 fl oz/½–⅔ cup of olivada to taste, correct the seasoning and serve.

FARM-FRESH STRAWBERRY MERINGUE

. . . .

Serves 6

3 egg whites, free range if possible

1 pinch salt

175 g 6¼ oz/¾ cup + 1 tbsp caster
    (superfine) sugar

1 tsp cornflour (cornstarch)

½ tsp white wine vinegar

225 g/8 oz small ripe strawberries, hulled
    and halved

1 tbsp icing sugar, sifted

¼ tsp orange zest, finely grated

300 ml/½ pint/1¼ cups double (heavy)
    cream

Mint leaves, to garnish

Preheat oven to 140°C/275°F/Gas Mark 1. Line a baking tray with greaseproof paper.

In a large clean bowl, place the egg whites and salt, and whisk to stiff peaks. Whisk in the sugar, one tablespoon at a time, to make a stiff, glossy meringue. Carefully whisk in the cornflour and vinegar.

Drop 6 even-sized spoonfuls of meringue onto the prepared tray, spacing them well apart. Flatten slightly with the back of a spoon, making a small dip in the centre. Bake in the middle of the preheated oven for 45 minutes. Then turn off the oven and leave them inside for 2 to 3 hours to go completely cold.

A half hour before serving, prepare the topping: in a mixing bowl, place the strawberries and gently fold in the icing sugar and orange zest. Loosely cover and set aside to let the flavours infuse.

In a large mixing bowl, whip the cream to soft peaks. Assemble by placing a small dollop of cream on each plate, topped with a meringue. Divide the remaining cream between the meringues, making an indentation in the middle. Top with strawberries, drizzling a bit of the juices over the dessert and around the plate. Garnish with mint leaves.

CHEF'S NOTE

If you are using a copper bowl to whip your egg whites for the meringues, you can skip the addition of vinegar. The ionic reaction between the sulphur in the whites and the copper will stabilise the structure of the proteins in the same way the acid does.

THE LONG TABLE

One of the best parts about food is sharing. It's why we curated thirty-two unique Burren menus from professional chefs and talented comers alike. But there are other ways to share a taste of the Fertile Rock. In fact, it's become fashionable to revive an old north Clare tradition of sharing food in a communal meal at Long Table suppers.

The Burren Food Trail played no small part in the reawakening of the custom. Through their members they offer unique dining experiences for locals and visitors alike. In caves, pubs, historic buildings or in the open air of a Burren summer, ingredients mingle with talent and are presented for all to enjoy.

For nine of our foodies – chefs, producers and keepers themselves – the idea of throwing a full-on dinner party was right out. Instead, they offered up speciality dishes for which they have some considerable renown, are oft asked to bring along to a communal meal or might have been offered at a Food Trail Long Table event. These dishes speak to person and place as fully and as finely as the dinner party menus have.

From scrumptious starters and mouth-watering main dishes to savoury sides and delectable desserts, these offerings are sure to make their way into your repertoire.

As with all of the recipes in previous sections of this book, each dish serves approximately six people.

STARTERS
Steamed mussels with white wine and cream

Local cheese board

Tomato and blood orange sorbet

Sloke cakes

MAINS
Roast fillet of hake with chorizo, mussels and clams

Hot-smoked salmon with spring onion mash, creamed cabbage and leeks with
mustard cream sauce

Roast rib of beef with Yorkshire puddings

Baked wild salmon with herb crust and sorrel sauce

SIDE
Burren Nature Sanctuary savoury scones with walnuts, spinach and cheddar

DESSERTS
Aunt Esther's apple pie with cheesy crust

Banana and maple upside-down toffee cake

BRÍD FAHY

CAFÉ LINNALLA

. . . .

Cruinniú na mBád (Gathering of the Boats) is a tradition still celebrated with the first spring tide of August on the north shore of the Burren. It acknowledges the time at the end of the turf-cutting season when Galway hookers would sail south from Connemara to Clare to trade fuel to keep Burren farmers warm in the winter in return for the foods for which the area continues to be celebrated.

The story of Cruinniú na mBád, as well as the traditions of the winterage of cattle on the mountains and how Henry VIII's favourite oysters came from a bay just below her husband's family farm, were all stories told to me by Bríd Fahy.

Originally from Meath, to where her grandfather had moved from Mayo during the Rural Resettlement Programme of the 1920s, Bríd studied nursing in Manchester in England. Though a fair number of her nursing colleagues stayed in England, Bríd was never the one who was going to be

A GOOD PLACE TO BE

gone for good. She always intended to return to Ireland. A job in Waterford city afforded that return and she happily worked in Waterford through much of the late 1980s.

Her next nursing post found her in Galway, where she met a man called Roger Fahy. The rest, as they say, is ice-cream history in the making.

The couple married in the traditional way in Meath: her father walked her up the aisle and they all danced with the straw boys to the céilí band afterwards. Bríd moved to Roger's family's 150-acre dairy farm in Finvarra, where they have raised their own family of three children.

The early noughties saw many dairy farmers encouraged to diversify. Bríd and Roger considered a few options, including cheesemaking, but given their unique location on a peninsula with the Flaggy Shore at the top and a Martello tower on the end, it seemed a shame not to take advantage of the natural beauty of the place.

What dairy product might tourists coming to the area enjoy as they take in the sights? Ice cream, made from the milk of the very cows they could see, was the decision. They added Dairy Shorthorns to their herd of Friesians. Holstein Friesians produce more milk, but the Shorthorns have a higher milk-fat content, which produces a more luxurious ice cream.

While they began by selling ice cream to some restaurants, it was always the intention to bring visitors up to Finvarra, to show them where the food comes from and experience why it tastes so unique. Today you can only get Linnalla ice cream by getting off the N67 and winding your way along the coast to their little shop. With tables and walking paths and views for days, there are fewer places better imagined for enjoying an ice cream – and it might very well be Bríd Fahy who scoops it for you.

THERE ARE FEWER PLACES BETTER IMAGINED FOR ENJOYING AN ICE CREAM

STEAMED MUSSELS WITH WHITE WINE AND CREAM

· ·

Serves 6

30 g/1 oz/2 tbsp butter

1 handful spring onions (scallions) or dill,
  finely chopped

800 g/1 lb 12 oz fresh mussels, washed
  and de-bearded

350 ml/12 fl oz/1½ cups dry white wine

300 ml/½ pint/1¼ cups cream

Crusty bread, to serve

In a large pot with a tight-fitting lid over high heat, add the butter and melt. Add the onion or dill and stir. Add the mussels and cover. Cook, shaking occasionally, for 5 minutes, then check to see if the mussels have opened. If not, an additional 2 to 3 minutes will do the trick.

Pour into a colander over a bowl to catch the juices (most of the juices can be reserved for another use, such as shellfish stock).

Return the pot to medium–low heat and add wine and 1 to 2 tablespoons of the cooking liquid. Simmer for 1 minute. Add the cream, bring to a simmer and add the mussels, tossing to coat. Place in a large heated dish and serve immediately with crusty bread.

SINÉAD NÍ GHÁIRBHITH

THE CHEESE PRESS

· ·

You will not meet many people in your life who nearly lost theirs for a cause in which they believe. Neither are you likely to meet many people like Sinéad Ní Gháirbhith. From the time of an epiphany at secondary school, she knew that she was set on a course of discovery and self-enlightenment. What she didn't know were the places it would take her nor the people she would help – and would help her – along the way.

First, if you think you may have heard the name, you probably have. Sinéad Ní Gháirbhith was the 'one woman' in the now famous 'One Woman Protest' of Xi Jinping's visit to the Cliffs of Moher.

CONNECTIONS

From 'Mighty, Mighty Inagh', Sinéad grew up in a family of supportive educators, but felt a bit betrayed by the guidance counsellors at her secondary convent school who dissuaded her from studying the arts, languages and physics she loved. Rather, she was sent down a university path of study in international marketing. What she knew deep down was that her truest desire was to study the workings of the mind and calming her inner self.

It was the drive towards inner peace that brought her to the Tibetan Buddhist Meditation Centre in Cavan, where she began her mindfulness training and practice. Her experience fund-raising for local schools and charities in Clare along with her love of languages prepared her for the major course change her life was about to take with the help of the Venerable Panchen Ötrul Rinpoche.

Going first to a Tibetan refugee camp in central India and then another in Mongolia, Sinéad eventually spent time in the high mountain country of Tibet, acting as intermediary between displaced refugees and their families.

It was experiences with numbing fatigue and crushing isolation during her first trip that led her to understanding the importance of connection and physical contact with others. The solemnity of the healing hands of a doctor as she awoke from a malaria-induced coma brought her to tears and it was that moment, she says, that has informed most of her subsequent decisions.

You can see how her discernment of our empirical need for connection forms the design of her seating space at The Cheese Press in Ennistymon. The two U-shaped seating areas put customers enjoying a coffee or a nibble from her offerings in direct contact with one another. It's almost impossible to be 'alone' there, even if you are not with another person. Conversations are sparked, stories and experiences shared and friendships renewed or engaged.

Truly it is a place where people come together for more than a loaf of their famed sourdough bread, a wedge of Irish-only cheese or a perfectly brewed Clare-roasted coffee. Sinéad Ní Gháirbhith – a woman like few others you'll find in the west of Ireland – has created a space the likes of which you'll be searching for well after you leave the Burren.

TRULY IT IS A PLACE WHERE PEOPLE COME TOGETHER

LOCAL CHEESE BOARD

Serves 6

6–8 x 250 g/9 oz local cheeses (a mixture of sheep, goat and cow, soft, medium and hard)

2 apples, cut into 6 wedges

2 pears, cut into 6 wedges

60 g/2 oz/½ cup mixed nuts, unsalted

12 gherkins

Arrange the cheeses, partly sliced, attractively on a board. Place the apples and pears around the cheeses. Serve nuts and gherkins in small bowls or pots. Serve with sloke cakes (page 271) and tomato and blood orange sorbet (page 270).

TOMATO AND BLOOD ORANGE SORBET

Serves 6

2.5 kg/5½ lb ripe tomatoes, chopped

1 tsp coarse sea salt

1 red bell pepper, deseeded and chopped

120ml/4 fl oz/½ cup blood orange juice

1 sprig tarragon

1 sprig basil

1 pinch red chilli flakes

50 g/1¾ oz/¼ cup caster (superfine) sugar

2 tbsp golden syrup

3 tbsp water

1 tbsp lemon juice

1 pinch white pepper, ground

CHEF'S NOTE

While it won't be exactly the same, a mixture of ⅔ orange juice and ⅓ lemon juice can be substituted for the blood orange juice in this sorbet.

Set a large colander, lined with a layer of cheesecloth, over a bowl. In a large bowl, toss half the tomatoes with salt and transfer to the colander. Place the remaining tomatoes in a ziplock bag, seal and refrigerate until needed. Cover the colander with cling film and refrigerate for at least 8 hours or preferably overnight.

Remove the colander from the bowl, measure 100 ml/ 3½ fl oz/⅓ cup + 4 tsp of the tomato water and reserve. Save the tomatoes and remaining tomato water for another use.

Working in batches, purée the diced tomatoes from the ziplock bag with the bell pepper in a blender until very smooth. Strain through a fine sieve into a large saucepan over medium–high heat, discarding the solids. Stir in the blood orange juice, tarragon, basil and red chilli flakes and cook, stirring occasionally. Reduce to 500 ml/18 fl oz/2 cups (about 35 to 40 minutes).

In a small saucepan over medium heat, add the sugar, syrup and water. Bring to a boil, stirring to dissolve the sugar. Remove from the heat and stir into the reduced tomato and blood orange juice, along with the lemon juice, white pepper and reserved 100 ml/3½ fl oz/⅓ cup + 4 tsp of tomato water. Strain into a pitcher, discarding the solids. Cover with cling film and refrigerate until cold (at least 4 hours).

Churn and freeze in an ice-cream maker to the manufacturer's instructions, until the sorbet is set but not rock hard, about 25 minutes, or put into a container and freeze, stirring every 2 hours until frozen. Place in a covered container and freeze until needed. Will keep for up to 5 days.

SLOKE CAKES

. . . .

Serves 6

1 large handful fresh sloke (aka nori, laver,
    sleaddaí), snipped

1 tsp dry pepper dulse (optional)

200 g/7 oz/2 cups organic oats

1–2 drops toasted sesame oil

Organic butter or coconut oil for frying

Into a saucepan over medium–high heat, snip the sloke
into very small pieces with sharp scissors. Add 1 litre/
1¾ pint/4 cups salted water and bring to the boil, then
reduce heat to medium and simmer for 55 minutes. Strain
the liquid into a large jug.

In a large bowl, mix the cooked sloke and pepper dulse (if
using) into the oats.

Add sesame oil to the cooking liquid and mix enough
liquid into the oats to make a porridge thick enough to
form into patties (start with 2 cups of liquid and work up
from there as needed). Divide the mixture into 12 equal
portions and flatten into 13 mm/½-inch thick discs.

In a non-stick skillet over medium heat, melt a knob of
butter or coconut oil. Fry the patties for 4 to 5 minutes
on each side until deep brown. You may need to turn
them more than once to cook all the way through without
browning them too much. Drain and cool on kitchen
paper. Repeat with the second (and third depending on
the size of your skillet) batch.

Serve with cheese and sorbet (page 270).

CONOR GRAHAM

LINNANE'S LOBSTER BAR

• •

The Graham family have been running pubs for four generations. Conor Graham's father, Vincent, ran several pubs in his native Galway before taking over the lease on a 300-year-old building in New Quay, which has been a pub for the last two-thirds of that time.

Conor's working life began in a way with which the son of many a publican will be quite familiar: he started in the yard, crushing cardboard. He went to a business university where international commerce was his course of study (as was it for his sister). He finished his degree and began searching for an entry-level job in his field … but he hated it. It wasn't obvious just to Conor that he'd not be content in the world of high finance; his mother took note and sat him down for a parental heart-to-heart.

It was decided that the food side of the business might suit the new graduate, so he was packed off to the illustrious Ballymaloe Cookery School where he studied for twelve weeks and obtained his certification. Then it was off to London to cut his teeth in a real working kitchen.

Perhaps a bit out of his depth, he felt he'd caught a tiger by the tail in the busy city restaurant where he secured his first job. He soon came to understand that he wouldn't attain his eventual goal of running his own restaurant if he were spending sixteen to eighteen hours a day working in someone else's kitchen.

He met his future business partner, Mark Commins, an accountant, and they became good friends. They talked of opening a restaurant in the city together. At the end of the day, however, Conor just couldn't see it happening in the high-rent city and he was also burnt out from the hours.

He returned to university in Galway for a master's degree in management before returning to London, to an office job. He committed to it for a few years to confirm what his gut was telling him: that he was pursuing the wrong career and in the wrong place.

The universe, then, told him where he was supposed to be.

It was in November, entering the final year of a lease on the business, that Vincent was doing the kind of maintenance required of a three-century-old building, fell off a ladder and injured himself quite severely. Conor returned home to find his father recovering but his mother ready to hand back the keys and close the place. It was his opportunity to take over and run his own restaurant in a place he knew, with a staff who knew him and a steady customer base year over year.

He took a week back in London to consider the idea. He knew he wanted to do it. He also knew the job was too big for one person. He made the commitment to reopen Linnane's the next spring, but only if Mark came back to help him run the place … which he did.

While they have tweaked a few things in the years since taking over the business, Linnane's is still a place for a great pint, a view of the sea whence your food came and one of the best lobster dinners you'll find in the Burren.

IT WAS HIS OPPORTUNITY TO TAKE OVER AND RUN HIS OWN RESTAURANT IN A PLACE HE KNEW

A TIGER BY THE TAIL

ROAST FILLET OF HAKE WITH CHORIZO, MUSSELS AND CLAMS

Serves 6

2 large fillets fresh hake (about 1100 g/ 2½ lbs)

Sea salt and freshly ground black pepper

2 cloves garlic, minced

30 g/1 oz/2 tbsp butter, softened

30 ml/1 fl oz/2 tbsp extra virgin olive oil

1 tbsp minced parsley

30 ml/1 fl oz/2 tbsp rapeseed (canola)

12 mussels, scrubbed and de-bearded

12 clams, scrubbed

60 ml/2 fl oz/¼ cup white wine

120 g/4 oz/½ cup chorizo, chopped

12 cherry tomatoes, halved

parsley, to garnish

1 lemon, cut into 6 wedges

Preheat oven to 200°C/400°F/Gas Mark 6.

Season the hake well and place in the refrigerator for 30 minutes to firm.

In a small bowl, mix the garlic, softened butter, olive oil and parsley together, then set aside.

In a large casserole (Dutch oven) over medium heat, add the oil and heat to shimmering. Carefully lay the fillets skin-side down and cook until the skin is crispy (2 to 3 minutes). Using a spatula, turn the fillets skin-side up. Add the mussels, clams, wine and reserved garlic butter. Cover and place in the middle of the preheated oven for 5 minutes. Add chorizo and cherry tomatoes and continue cooking until the shellfish open, about 4 to 5 minutes. Once the mussels and clams are opened and the hake is cooked through, remove from the oven. Garnish with parsley and lemon wedges and serve in the casserole.

KIERAN O'HALLORAN

KIERAN'S KITCHEN IN THE ROADSIDE TAVERN

• •

When ten-year-old Kieran O'Halloran of Lisdoonvarna ate at a restaurant for the very first time, it was with an aunt, in Doolin's original Bruach Na hAille. He read of foods on the menu and tasted foods on his plate that he'd never even imagined, let alone eaten. Kieran jovially blames Helen and John Browne, the founders of that restaurant, for the culinary voyage he took over the next thirty-five years.

Not one for the traditional education route, he left secondary school for technical school. He left technical school for the Cert chef's training programme. When that didn't suit his learning style, he set off to learn the way Kieran had discovered he learns best: by doing.

THE VOYAGER RETURNED

That part of the voyage began with a little white lie to the manager of a hotel outside Edinburgh. Kieran lied about his age and his qualifications to get an entry-level job. He thought he might want to cook, but it was a front-of-house job he got. At the tender age of sixteen and with little more than a few Cert classes under his belt, he knows well that he was lucky to have been given a job at all.

HE FEELS LIKE HE'S NOT ONLY HOME, BUT HOME FOR GOOD

Kieran's next decade on the job ladder was more like running up an escalator.

Within a few short years he'd opened an Irish-themed pub in Aberdeen, which became so popular that a major UK brewery bought him out and then put him on the management team that created an entire chain of pubs themed in its likeness. They opened over 120 of those pubs in the UK and one of the largest chain pub companies now manages the fifty-odd still remaining. All sprouted from the lone Irish pub Kieran and a mate started in the Gaelic Lane.

Wrung out from the stress of it all, he set off for Africa on a charitable mission, which found him spending his spare time helping a local restaurateur redefine his market and his dining concept. He just couldn't get it out of his blood.

The people of Lisdoonvarna don't mind so much that the hospitality business has seated itself so firmly into Kieran's life. They, as well as the thousands of tourists that come through the spa town each year, benefit from his expertise. He hires residents of the town, he spearheaded the efforts to use local farmers, foragers and fishermen in Burren restaurants, and he has raised the bar for the standard of pub food and service in the whole of County Clare.

Though Kieran's parents – from west Galway and Mount Callan in Clare – met in London, they returned to Ireland and the Burren before he and his twin brother were born. He feels a strong connection to Lisdoonvarna where he was raised. Returned after his 21-year voyage of work and travel abroad, he feels like he's not only home, but home for good.

With all the work that he has done in the area to help create a buzz about the place, it's safe to say that it's good for his home as well.

HOT-SMOKED SALMON WITH SPRING ONION MASH, CREAMED CABBAGE AND LEEKS WITH MUSTARD CREAM SAUCE

Serves 6

1 side (approximately 1 kg) hot-smoked salmon

For the potatoes
2 kg/4½ lb rooster potatoes, scrubbed, peeled and cut into eighths
60 g/2 oz/4 tbsp butter
100 ml/3½ fl oz/⅓ cup + 4 tsp cream
Sea salt and freshly ground black pepper
1 bunch spring onions, sliced

For the mustard cream sauce
400 ml/14 fl oz/1⅔ cups cream
3 tbsp, rounded, wholegrain mustard
2 tbsp lemon juice

For the cabbage
1 head green cabbage, finely chopped
75 g/2½ oz/5 tbsp butter
1 onion, peeled and sliced
2 leeks, washed and thinly sliced
150 ml/5¼ fl oz/⅔ cup cream
Baby rocket leaves, to garnish

Preheat oven to 180°C/350°F/Gas Mark 4.

Slice the salmon into 6 equal portions, place on a baking tray lined with greaseproof paper and set aside.

Place the potatoes in a large saucepan of cold, salted water over medium–high heat and bring to a boil. Reduce heat to medium and simmer until just tender. Strain and return to heat to dry for 1 minute. Mash with a hand masher then add the butter and cream. Season to taste and fold in the spring onions. Cover and keep warm.

For the mustard cream, combine the cream, mustard and lemon juice in a saucepan over medium heat. Simmer to reduce by half.

In a large pot of boiling salted water, cook the cabbage for 5 to 6 minutes until tender. Drain and refresh in cold water. In a heavy-bottomed pot over medium heat, melt butter and sweat onion for about 5 minutes until soft. Add the leeks and cook, stirring, for 2 minutes. Add the cabbage and cream, bring to the boil then turn heat to low and reduce for 3 to 4 minutes. Season to taste.

To serve, first place the salmon in the preheated oven for 6 to 8 minutes while you assemble the plates. Spoon a large mound of mashed potatoes onto each warmed plate. Surround the potatoes with the creamed cabbage and leeks. Place the salmon atop the potatoes and ladle the mustard cream over the salmon. Garnish with rocket leaves and black pepper.

NEIL HAWES

THE BURREN CRAFT BUTCHER

• •

You might as easily expect the name on Neil Hawes's shop in Lisdoonvarna to be 'The Sports Butcher' as you would 'The Burren Craft Butcher'. With Sky Sports on the telly, sports-related newspaper clippings here and there, photos of inter-county GAA legends on the walls and scores from the latest match on everyone's lips, it's like a sports bar without stools or taps.

And Neil is not just some punter who likes sport: Neil Hawes lives and breathes sport.

He met his wife, Paula, when she and her friends were over from Dublin on a kayaking and surfing holiday. He used his love of any event at Croke Park to make regular trips to Dublin to see her – often after a long day working on a Saturday and with an early Monday awaiting him back in Clare.

When taking an advanced butchery course four days per week, he'd sometimes sneak off from an abattoir trip to catch a match at Lansdowne Road. Though he no longer plays at the county senior level, he is involved in playing and coaching the young lads for his local club, Naomh Breacáin (St Breckan's) in Lisdoonvarna.

WOULD YOU EAT IT YOURSELF?

Though not a butcher himself, Neil's father, Francis, did a bit of pick-up work for a local butcher. That and a bit of a nudge from his late grandmother set Neil on the path that brought him to owning his own shop since early in 2007 and winning the prestigious Rural Craft Butcher of the Year award in 2016.

NEIL WORKED HARD AND HE WORKED SMART TO KEEP HIS CORE CUSTOMER BASE HAPPY

At the age of thirteen he took a summer job in one of the three butcher's shops the small town once supported. A professional retail butcher's course at Galway-Mayo Institute of Technology was where he got his formal training. He was a natural at the trade and his instructors were keenly aware of that fact. He graduated with top honours and went on to hone his skills for a number of years in other butcher's shops and busy supermarket butcheries. These dozen or so years were invaluable for Neil, as he was able to see where customer trends were headed and where quality gaps in the market had opened.

When the lease on a shop back in his home town of Lisdoonvarna became available, Neil's family helped him to open his own business. With six brothers and sisters, aunts, cousins and his parents still living in the town, Neil had a built-in customer base in family alone. But it wasn't just family who gave Neil their custom. The shop was abuzz from the first day he opened his doors, keeping Neil and his colleague at the time, Fergus Crowe, hopping. That was, of course, until the economic downturn of 2008, which changed much for the lives of small shops across the country.

With the tenacity of a midfielder down by two points and into injury time, and now single-handedly, Neil worked hard and he worked smart to keep his core customer base happy and remain open for those who could afford Neil's quality only for special occasions. It was a tough old haul, those years, and many of the regulars from those early days have passed away or continue to shop at multinationals even after the economy has returned to strength.

No matter what the economy holds for the Burren, Neil holds true to something an instructor said to him in his first months of training. 'Would you eat it yourself?' the professor asked.

If he wouldn't put it on his own plate, it's not in the case. If he wouldn't serve it to his growing family, he wouldn't sell it to yours. It is not an easy business – a craft butcher in a small town in rural north Clare, Ireland – but a GAA man knows that there is no easy way to the Sam Maguire Cup. Neil keeps his eyes on the prize.

ROAST RIB OF BEEF WITH YORKSHIRE PUDDINGS

Serves 6

2.7 kg/6 lb bone-in rib of beef

30 g/1 oz/2 tbsp butter, softened

1 tbsp flaked sea salt

For the puddings

3 large eggs, at room temperature

370 ml/13 fl oz/1½ cups full-fat (whole)
   milk, at room temperature

225 g/8 oz/1½ cups plain (all-purpose)
   flour

¾ tsp table salt

3 tbsp beef fat from roast

For the jus

2 tbsp cornflour (cornstarch)

1 litre/1¾ pints/4 cups rich beef stock

The easiest way to approach this is to prepare the Yorkshire pudding batter after the beef has roasted for 30 minutes. Then, while the roast rests, add the beef fat to the batter and get the puddings into the oven. While the puddings bake, complete the jus.

Preheat oven to 230°C/450°F/Gas Mark 8.

Place the beef on a rack in a deep roasting tin, rub it completely with butter and season well with salt. Roast in the middle of the preheated oven for 20 minutes, then reduce heat to 160°C/320°F/Gas Mark 3.

To prepare the Yorkshire pudding batter, whisk the eggs and milk in a large bowl for about 20 seconds. In a second bowl, whisk the flour and salt, then add the dry ingredients to the wet, whisking quickly until the flour is just incorporated and the mixture is smooth (about 30 seconds). Cover the batter with cling film and let it stand at room temperature for at least 1 hour (can be made up to 3 hours in advance of use).

Roast the beef for approximately 1½ hours for medium-rare (reduce by 15 minutes for rare or add 15 minutes for medium-well). Remove the beef, set over a platter to collect the juices and loosely tent with tinfoil.

Increase the oven temperature to 230°C/450°F/Gas Mark 8. Defat the cooking juices and reserve the fat for the puddings.

Whisk 1 tablespoon of beef fat into the pudding batter until bubbly and smooth (about 30 seconds). Transfer batter to a measuring jug. Measure a half teaspoonful of beef fat into each cup of a standard 12-cup muffin tray.

Place the tray in the middle of the preheated oven for 3 minutes (the fat will smoke a bit). Working quickly, remove the tray from the oven, close the oven door and divide the batter evenly among the 12 muffin cups, filling each about two-thirds full. Immediately return the tray to the oven and bake without opening the oven door for 20 minutes.

Meanwhile, place the roasting tin over medium–high heat and whisk in the cornflour until it is dissolved. While whisking, add the stock in a thin stream, bring to a hard simmer and reduce heat to medium. Simmer for 10 minutes until the jus is thick and glossy. Transfer to a heated jug.

When the puddings have baked for 20 minutes, reduce the temperature to 180°C/350°F/Gas Mark 4. Bake until deep golden brown, about 10 minutes longer. Remove the tray from the oven and pierce each pudding with a skewer to release steam and prevent collapse. Using hands or a dinner knife, lift each pudding out of the tray and prepare to serve immediately.

To serve, carve the beef from the bone, then slice thinly and cut between the bones. Arrange the beef slices on a heated platter with the bones, with jus and Yorkshire puddings on the side.

HELEN BROWNE

DOOLIN CAVE

• •

One would be forgiven for being surprised by the story of Helen Browne's entry into the food business. A schoolteacher by training, the Kilmaley woman grew up on a mixed farm southwest of Ennis and decided along with her best friend – also a schoolteacher – to leave the profession and start a restaurant in Doolin.

While this mightn't sound too far-fetched, neither Helen nor her friend had ever even worked in a restaurant when they decided on the switch. They'd not waited on a table, bussed dishes or made an Irish coffee, let alone cooked professionally. Oh, and it was the early 1970s in rural north Clare where hotel dining rooms were about the only places one could purchase a dinner.

It didn't stop the two from opening the first, and arguably most successful, restaurant in the area,

FORGING THE WAY

Bruach Na hAille, in a historic cottage on the banks of the River Haille.

While the building still stands and Helen and her husband, John, still own it, the business is now rented out to others who continue to run it as a restaurant under that name. Helen and John called time on running it themselves after thirty-five years.

Each winter, the couple closed to get a break after the busy season and found solace in the Caribbean, South America, Africa, Spain and Australia. Though Bruach Na hAille had been founded on the concept of local ingredients used in the cooking of traditional Irish cuisine, those travels flavoured the menu as the years progressed.

GARLIC WAS AN EXOTIC INGREDIENT FOR THE TIME AND PLACE THAT WAS IN IT

Helen and John – a local farmer himself – grew many of the more 'international' ingredients that were required to make dishes inspired by the couple's travels. Helen remembers being told at a market in Lisdoonvarna while searching out garlic that she might (*might*) be able to find it in Limerick. Never mind the likes of coriander, root ginger or fresh chilli, which might be required to emulate a dish from their holidays. Garlic was an exotic ingredient for the time and place that was in it.

It was after one of their extended trips away that the couple decided to move on from the restaurant and open a tourist attraction at Poll an Eidhneáin – the limestone cave now known as Doolin Cave. Ever mindful of the delicate balance of life in the Burren, they worked closely with the county council, An Bord Pleanála, conservationists, geologists and their neighbours to ensure that the Great Stalactite – the largest free-standing stalactite in Europe – was properly preserved for visitors well into the future.

They've built an eco-friendly visitor centre and café on the site, as well as a nature trail with thousands of native plants lovingly transplanted to make the experience complete. On the misty day I arrived at Doolin Cave to chat with Helen, a few of the goats from their farmyard menagerie were on top of the building making a breakfast of grasses growing on the centre's sod roof.

Helen loves to walk the nature trail and have a chat with her animals. She'll occasionally forage wild berries, mushrooms or herbs she finds along the way. The sorrel in the sauce for her addition to our Long Table grows in abundance in the fertile soil that leads from the Burren to the sea.

BAKED WILD SALMON WITH HERB CRUST AND SORREL SAUCE

Serves 6

6 x 150 g/5 oz wild salmon fillets, skinned

Sea salt and freshly ground black pepper

1 lemon, juiced and zested

60 g/2 ozs/4 tbsp butter, melted

50 g/2 oz fresh white breadcrumbs

50 g/2 oz/½ cup Parmesan, coarsely grated

2 tbsp wild garlic, chopped (or parsley or chives and 1 small clove garlic, crushed)

For the sorrel sauce

1 shallot, minced

400 ml/14 fl oz/1⅔ cups fish stock

150 ml/5¼ fl oz/⅔ cup dry vermouth

200 ml/7 fl oz/¾ cup + 4 tsp double (heavy) cream

Sea salt and freshly ground black pepper

1 tbsp lemon juice

1 bunch sorrel leaves, torn

Parsley, to garnish

Preheat oven to 200°C/400°F/Gas Mark 6. Line a baking tray with greaseproof paper.

Season both sides of the salmon fillets and place on the prepared baking tray. Sprinkle with half the lemon juice and zest, and brush with melted butter.

In a bowl, mix the breadcrumbs, Parmesan, wild garlic (or garlic and herbs) and season. Pour in any remaining butter and mix well. Spread the crumb topping thickly on top of the salmon, pressing firmly. Bake in the middle of a preheated oven for about 15 minutes or until nicely browned. When the salmon is done, it will have changed from translucent to an opaque pink.

To make the sorrel sauce, add the shallot, stock and vermouth to a saucepan over medium–high heat. Bring to the boil and reduce by half. Add the cream and reduce again by half. Season with salt, pepper and lemon juice. Fold in the torn sorrel.

To serve, spoon the sorrel sauce onto a warmed platter. Using two spatulas to support the fillet, remove from the tray and place on top of the sauce. Garnish with chopped parsley.

ROY BERMINGHAM

THE BURREN NATURE SANCTUARY

· ·

Roy Bermingham's maternal grandfather was a very good hurler, but he was in An Garda Síochána so was moved around quite often. Thus his collection of hurling medals included club and county championships from Limerick, Tipperary, Clare and Dublin. He won an All-Ireland medal as a junior, while as a senior hurler his honours include a Corn an Iarnróid (the interprovincial championship Railway Cup) and an All-Ireland championship.

Roy, on the other hand, hopes never to have to move from Kinvara, the village of his birth and of his domicile since he was born.

His mother, father, Roy and all of his siblings all hail from the tidy seaport village. Roy remembers stories of his family trading for turf and grain with the people of Connemara during Cruinniú na mBád (the Gathering of the Boats). His people were not farmers; rather they were local business people who helped bring electricity and modern conveniences into the homes of the village. Still, a bag of turf can go a long way at taking the chill off a long Burren winter's night.

NO FRY, NO FIZZ

A mechanic by training and trade, Roy stumbled into the food business the way he has fortuitously stumbled into several pretty good things in his life. While working at a speciality stonecutter's in Galway, for example, he stumbled upon a beautiful English woman working in the front office. That woman is now his wife, Mary. There's a funny story Roy tells me about how he proposed to Mary: with his grandmother's ring he walked into the room where Mary was sitting. Mary, at the same time, decided to walk into the kitchen to talk to Roy. The two ran into one another, bumped their heads together and that, Roy tells me, is how they got engaged. If that's not stumbling into something good, I don't know what is.

While on holidays in the south of England with their children, the couple also stumbled upon the thin end of the wedge that would lead to the eventual opening of the Burren Nature Sanctuary on their 50-acre organic farm just three minutes' drive from the centre of the village.

Their sanctuary is not at all like that holiday centre they visited, but not all that far from it either. The Burren Nature Sanctuary offers families a space to come and play outside when the weather is fine or inside while they wait for a break in the clouds. Children get the chance to meet a wide assortment of animals – from native Burren goats to alpacas and llamas from South America – and just get out into the fresh air. It's a complete introduction to the flora and fauna of the Burren, including an audio tour and interpretive signage.

Always with a mind to a healthier lifestyle for themselves as well as for their guests, Mary and Roy adopted a radical 'no fry, no fizz' ethos upon opening in 2014. Nothing from the Sanctuary's kitchen is ever fried in a deep-fat fryer, and you'll find no fizzy drinks in the café either. It's a decision that has pleased many parents and is yet another way the Sanctuary sets itself apart from other family attractions.

Only in their pre-teen years, the couple's two youngest children, Grace and Lorna, have seen more of the world than Roy has visited. He likes that. He says that his hope is for the girls to travel the world to visit and experience several cultures. Only by leaving, he reckons, can they unequivocally understand the uniqueness of the place they consider 'home' in the nonchalant manner every generation regards the place they came up.

Then he wants them to come back to Kinvara – the place he hopes that his grandchildren will call home.

IT'S A COMPLETE INTRODUCTION TO THE FLORA AND FAUNA OF THE BURREN

BURREN NATURE SANCTUARY SAVOURY SCONES WITH WALNUTS, SPINACH AND CHEDDAR

Makes 8–12

800 g/1 lb 12 oz/5⅓ cups self-raising flour

100 g/3½ oz/½ cup margarine

50 g/1¾ oz/½ cup chopped walnuts

100 g/4 oz spinach, roughly chopped

100 g/4 oz/1 cup cheddar cheese, grated

2 eggs, beaten

100 ml/3½ fl oz/⅓ cup + 4 tsp milk

CHEF'S NOTE

This recipe is perfect the way it is but you can try different nuts and cheeses. Toasting the nuts will also change both flavour and texture.

Preheat oven to 200°C/400°F/Gas Mark 6. Line a baking tray with greaseproof paper. Reserve a few pinches of walnuts and cheese for topping.

In a large bowl, rub the margarine into the flour with your fingers until it looks like coarse meal. Stir in the walnuts, spinach and cheese until well mixed.

In another bowl, beat the eggs into the milk. Slowly add the wet ingredients to the dry until it comes together to form a nice dough, reserving any extra egg and milk mixture. Turn the dough onto a floured surface and form into a ball. Pat flat and then roll to an even thickness of 2 cm/¾ inch and cut with a round biscuit cutter.

Transfer the scones to the prepared baking tray. Brush the tops with the reserved egg and milk mixture and place a little cheese and a few walnut pieces on top of each. Bake in the middle of a preheated oven for approximately 30 minutes, until golden. Transfer to a wire rack to cool. Lovely served with a slice of Burren Gold cheese and country relish.

DIARMUID O'CALLAGHAN

BURREN GOLD CHEESE

· ·

When first doing research for *Burren Dinners*, I was made aware of the cheesemaker up at Aillwee Caves. I was told that he's up every morning to milk the cows for 6 a.m., then hauls the milk behind his own car down to the caves to make the cheese. This was a story ripe for the telling.

Little did I know that it was only a wedge of the wheel.

Diarmuid O'Callaghan grew up on his mother's family farm in Cohey, Kilfenora. He and his brother John worked on the dry-stock farm from as early as he can remember. Summers found him heading south to Doonbeg to his uncle's farm to help with the making of hay and the cutting of turf. Nothing particularly noteworthy until he was in his twelfth spring, in 1999.

That year his father took ill and needed Diarmuid around to help with the cattle and sheep. A summer job was arranged for him with Roger Johnson, the founder of the business at Aillwee Caves, but a hand was needed at Easter. For three days, Diarmuid hid what he remembers as 'thousands of

LOOKING FOR THE HILLS

Creme Eggs' in the woodlands around the cave. He assures me that after being a twelve-year-old with access to cases upon cases of the seasonal treat, he can't remember eating another since.

Diarmuid's career path touched just about every base in the operation: gift shop, pot washing, helping out in the tea room, a good few years in maintenance, a bit of cooking and baking in the kitchens. Then, in the spring of 2011, the head cheesemaker left and a replacement was needed. Diarmuid got the tap to take over.

HE FINDS COMFORT IN THE EXACT ROUTINE OF THE PROCESS

He'd been milking the cows and hauling the milk down for the cheesemaker ever since he was licensed to drive. He knew the process of getting the milk from the cows to the can and from the can into the pasteurisation tank. Beyond that, however, he knew nothing of the cheesemaking process.

On day one of his training, he watched the whole process as the milk went beyond his former grasp of the procedure. Day two had him repeating the steps he'd watched the master perform the day before. Day three …

It was like no other day, even those before he began training. He transferred the milk from the can behind his car to the tank. However, he now knew how to start the next step and began pasteurisation. Thinking his supervisor might have had a bit of a lie-in, he completed that step, began cooling down the milk and then rang the cheesemaker's mobile.

Answering the foreign ringtone on the other end of the line, his mentor explained they had found Diarmuid's work satisfactory and headed off to France for a holiday. Nothing like on-the-job training – and he has never looked back.

He finds comfort in the exact routine of the process. Times, temperatures, proportions and formulas all play integral roles in the making of all six varieties of Burren Gold Cheese. He still looks for ways to shave off a minute or two here and there to keep his head in the game. It's not unlike his hobby of competitive cycling.

A small man himself, Diarmuid knows that he'll never win a race in the downhill stages. He tells me he's 'always looking for the hills'. It's where his skills, training and tenacity can win the day and win the race. He has won his fair share, including the county championship.

For Diarmuid, food is fuel. If it's not going to help him cycle faster or farther, it's of no use to him. On the rare occasion he splurges, however, it is his Aunt Esther's apple pie. If he has won a race, he might even have a scoop of ice cream with it.

AUNT ESTHER'S APPLE PIE WITH CHEESY CRUST

Serves 6

For the pastry

300 g/10½ oz/2 cups plain (all-purpose)
  flour

½ tsp salt

200 g/7 oz Gouda-style cheese (Burren
  Gold, if possible), grated

275 g/9 oz/1¼ cups + 1 tbsp unsalted
  butter, cubed

6–7 tbsp ice cold water

For the filling

1 kg/2 lb 4 oz Bramley apples, peeled,
  cored and sliced

150 g/5¼ oz/¾ cup caster (superfine)
  sugar

3 tbsp plain (all-purpose) flour

1 tbsp lemon juice

½ tsp cinnamon

½ tsp salt

30 g/1 oz/2 tbsp unsalted butter

1 egg, beaten

2 tsp sugar

In a large bowl, mix together the flour, salt and cheese. Add the butter and rub with your fingertips until it resembles coarse breadcrumbs. Add the iced water, one tablespoonful at a time, until the mixture comes together into a dough.

Turn onto a lightly floured surface and form into a ball, flatten a bit and cut in half. Gently form each half into a ball, flatten into a 13 mm/½-inch disc and wrap in cling film. Refrigerate for a minimum of 1 hour (can be made a day ahead).

Preheat oven to 200°C/400°F/Gas Mark 5. Remove the dough from the refrigerator to temper as you make the filling.

In a large bowl, mix the apples, sugar, flour, lemon juice, cinnamon and salt. Set aside.

Roll out both pieces of dough on a lightly floured surface. Place one piece onto a 23 cm/9-inch pie tin, gently pressing into the bottom and sides. Pour the apple mixture into the pie tin and dot with the butter. Cover the mixture with the other half of the pastry dough. Crimp the edges together to seal and make a slit on the top to let out the steam. Whisk the egg with 1 tablespoonful of water and brush over the top, then sprinkle with sugar.

Place on a baking tray in a preheated oven for 45 to 50 minutes until golden in colour. Remove to a wire rack to cool for at least 20 minutes. Serve warm with freshly whipped cream, ice cream or a thin slice of Burren Gold cheese.

KAREN COURTNEY

STONECUTTERS KITCHEN

• •

She might not have known she was amassing pieces of the eventual jigsaw puzzle of her professional life when she competitively sailed out of Howth Harbour and around Ireland with an all-woman crew in 1988. Days (and nights) of tacking and gybing around the island on her father's 37-foot Swan, called *Bandersnatch*, taught the teenager much about herself as well as how people work in different situations.

One piece in place.

Throughout her teens and early twenties, Karen worked her way up the ladder in catering and nightclub establishments, which gave her knowledge about the business – knowledge she didn't consider important at the time. Likewise for the understanding she gained acting as first secretary

PIECES OF THE PUZZLE

then the payroll supervisor for her father's company.

Both were skills required to make it in the catering trade.

Karen's husband, Myles Duffy, also had a series of jobs and careers that set the couple up for success. He has worked in a number of manufacturing and fabrication trades, from spray painting to stained-glass art and everywhere in between. There's little Myles can't fix, and his easy-going manner is an underappreciated asset when you own the building and equipment and manage a seasonal staff.

'LIKE A HUG FROM THEIR MAMMY' IS HOW KAREN HOPES THEIR CUSTOMERS FEEL ABOUT THE FOOD AND EXPERIENCE AT THEIR RESTAURANT

The couple decided to leave Dublin and the east coast to avail of the quieter lifestyle and lower expenses that other parts of the country might afford. That her sister had moved to Clare and opened a pottery didn't feel like a piece to the puzzle at the time, but when property directly across the street became available, that piece clicked nicely into place. It was from there that the couple set up house and moved a hotdog cart to the Doolin pier in 1992.

The final piece snapped into position when their offer on the building and property adjacent to theirs was accepted.

With all the pieces arranged, the Stonecutters Kitchen was set on course.

The couple made the conscious decision to pursue a casual dining atmosphere for families, which they felt missing from the area. 'Like a hug from their mammy' is how Karen describes how she hopes their customers feel about the food and experience at their restaurant.

Like most people in the food business, they both laughed when I asked what they did in their spare time. While they have little of it, they fill it with coaching their sons' swimming teams, scouting and volunteer work with the local coastguard. Time is precious when you're running a busy restaurant and raising two boys. Karen Courtney and Myles Duffy offer as much of the time they do have to make their little piece of Burren life better for everyone.

Their days of sailing are most likely over for now. From their clifftop home and business, however, the view of the changing sea is their constant and there is always a bit of salt in the air – 'and on the windows!' Karen says, reminding Myles that it's his turn to give them a wash.

BANANA AND MAPLE UPSIDE-DOWN TOFFEE CAKE

∙ ∙

Serves 6

For the toffee

60 g/2 oz/4 tbsp butter

30 g/1 oz/2 tbsp brown sugar

60 ml/2 fl oz/¼ cup maple syrup

1 tbsp lemon juice

For the cake

100 g/3½ oz/½ cup butter, softened

60 ml/2 fl oz/¼ cup maple syrup

100 g/3½ oz/½ cup brown sugar

1 banana, mashed

3 eggs, beaten

170 g/6 oz/1⅓ cups self-raising flour

3 bananas, peeled, halved and sliced in half
    lengthwise

Whipped fresh cream, to serve (optional)

Preheat oven to 180°C/350°F/Gas Mark 4.

To make the toffee, place a 25 cm/9¾-inch sauté pan over medium heat. Add the butter, brown sugar and maple syrup. Cook, stirring occasionally, for 4 minutes until the toffee has thickened slightly. Remove from the heat and sprinkle with lemon juice.

To make the cake, cream the butter in the bowl of a stand mixer. While still running, add the maple syrup and brown sugar. Add the mashed banana and eggs, bit by bit, then stir in the flour.

Arrange the sliced bananas in a fan shape in the pan with the toffee sauce. Spread the batter over the bananas and place in the centre of a preheated oven for 35 minutes or until the cake feels set in the centre.

Remove to a work surface, slide a knife around the sides of the pan, place a plate on top and turn it over (the pan must still be warm). If too much toffee remains, place the pan over medium heat with 1 tablespoonful of water and whisk until the toffee dissolves, then spoon over the cake. Slice into wedges and serve with whipped cream, if desired.

ACKNOWLEDGEMENTS

This author would be crushed by the mass of a list including everyone who should be acknowledged for their contributions to the book you hold.

At the top, bottom and middle of the list are the chefs, producers and keepers of shops and inns who suffered a season of phone calls, e-mails, and intrusion in order to get their stories and menus to you. It's been an honour to be entrusted by the hard-working, food-loving stars of the Burren to tell their story.

For her end of all those calls and contacts, many thanks to Jill Lever – likely the most over-qualified production assistant in publishing history.

We got the band back together! Jette Verdi, Joanne Murphy and Niamh Browne were all back for the food – prep, cooking, styling and photography. We also called upon Clare Wilkinson's adept hands for the project. The photos mightn't show it, but the kitchen craic was 90!

Carsten Krieger's eye for the Burren is famous. We were fortunate that his busy schedule allowed for him to shoot not only the Burren, but also the hands and faces of those who turn its produce into astounding food.

Both The Collins Press and The O'Brien Press played significant roles in this book's genesis and revelation. To Con, Michael and Ivan: go raibh maith agaibh.

The Clifford family had far more hand in *Burren Dinners* than allowing me to dedicate the book to the memory of Keady. All-star champions of Irish food, I thank Artie, Linda, Fallon and Rachel beyond words.

Paula Elmore, Emma Dunne and Emma Byrne squished, squeezed, moulded and shaped the project from a bunch of words, recipes and photographs into a tome of which I am very proud. Accolades all around.

Chefs Neven Maguire and Brian McDermott have both, once again, been an important part of a *Dinners* book. Many thanks to both of these immensely talented (and immensely busy) chefs for their time and talent.

The Burren is a mystical, magical place without doubt. I fell under its spell while spending the spring, summer and autumn researching *Burren Dinners*. To write it off to mysticism and magic, however, would be unfair and incomplete. The people, I have come to know, outshine even this thoroughly unique place.

Finally, my wife, Caryn, has been supportive throughout the birthing process of this work in a way that only writers can understand, only the most fortunate ever experience and of which only saints (and surely not this chef) are worthy. Thank you, Petal.

INDEX

A

almonds
    'Craggy Island' lamb and almond tagine, 22
    blackberry, almond and cardamom cake with black fruits, 183
    pear and almond tart, 90
apples
    berry and hazelnut crumble, 162
    apple fritters with spiced orange syrup, 247
    apple, berry and hazelnut crumble, 162
    Aunt Esther's apple pie with cheesy crust, 293
    baked chutney apples, 25
    blackberry and apple compote, 56
    Mum's apple crumble, 36
    roast Glencarn suckling pig with herb and apple pan sauce, 23
Argentine chimichurri sauce, 181
aubergine dip, roasted, 196
Aunt Esther's apple pie with cheesy crust, 293
avocado, chilli shrimp with guacamole salad, 229

B

bacon
    bacon-roasted Brussels sprouts, 88
    bacon-roasted rabbits, 220
    goat cheese panna cotta with bacon syrup, 211
baked chutney apples, 25
baked wild salmon with herb crust, 286
banana and maple upside-down toffee cake, 296
barley, farmhouse lamb stew, 169
beef
    beef cheeks in red wine, 230
    braised feather blade of beef in red wine, 146
    braised shin of beef with rocket gremolata, 256
    grilled rib-eye steaks with duck-fat chips, 179
    roast rib of beef with Yorkshire puddings, 282
'beer-pura' fried cabbage, 99
beetroot
    buckwheat and beetroot risotto, 115
    homemade lemon ricotta with golden beetroot salad, 72
    mackerel salad with beetroot and dill crème fraîche, 178
    wild crudités of beetroot carpaccio, samphire salsa verde and radishes, 216
biscotti, pistachio-cranberry, 76–7

blackberries
    apple, berry and hazelnut crumble, 162
    blackberry and apple compote, 56
    blackberry bread and butter pudding, 222
    blackberry crème brûlée with blackberry and Cointreau sorbet, 140–1
    blackberry crème brûlée with hazelnut shortbreads, 44–5
    blackberry, almond and cardamom cake, 183
    lamb shanks in spiced blackberries and port, 53
boulangère potatoes, 89
braised feather blade of beef in red wine with purée of braised vegetables, 146
braised red cabbage, 89
braised shin of beef with rocket gremolata, 256
bread
    Don's treacle bread, 51
    Dooliner brown bread, 127
    railway cake, 219
broccoli, oven-roasted, 150
Brussels sprouts, bacon-roasted, 88
buckwheat and beetroot risotto with goat cheese and duck egg, 115
Burren Nature Sanctuary savoury scones with walnuts, spinach and cheddar, 290
buttered mashed potatoes, 148

C

cabbage
    'beer-pura' fried cabbage, 99
    braised red cabbage, 89
    hot-smoked salmon with spring onion mash, creamed cabbage and leeks, 278
    Romanian cabbage slaw, 198
cakes
    banana and maple upside-down toffee cake, 296
    blackberry, almond and cardamom cake with black fruits, 183
    chocolate cheesecake, 200
    Mary's ultimate chocolate celebration cake, 232
    pecan and maple baked cheesecake, 100
carpaccio of smoked haddock and kumquat, 65
carrots and parsnips, honey roasted, 138
celeriac salad, 106
cheese
    cheese scones, 170

Aunt Esther's apple pie with cheesy crust, 293

buckwheat and beetroot risotto with goat cheese, 115

Burren Nature Sanctuary savoury scones with walnuts, spinach and cheddar, 290

goat cheese panna cotta, 211

grilled oysters with chorizo and Parmesan, 160

heirloom tomato and buffalo mozzarella salad, 134

homemade lemon ricotta, 72

kale and quinoa salad with feta, 145

local cheese board, 268

Niall's goat cheese frittata, 248

smoked mackerel and goat cheese pâté, 50

chicken

Folk Festival jambalaya, 126

lemon-garlic roasted chicken with lemon and thyme stuffing and Madeira jus, 136

chilli-lime butter, 195

chilli shrimp with guacamole salad, 229

chocolate

chocolate cheesecake, 200

Doolin bog pie, 129

Mary's ultimate chocolate celebration cake, 232

Szechuan pepper chocolate fondant with eucalyptus cream, 67

chorizo

Folk Festival jambalaya, 126

grilled oysters with chorizo and Parmesan, 160

roast fillet of hake with chorizo, mussels and clams, 275

chowder, Gran's smoked haddock and potato, 97

chutney

baked chutney apples, 25

Darra's tomato chutney, 250

cider-glazed potatoes, 24

clams

garlic breaded clams, 158

roast fillet of hake with chorizo, mussels and clams, 275

shellfish boil with garlic butter, 188

shellfish linguini in white wine cream, 161

coconut panna cotta with passion fruit and mango mousse and cocoa-ginger shortbreads, 118

cod, herb-crusted fillet with mussels and peas, 42

confit of pork belly with rhubarb and rose-petal subh, 208

courgette

soup with seaweed crackers, 206

tian of summer vegetables, 54

sweet potato and courgette fritters, 74–5

crab and smoked salmon salad, 239

'Craggy Island' lamb and almond tagine, 22

crème brûlée

blackberry crème brûlée with blackberry and Cointreau sorbet, 140–1

blackberry crème brûlée with hazelnut shortbreads, 44–5

crispy braised pork belly with pan-seared scallops, 116

crumbles

apple, berry and hazelnut crumble, 162

Mum's apple crumble, 36

rhubarb crumble, 243

cucumber salad, 41

cupcakes, Irish coffee, 172

D

dandelion oil, 216

Darra's tomato chutney, 250

Don's treacle bread, 51

Doolin bog pie, 129

Dooliner brown bread, 127

duck

duck sausages with Puy lentils, 66

slow-cooked leg of duck with celeriac salad, 106

dukkah spice, 74–5

F

farm-fresh strawberry meringue, 258

farmhouse lamb and barley stew, 169

feta, with kale and quinoa salad, 145

figs, spiced, with marmalade ice cream, 251

fish

baked wild salmon with herb crust, 286

carpaccio of smoked haddock and kumquat, 65

crab and smoked salmon salad, 239

Gran's smoked haddock and potato chowder, 97

grilled mackerel with smoked salmon and cucumber salad, 41

herb-crusted fillet of cod with mussels and peas, 42

hot-smoked salmon with spring onion mash, creamed cabbage and leeks, 278

mackerel salad with beetroot and dill crème fraîche, 178

oyster and smoked salmon rumaki, 33

roast fillet of hake with chorizo, mussels and clams, 275

smoked mackerel and goat cheese pâté, 50

smoked salmon and shrimp 'ravioli', 168

Folk Festival jambalaya, 126

foraged periwinkles with chilli-lime butter, 195

fresh tomato soup, 255

frittata, Niall's goat cheese, 248

G

game sauce, 84–7

garlic

    garlic breaded clams, 158

    shellfish boil with garlic butter, 188

    smoked-garlic fondant potatoes, 139

goat cheese *see* cheese

goat, yogurt-marinated kebabs with roasted aubergine dip, 196

gorse-flower sorbet, 222

Gran's smoked haddock and potato chowder, 97

gravy

    sloe-gin giblet gravy, 220

    vegetable gravy, 240

gremolata, rocket, 256

grilled lobsters with lemon mayonnaise, 34

grilled mackerel with smoked salmon and cucumber salad, 41

grilled oysters with chorizo and Parmesan, 160

grilled rib-eye steaks with duck-fat chips, 179

H

hake, roast fillet with chorizo, mussels and clams, 275

Hasselback potatoes, 210

hazelnuts

    apple, berry and hazelnut crumble, 162

    blackberry crème brûlée with hazelnut shortbreads, 44–5

    goat cheese panna cotta with bacon syrup and toasted hazelnuts, 211

heirloom tomato and buffalo mozzarella salad with soused vegetables, 134

herb-crusted fillet of cod with mussels and peas, 42

herb-crusted rack of lamb with confit belly, 107–9

homemade lemon ricotta with golden beetroot salad, 72

honey roasted carrots and parsnips, 138

honeysuckle-lavender syrup, 56

horseradish crème fraîche, 41

hot-smoked salmon with spring onion mash, creamed cabbage and leeks with mustard cream sauce, 278

I

ice creams

    marmalade ice cream, 251

    meadowsweet ice cream, 76–7

Irish coffee cupcakes, 172

Irish whiskey and sherry trifle, 191

K

kale and quinoa salad with feta, 145

kumquat, carpaccio of smoked haddock and, 65

L

lamb

    'Craggy Island' lamb and almond tagine, 22

    farmhouse lamb and barley stew, 169

    herb-crusted rack of lamb with confit belly, 107–9

    lamb shanks in spiced blackberries and port, 53

    roast leg of lamb with vegetable gravy, 240

    slow-roasted lamb belly with potato-sage stuffing, 98

leeks, creamed cabbage and, 278

lemon

    grilled lobsters with lemon mayonnaise, 34

    homemade lemon ricotta, 72

    lemon and redcurrant posset, 27

    lemon posset, 110

    lemon-garlic roasted chicken with lemon and thyme stuffing, 136

lentils, Puy, with duck sausages, 66

lobster

    grilled lobsters with lemon mayonnaise, 34

    shellfish boil with garlic butter, 188

local cheese board, 268

M

mackerel *see* fish

mango, 118

Mary's ultimate chocolate celebration cake, 232

mayonnaise

    grilled lobsters with lemon mayonnaise, 34

    prawns with fresh mayonnaise, 82

meringues, farm-fresh strawberry, 258

minted marrowfat peas, 241

mozzarella, buffalo, and heirloom tomato salad, 134

Mum's apple crumble, 36

mushrooms

    Niall's goat cheese frittata, 248

    venison Wellington with game sauce, 84–7

mussels

    herb-crusted fillet of cod with mussels and peas, 42

    roast fillet of hake with chorizo, mussels and clams, 275

    shellfish boil with garlic butter, 188

    shellfish linguini in white wine cream, 161

    steamed mussels with white wine and cream, 264

wild garlic and bacon stuffed mussels, 124
mustard cream sauce, 278

N

nettle colcannon, 221
Niall's goat cheese frittata, 248

O

olivada mash, 257
onions, caramelised, 248
oranges
    apple fritters with spiced orange syrup, 247
    tomato and blood orange sorbet, 270
oven-roasted broccoli, 150
oysters
    grilled oysters with chorizo and Parmesan, 160
    oyster and smoked salmon rumaki, 33
    Pouldoody Bay oysters au naturel, 187

P

panna cotta, goat cheese with bacon syrup, 211
parsnips
    glazed, 88
    honey roasted carrots and parsnips, 138
    smoked parsnip purée, 117
passion fruit, 118
peaches, roasted with meadowsweet ice cream, 76–7
pears
    braised red cabbage, 89
    pear and almond tart, 90
peas
    herb-crusted fillet of cod with mussels and peas, 42
    minted marrowfat peas, 241
pecan and maple baked cheesecake, 100
peperonata stew, 74–5
periwinkles, foraged, with chilli-lime butter, 195
pineapple pudding, 151
plums, pickled, 106
pork
    confit of pork belly with rhubarb and rose-petal subh, 208
    crispy braised pork belly with pan-seared scallops, 116
    roast Glencarn suckling pig with herb and apple pan sauce, 23
potatoes
    boulangère potatoes, 89
    buttered mashed potatoes, 148
    cider-glazed potatoes, 24
    Gran's smoked haddock and potato chowder, 97

    grilled rib-eye steaks with duck-fat chips, 179
    Hasselback potatoes, 210
    hot-smoked salmon with spring onion mash, 278
    nettle colcannon, 221
    olivada mash, 257
    potato salad, 199
    potato-sage stuffing, 98
    rosemary-roasted potatoes, 242
    scallion mashed potatoes, 231
    smoked-garlic fondant potatoes, 139
    tian of summer vegetables, 54
Pouldoody Bay oysters au naturel, 187
prawns with fresh mayonnaise, 82

Q

quinoa, and kale salad with feta, 145

R

rabbit, bacon-roasted with sloe-gin giblet gravy, 220
railway cake, 219
red pepper pickle, 128
redcurrant, and lemon posset with Scottish shortbreads, 27
rhubarb
    rhubarb and rose-petal subh, 208
    rhubarb crumble, 243
ricotta, homemade lemon, 72
roast fillet of hake with chorizo, mussels and clams, 275
roast Glencarn suckling pig with herb and apple pan sauce, 23
roast leg of lamb with vegetable gravy, 240
roast rib of beef with Yorkshire puddings, 282
roasted peaches with meadowsweet ice cream and pistachio-cranberry biscotti, 76–7
rocket gremolata, 256
Romanian cabbage slaw, 198
rose petal subh, rhubarb and, 208
rosemary-roasted potatoes, 242

S

salads
    crab and smoked salmon salad, 239
    heirloom tomato and buffalo mozzarella salad, 134
    kale and quinoa salad with feta, 145
    mackerel salad with beetroot and dill crème fraîche, 178
    potato salad, 199
salmon *see* fish
samphire salsa verde, 216
sausages, duck, with Puy lentils, 66

scallion mashed potatoes, 231

scallops, pan seared with crispy braised pork belly, 116

scones

    Burren Nature Sanctuary savoury scones, 290

    cheese scones, 170

seaweed

    seaweed butter, 216

    seaweed crackers, 206

    sloke cakes, 271

shellfish

    chilli shrimp with guacamole salad, 229

    crab and smoked salmon salad, 239

    crispy braised pork belly with pan-seared scallops, 116

    Folk Festival jambalaya, 126

    foraged periwinkles with chilli-lime butter, 195

    garlic breaded clams, 158

    grilled lobsters with lemon mayonnaise, 34

    grilled oysters with chorizo and Parmesan, 160

    herb-crusted fillet of cod with mussels and peas, 42

    oyster and smoked salmon rumaki, 33

    prawns with fresh mayonnaise, 82

    roast fillet of hake with chorizo, mussels and clams, 275

    shellfish boil with garlic butter, 188

    shellfish linguini in white wine cream, 161

    smoked salmon and shrimp 'ravioli', 168

    steamed mussels with white wine and cream, 264

    wild garlic and bacon stuffed mussels, 124

shortbreads

    cocoa-ginger shortbreads, 118

    hazelnut shortbreads, 44–5

    Scottish shortbreads, 27

shrimp

    chilli shrimp with guacamole salad, 229

    Folk Festival jambalaya, 126

    shellfish boil with garlic butter, 188

    smoked salmon and shrimp 'ravioli', 168

sloe-gin giblet gravy, 220

sloke cakes, 271

slow-cooked leg of duck with celeriac salad and pickled plums, 106

slow-roasted lamb belly with potato-sage stuffing and Madeira cream, 98

smoked haddock see fish

smoked mackerel and goat cheese pâté, 50

smoked parsnip purée, 117

smoked salmon see fish

smoked-garlic fondant potatoes, 139

sorbets

    blackberry and Cointreau sorbet, 140–1

    gorse-flower sorbet, 222

    tomato and blood orange sorbet, 270

sorrel sauce, 286

soups

    courgette soup with seaweed crackers, 206

    fresh tomato soup, 255

    Gran's smoked haddock and potato chowder, 97

spiced figs with marmalade ice cream, 251

spicy tomato sauce, 181

steak

    sauces, 181

    grilled rib-eye with duck-fat chips, 179

steamed mussels with white wine and cream, 264

strawberry, farm-fresh meringue, 258

suckling pig, 23

sweet potato and courgette fritters, peperonata stew and dukkah spice, 74–5

Szechuan pepper chocolate fondant with eucalyptus cream, 67

T

tian of summer vegetables, 54

tomatoes

    Darra's tomato chutney, 250

    fresh tomato soup, 255

    heirloom tomato and buffalo mozzarella salad, 134

    Niall's goat cheese frittata, 248

    spicy tomato sauce, 181

    tian of summer vegetables, 54

    tomato and blood orange sorbet, 270

trifle, Irish whiskey and sherry, 191

V

venison Wellington with game sauce, 84–7

W

whiskey-peppercorn sauce, 181

wild crudités of beetroot carpaccio, samphire salsa verde and radishes with seaweed butter and dandelion oil, 216

wild garlic and bacon stuffed mussels, 124

Y

yogurt-marinated kid goat kebabs with roasted aubergine dip, 196

Yorkshire puddings, 282

BURREN